T0301614

Teaching Pluralism in Economics

Teaching Pluralism in Economics

Edited by

John Groenewegen

Delft University of Technology, the Netherlands

BELGIAN–DUTCH ASSOCIATION FOR INSTITUTIONAL AND
POLITICAL ECONOMY

Edward Elgar
Cheltenham, UK • Northampton, MA, USA

Published by
Edward Elgar Publishing Limited
Glensanda House
Montpellier Parade
Cheltenham
Glos GL50 1UA
UK

Edward Elgar Publishing, Inc.
William Pratt House
9 Dewey Court
Northampton
Massachusetts 01060
USA

A catalogue record for this book
is available from the British Library

Library of Congress Control Number: 2006940754

ISBN 978 1 84542 305 6

Printed and bound in Great Britain by MPG Books Ltd, Bodmin, Cornwall

Contents

v

Figures and Tables

Contributors

Hendrik P. van Dalen is Senior Research Associate at the Netherlands Interdisciplinary Demographic Institute, The Hague, Research Fellow of the Tinbergen Institute and Erasmus Competition and Regulation Institute of the Erasmus University Rotterdam, and Secretary of the Dutch Council of Economic Advisors.

Sheila C. Dow is Professor of Economics at the University of Stirling, and Director of the Stirling Centre for Economic Methodology (SCEME).

Wolfram Elsner is Professor of Economics at the Faculty of Economics and Business Studies, and the Institute of Institutional and Social-Economics (IISO) at the University of Bremen, Germany.

John Groenewegen is Professor of Economics of Infrastructures at the Faculty of Technology, Policy, and Management at the Delft University of Technology, and of Institutional Economics at Erasmus University Rotterdam.

Henk Jager is Professor of International Economics at the University of Amsterdam.

Albert Jolink is Editor in Chief of the ESB (*Economisch Statistische Berichten*) journal, and an Associate Professor of History of Management and Economics, at RSM Erasmus University Rotterdam.

Ruud Knaack is Associate Professor of Comparative Economics at the University of Amsterdam.

Wolter Lemstra is Senior Research Fellow of the Economics of Infrastructures section at the Delft University of Technology, and a Lecturer in Strategy at the Strategy Academy in Rotterdam, the Netherlands.

Roberto Simonetti is Senior Lecturer in Economics in the Faculty of Social Sciences and Innovation, Knowledge, and Development (IKD) at the Open University, Milton Keynes, UK.

Daniel Underwood is Professor of Economics and Environmental Science at Peninsula College, Port Angeles, WA West, USA.

Jack Vromen, is Professor in Philosophy of Science and Methodology, in particular of Economics, at Erasmus University Rotterdam.

Rifka Weehuizen, is Researcher at UNU-MERIT, a joint research and training centre of the United Nations University and Maastricht University, the Netherlands.

Acknowledgements

This publication and its preparatory conference of the Belgian-Dutch Association for Institutional and Political Economy (AIPE) could not have been realized without the financial support of the *Vereniging Trustfonds* of Erasmus University Rotterdam and the section 'Economics of Infrastructures' (Faculty Technology, Policy and Management) of the Delft University of Technology.

Many thanks to the authors for their patience and for bearing with editorial requests. A special word of thanks to Daniel Sutjahjo for turning the manuscript of the book into a camera-ready copy.

1. On Pluralism and Interdisciplinarity in Economics

John Groenewegen

1.1 THE ISSUE

This volume is about different schools within the discipline of economics (theoretical pluralism) and about the relation of economics with other disciplines, such as sociology, political science, and the like (interdisciplinarity). This volume addresses the implications of pluralism and interdisciplinarity for teaching economics at undergraduate and graduate level.

The question of pluralism is raised more and more in relation to the teaching of economics, because especially with the growing importance since the 1970s of Post Keynesian Economics and institutional and evolutionary economics (Hodgson, 2002), pressure was put on the economics curriculum to pay equal attention to those new perspectives compared to the traditional neoclassical mainstream.

The generally felt need for a more open system of research and teaching in economics led to a petition in the *American Economic Review* titled 'Plea for a Pluralistic and Rigorous Economics' (May, 1992). The initiative was taken by Geoffrey M. Hodgson, Uskali Mäki and Deirdre McCloskey and signed by forty-four well-known economists including Nobel laureates such as Herbert Simon, Jan Tinbergen, Paul Samuelson and Franco Modigliani. Without doubt later Nobel laureates such as Ronald Coase and Douglass North would have supported the petition too. Central in the petition is the need to recognise that different theoretical approaches should live respectfully together under the umbrella of the one discipline of economics, that there should be a constructive conversation among the different perspectives and that such greater openness should not come at the cost of a less rigorous type of economics.

That broadly supported plea for pluralism in economics was preceded by the establishment of the European Association for Evolutionary and Political

1

Economy (EAEPE) in 1988. Later the International Confederation of Associations for Pluralism in Economics (ICAPE) was created, as well as the International Society for New Institutional Economics (ISNIE) in 1997. EAEPE and ISNIE, together with the (much earlier established) Association for Evolutionary Economics (AFEE) and the Association for Institutional Thought (AFIT), now form with the European Group for Organization Studies (EGOS), the Schumpeterian Society, and the Society for the Advancement of Socio-Economics (SASE), a rich pluralistic forum. Some stay close to the world of mainstream economics (like ISNIE), others cross the boundary of the economics discipline (like SASE).

More recently a strong student movement, which started in France in 2000 and is now the well-established worldwide movement of 'Post Autistic Economics', further pushed the plea for pluralism in economics (Fullbrook, 2003)

In the following we first discuss the issue of pluralism in a general sense: what would pluralism be and why should there be pluralism in economics? In the third section attention is paid to pluralism within the economics discipline: New Institutional Economics, including game theory, as well as experimental economics are now well established branches of economics. Also the work of Masahito Aoki (Comparative Institutional Economics) is worthy of special attention, because it bridges the static approaches and the more evolutionary ones. In the fourth section evolutionary and original institutional economics is discussed. Here a dynamic process analysis is central including complexity with interesting contributions of Douglass North. From pluralism to interdisciplinarity is the subject of the fifth section. This chapter ends with some conclusions and remarks on the barriers to changing the economics curriculum and how in practice these barriers could be circumvented. A short summary of the contributions to this volume concludes this chapter.

1.2   PLURALISM: WHAT AND WHY

Theoretical pluralism is about the question whether several theories in one discipline can meaningfully exist together[1].

Mäki (1997) takes the existence of 'one world' as point of departure and explores the question of the existence of a pluralism of theories to explain that one world. The many theories we hold do then not create each a world of its own, but each illuminates an aspect or one feature of the world. Two reasons for the possibility of the 'one world and the many theories' stand out: an ontological and an epistemological one[2].

Pluralism at the ontological level involves the belief that reality constitutes a plurality of entities. In its pure form it denies any unifying force in nature and hence no scope for any general theorizing exists. The opposite of pure pluralism would be the position held by mainstream economics: its scope is defined by universal regularities.

In this volume Sheila Dow pleads for a middle ground: there are regularities in nature that are to be identified by science, but these regularities are of process rather than event type (Lawson, 1994).

> How far regularities, if they exist, can be perceived, is an epistemic issue. Epistemic pluralism entails a plurality of understandings of reality; there is no best way of establishing what constitutes true knowledge. Logical positivism entails a unitary understanding of facts by agents and a corresponding unitary understanding by economists. In contrast: post modernists and rhetoric approaches deny a basis for choosing between understandings of agents or economists. (Dow, 1997)

> If reality derives from a unity in nature, then, as long as that unity were accessible, there would be one best way of constructing knowledge about it, so that science would have one best methodology which in turn would specify the best theories and methods to be used to derive and assess them. In other words monism in nature feeds through monism at all other levels: one best epistemology, methodology, theory and method. If nature is understood to be pluralist then pluralism at different levels may be something to be welcomed. (Dow, in this volume: 26)

1.3   PLURALISM IN ECONOMICS

Economics in the twentieth century is generally called neoclassical economics. However, such characterization is incorrect in that it does not pay attention to the dominance of the transition from more descriptive, institutional economics before the 1940s to the more formal modelling that dominated economics from the 1950s onwards (Colander, 2000).

In this volume several authors point to the transition of economics in the twentieth century from a discipline with a clear subject matter to a discipline with a specific method to be applied to any subject. Reasons for this model-building focus were the problems the older discursive approach had with objectivity and the testing of deductively derived hypothesis positioned economics close to the assumed objectivity of physical science. Moreover, policy-makers demanded more and more quantitative answers from the economist advisers: if the interest rate increases by 1 percent what happens then with the number of unemployed? Also the arrival of the computer allowed for analysing larger sets of data, which stimulated the development of economics as a 'box of tools' (Colander, 2000). This had large consequences for the economics curriculum. The focus became more and more on (mathematical) methods and (econometric) tools, which resulted in what Solow (1997) called 'the overeducated in pursuit of the unknowable'.

In other words: the focus on the subject matter before the 1940s was replaced by a focus on instruments suitable for any question of optimization. Economic researchers would typically start with a set of principles: utility-maximizing consumers, profit-maximizing firms, rational actors, and focus on equilibrium end states. The interactions and relations between actors are well structured and the micro foundations of macroeconomics are such that macro is just a matter of aggregation, of 'blown-up individuals'.

Well-recognized experts in the field, among them Nobel laureates such as Friedrich von Hayek, Kenneth Arrow, Herbert Simon, Gunnar Myrdal, Ronald Coase, and Douglass North, criticized the narrow focus on methods. Ronald Coase (1998) for instance characterized mainstream economics as 'blackboard economics' with hardly a relation to reality. Coase (1999) quoted Ely Devos, an English economist: 'If economists wished to study the horse, they wouldn't go to look at horses. They'd sit in their studies and say to themselves. "What would I do if I were a horse?"'

According to Coase, mainstream economics has made a mistake in developing economics as a method, a technique of thinking to be applied to any subject matter instead of analysing a subject matter. 'What it comes down to is that economists think of themselves as having a box of tools but no subject matter ... Studying the circulation of the blood without the body' (Coase, 1998: 73).

The point is that the focus on equilibrium and the ambition to create a universal theory of markets and economic interactions with homogeneous actors, who react to exogenous changes in an identical way making predictions universal, ignores the specificities of time and place. It ignores the possibility and existence of different development paths of markets and economic systems. Life was taken out of economics (Hodgson, 1993). To understand the economic subject matter (the working of the economic system: Coase, 1997)[3] it is important to study the institutions in which actors are embedded and which largely determine, or at least to a large extent influence, the outcomes of their behaviour.

In several of the chapters in this volume the trade-off between rigour and relevancy is pointed out: with the focus on methods and tools, often accompanied by an excessive use of mathematics, economics as a science is 'rigorous' and to be compared with the 'hard' sciences[4]. The need to focus and to isolate behaviour of actors in the models from 'reality' has raised questions about the 'relevancy' of economics. In 1991 the US Commission on Graduate Education in Economics, composed of very distinguished mainstream economists, reported that tools and theory were overemphasized at the expense of creativity and problem solving.

> 'The weakness of [graduate education in economics] is not an excessive use of mathematics. If there is a central theme of our concern, it is that we believe there is considerable scope for improvement in ensuring that students' knowledge of economic problems and institutions enables them to use their tools and techniques on important problems.'
> (Quoted from Streeten, 2002: 14)

1.3.1 Recent developments in mainstream economics: game theory and experimental economics

The neoclassical 'synthesis of micro and macro economics' was unchallenged until the 1970s. The equilibrium framework ran into fundamental difficulties from the mid-1970s onwards (Kirman, 1989). Internal and external pressure has also changed the landscape of mainstream economics (see Jack Vromen in this volume). Especially from within new institutional economics, including game theory and experimental economics, forced the mainstream to pay more explicit attention to the role of institutions in economic life[5]. From the outside pressure is put on economics from the reducing number of students, reports of official committees, student protest movements and of course from critics from other social sciences.

Game theory

Game theory has become the core of modern mainstream economics. Although most of the traditional economic methods and tools can still be applied, game theory has given a strong push to the conviction that 'institutions matter'. Indeed, the neoclassical world of actors operating in a vacuum is in game theory replaced by a structured world, in which the rules of the game are well specified. In other words: the importance of institutions like conventions and rules (Schotter, 1981) becomes clear in a game theoretic analysis. This has led to the idea that the differences between institutional structures are relevant to the understanding of differences in economic performances. A specific institutional structure has for instance consequences for the information available to the actors, the asymmetry of information, the power base of actors, and the like. Specific institutional settings provide specific communication structures. Related to this, rationality gets another meaning in different institutional contexts. This view has fundamental implications for the neoclassical synthesis: macroeconomics cannot be treated anymore as a 'neutral' aggregation of individuals. The understanding of the result of interaction of individuals in a specific institutional context implies that also in macroeconomics different institutional structures should be introduced (see Underwood in this volume).

We do not suggest that game theory has fully incorporated these insights into their theoretical framework, but at least game theory has opened the minds of researchers in mainstream economics to the idea that institutions matter.

Experimental economics

The work of Nobel laureates Vernon Smith and Daniel Kahneman has challenged the rationality concept of mainstream economics and has shown the importance of institutions in the arena of economic agents. A market cannot be treated as an abstract set of relations of universal nature without any embeddedness in an institutional context. For experiments to work markets have to be specifically designed with explicit structures and rules both formal and informal. Rationality then becomes contextual and individuals demonstrate interactions instead of simply reacting to exogenous shocks: economics becomes a discipline about relationships.

1.3.2 New Institutional Economics

In our view, New Institutional Economics (NIE) is composed of a group of theories, in which the question about the efficiency of different modes of governance is studied. It is a world of individual actors aiming at the maximization of their utility, bounded in their rationality and opportunistic in their behaviour. Mostly three groups of theories are listed under the heading of NIE: property rights theory, principal agent theory and transaction cost economics[6]. Researchers working in this tradition can be found in economics (for an overview see Ménard, 2000; Richter, 2005), but also in political science and sociology addressing issues such as political, bureaucratic and corporate governance and behaviour inside and between organizations. The general hypothesis of TCE as developed by Oliver Williamson (1975, 1985), matches transactions with governance structures: if the transaction has specific characteristics (asset specificity, frequency and uncertainty), then the efficient governance structure that matches is a market contract, a hierarchy, or a hybrid. In other words, actors with bounded rationality and minimizing transaction costs behaviour, select the fitter[7] governance structure and this equilibrium holds until an exogenous variable changes (technology, legal rules of the game, values, norms and preferences of actors). See the layer model of Figure 1.1.

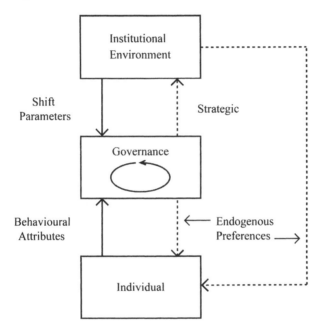

Source: Williamson (1985)

Figure 1.1: Three layer model

Oliver Williamson presents the relation between the individual actors, mode of governance and the institutional environment as an interactive one, but the dynamics in TCE are generally considered limited. Also the role of technology and the cognitive structure (the 'mind') of individuals is limited, although Williamson (2000) pleads for more dynamics, a larger role for technology and a link with cognitive science[8]. He also explicitly pleads for a pluralistic approach in which transaction costs economics is only one lens through which issues of governance can be studied, albeit it incorporates in his opinion the 'main issue' in explaining institutions of governance, namely efficiency. As explained elsewhere (Groenewegen and Vromen, 1996) the approach of Oliver Williamson is a clear example of the trade-off between 'rigorousness and relevancy': NIE prefers to preserve rigorousness and is willing to pay the price of relevancy.

Comparative Institutional Analysis

The Comparative Institutional Analysis (CIA) of Masahiko Aoki (2001) builds upon the framework of TCE and evolutionary game theory and attempts to answer the question why, on the one hand, multiple equilibria exist and how, on the other, the process towards equilibrium can be understood. Aoki's contribution lies in his analysis of the process of institutionalization by means of evolutionary game theory, in which actors maximize their trade-offs. This takes the analysis of the evolution of institutions a step further than Oliver Williamson's model, which only assumes a competitive process to select the 'fitter'. In Aoki's analysis individual actors minimize costs in selecting institutional arrangements and that selection process drives the system towards equilibrium. In contrast to traditional game theory, players in CIA do not have complete knowledge of the objective structure of the game. In fact, actors have incomplete and subjective cognitive views. During the interaction process, the players of the game create shared beliefs about the structure of the game. That is to say, agents' beliefs and actions become mutually consistent over time in a sort of self-organizing process. Aoki formulates the notion of the institution in terms of the establishment of an equilibrium: players can freely select the strategies from a choice set and when none of the players has an incentive to change his or her strategy any more, an equilibrium is established. In this 'institutions-as-an-equilibrium-approach', institutions are defined as the outcome of interactions of individual actors who maximize their pay-offs. Then institutions are the result of a long-term learning process by and among mutually dependent actors. They become 'objective' in the sense that they are shared by groups of actors as being a 'reality', while at the same time they remain endogenous in the sense that the actors themselves initiate the changes departing from subjective perceptions and preferences[9].

In contrast to the early versions of NIE (see especially Willliamson, 1975), the theoretical framework over the years has developed in such a way that the concepts provide possibilities to cope with the existence of multiple equilibria and the question of the evolution of institutions to a certain extent. This being to the extent to which the 'rigour' of the analysis is not too seriously damaged; after all it is economics and as such it should stick to a form of analysis allowing for predictions to be tested deductively.

Aoki has extended the analysis of Williamson: the interest is also focused on the process towards equilibrium, on the learning that takes place among interacting agents. The analysis of the process of institutional change is even more central in the so-called evolutionary economics with roots in the American school of Original Institutional Economics (OIE) (Rutherford, 1994).

1.4   EVOLUTION AND INSTITUTIONS

Coriat and Dosi (1998) identify seven broad methodological building blocks of evolutionary economics:

- a good explanation of why something exists rests on how it came to be as it is: the methodological imperative is dynamics first!
- theories should be microfounded: what agents do and why should be the foundation of dynamic theory
- those agents have an imperfect understanding of their environment: bounded rationality
- agents are not only imperfect in their understanding, but also learn along different path-dependent trajectories, which provides for the heterogeneity among agents
- agents are capable of discovering new techniques, are creative, bringing novelty into the system
- out of the resulting variety collective action selects inside and outside markets
- resulting from the selection mechanisms aggregate phenomena emerge as the collective outcome of 'far-from-equilibrium-inter-actions and heterogeneous learning'

Douglass North (2005) has presented an outline of a theoretical framework to study economic and institutional change, which he considers 'an extension of NIE' (for a summary see Mantzavinos et al., 2004). Building on his earlier studies (North, 1990) and especially on his work with Denzau (Denzau and North, 1994), he developed a theoretical framework that shows many similarities with the models and concepts of the original American institutionalists (Bush and Tool, 2001; Groenewegen et al., 1995) The Northian approach also corresponds well to the seven building blocks of Dosi and Coriat.

According to North neoclassical models, or in more general terms 'closed system models', are relevant for a so-called ergodic world, that is a world:

> ... in which the fundamental underlying structure of the economy is constant and therefore timeless. But the world we live in is non-ergodic – a world of continuous novel change; and comprehending the world that is evolving entails new theory, or at least modification of that which we possess. (North, 2005: 16)

In Denzau and North (1994) it is explained that substantive rationality is only a relevant concept in situations that are not complex, where agents have the relevant information and where the right motivation is present through an adequate system of incentives. When these conditions are not present then 'procedural rationality' (the world of Herbert Simon) becomes relevant. We then enter the world of learning, of endogenous preferences, and of changing shared mental maps. In short, the world that Williamson referred to as the 'mind of actors' and the interaction with technology (see note 8).

As depicted in Figure 1.2 the institutional environment can be separated into informal and formal institutions; this layer model allows us to briefly summarize the recent contributions of Douglass North. In the analysis of North the formal institutions can be considered an extension of the informal ones; formal institutions are the manifestations of the underlying values and norms. The institutions reinforce the mental maps of the individual actors in the system, which have a positive feedback on the institutions. The logic of the system, the consistency between the layers, becomes stronger through a learning process which drives the system to perfection (North, 1990: 6). In Denzau and North (1994) the 'intimate relationship' between mental models and institutions is discussed. With mental models (internal) individuals interpret the environment, whereas institutions (external) are created by individuals to structure and order the environment.

> We must understand the relationships of the mental models that individuals construct to make sense out of the world around them, the ideologies that evolve from such constructions, and the institutions that develop in a society to order interpersonal relationships. (Denzau and North, 1994: 4)

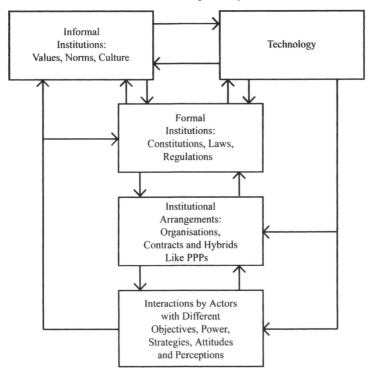

Source: Adapted from Williamson (1993 and 1998).

Figure 1.2: A dynamic layer model of technological, socio-economic systems

> Both direct learning and the culturally mediated learning show patterns of punctuation, of development as anti-gradualistic, which does not mean that the past was uninfluential (or that anything is possible at any point of time), rather that the influence of the past depends on a variety of events and may be broadly diversified. (Fiori, 2002: 1036)

1.5 INTERDISCIPLINARITY

So far I have discussed changes within mainstream economics (game theory, experimental economics and new institutional economics) and developments in institutional economics that aim at explaining the process of institutional change (CIA and the more evolutionary approach of Douglass North with connections to OIE). A fundamentally different step would be to connect the economics curriculum to other social sciences in order to present the student with at least a multidisciplinary, but preferably an interdisciplinary approach. Why would that be necessary?

When Ronald Coase (1998: 72) discussed the subject matter of economics, being the understanding of the working of the economic system, he remarked:

> That is why economists need the help of lawyers, political scientists, sociologists, anthropologists and other social scientists. Not in the sense that economists impose their method on the work of other social scientist (economic imperialism), but enlisting the help of those in other social sciences to enable us to understand better how the economic system works.

When Douglass North made an attempt to formulate a theoretical framework to understand economic change in general and institutional change in particular he remarked:

> A theory of economic change integrates theories of demographic, stock of knowledge and institutional change. The economic concern is on scarcity. Humans strive for a reduction of uncertainty, for control over their lives ... The way we perceive the world and construct our explanations about the world requires that we delve into how the mind and brain work – the subject matter of cognitive science. (North, 2005: 5)
> ... knowing how learning takes place in the mind is essential for understanding how humans deal with uncertainty. (North, 2005: 15)

However, as in most disciplines, in economics the pressures are towards a mono-disciplinary approach. The pressure of the university system in appointing young professors, promoting them and giving tenure, are such that the drive to specialize in narrow fields of the discipline has become very strong, too strong according to many of the contributors to this book. Wolter Lemstra in this volume further elaborates on the idea of inter-disciplinarity:

However, real world problems require holistic solutions. This means an increasing need for building bridges or closing gaps that are growing between disciplines. A first step is bringing disciplines together, an important next step is providing some form of integration of the underlying theories.

Multidisciplinarity is then defined as cooperation between sciences, which remain independent from each other in terms of theories, methods and tools. In the case of interdisciplinarity, the goal is integration between the disciplines resulting in a new (inter-) discipline (see also Weehuizen in this volume). Then existing concepts can get a new meaning, or even new concepts are created. This is far from the idea of one discipline imposing its concepts and tools upon other disciplines (as in the case of 'economic imperialism'). Interdisciplinarity is about going beyond cooperation between disciplines towards new concepts and models. The need for disciplines to cooperate or even to integrate is based on the idea that Gunnar Myrdal paraphrased as 'there do not exist economic and non-economic problems, but only problems'. Because the universe is not divided along the lines of the university (Streeten, 2002), it should not come as a surprise that problems dealt with in a mono-disciplinary way, are not only not solved, but most of the time create unexpected, more severe new problems.

1.6   CONSEQUENCES FOR THE ECONOMICS CURRICULUM

What are the implications of the above for the economics curriculum? The authors in this volume not only plead for bringing life back into economics, but also for a solid understanding of the philosophy and methodology of the discipline, more attention to the study of institutions, the history of economic thought, and economic history, the philosophy of economics, as well as a solid training in quantitative and qualitative methods of research, in which students learn which method is appropriate for which questions.

Economic history will make the student aware that real world issues are not about equilibrium, but about change, and that the dictum 'bygones are bygones' completely misses the point (see Jolink in this volume). Moreover, the economists should also have some training in adjacent social sciences such as politics. We agree with Paul Streeten (2002: 15): 'So I conclude that the economist, qua economist, is a better theorist for knowing philosophy, and a better applied and empirical economist for knowing political science and history.'

This being said the question is where to find space in the curriculum and how to get the change of the curriculum made. We take the position that in the curriculum some of the more detailed technical aspects of the methods and tools should be sacrificed in favour of more attention to the philosophy of economics, history of economic thought and economic history. The creation of more possibilities for students to choose in the curriculum will provide them the opportunity to make acquaintance with other social sciences of their interest.

Changing the curriculum is a complicated process similar to that of changing institutions in general: the path is full of lock-ins, of interests of specific groups and individuals, of information asymmetry, strategic behaviour, of power, and the like. The issue of how the economics curriculum should be designed and who decides on changing the curriculum is a matter of 'academic power'. What is the amount of resources (publishing, promotion, prestige) controlled by the endorsers of particular theories (Mäki, 1997)? There is no doubt that mainstream economics, meaning here neoclassical price theory, controls the economic textbooks and professional careers in most of the economics departments.

To understand the lock-ins in the process of adapting economics textbooks David Colander rightly points to the nature of the reviewing process. Textbooks are heavily reviewed (50 – 100 reviews for a principles text), not to see that the book is accurate and up to date, but to find out whether the professors who teach the course are comfortable with the approach taken. The selection mechanisms are such that successful textbooks cover what most professors are familiar with. So Colander's advice is to hook up with the existing concepts and models and to take first the professor and later the student to the more relevant and exciting economic issues. The concept of equilibrium can serve as an example. When introducing multiple equilibria the student will recognize the importance of institutions in choosing among the equilibria. Introduction to evolutionary game theory more or less automatically raises the question of moving from one equilibrium to another and will offer the opportunity to explore in a more detailed manner how the competitive process works under specific institutional and historical conditions. The difficulty lies in presenting a combination of mainstream economics with more heterodox approaches in such a way that the student is not confused, but better understands the possibilities and limitations of different schools in economics (pluralism), how to apply these different approaches and when the boundaries of the economics discipline have been reached and a more interdisciplinary approach is needed. This requires insights in philosophy, economic history and history of economic thought, insights that should ideally not be taught in separate courses, but should be integrated into the different principles, intermediate and advanced courses. Only then will the economics curriculum ensure that 'students' knowledge of economic problems and institutions enables them to use their tools and techniques on important problems. This volume attempts to offer insights into the question of the content of such a revised curriculum and into to the process of how to get there.

1.7   CONTRIBUTIONS TO THIS VOLUME

Sheila C. Dow discusses pluralism at different levels and how it contrasts with monism. The distinction between closed and open systems is essential. In closed systems the type of closed mainstream modelling is appropriate, whereas in open systems the evolutionary, institutional approach is warranted. This is related to North's ergodic and non-ergodic worlds. In her contribution Dow defends the middle ground between pure pluralism and monism, in which scientific communities develop different views on the nature of economic processes as to how best to build up knowledge about reality. Dow discusses the implications of her conceptualization of open systems for policy-makers and economics education.

Hendrik P. van Dalen asks the question whether pluralism in economics would be a public good or bad. For him science is first of all about social interaction. It follows then that pluralism is only a good thing when connection between the different 'organizing principles' exists. For that a common language is needed, a language that should evolve when insights grow or reality changes. Confronting theory with economic reality should be central in every economics curriculum: 'teach reality economics'. 'The real problem with economics starts when people really believe that with a "beautiful mind" you can solve all problems in the world' (van Dalen, in this volume: 57). According to van Dalen, price theory as we all know it can be a good starting point.

Jack Vromen also cherishes the theoretical virtues of the economics discipline: analytical tractability, rigour, precision, generality, parsimony, simplicity and elegance. He explains that nowadays economics is dominated by schools of thought that can no longer be characterized in the standard terms of self-interested, fully informed, rational individuals, the behaviour of whom can be aggregated into static equilibria. 'All in all it can be concluded that, even though things may not be moving very quickly and drastically, the boundary lines between orthodoxy and heterodox economics have increasingly become blurred. Economics is no monolithic bloc anymore' (Vromen, in this volume: 73).

A solid training in the basics of economics runs the danger of dogmatic thinking. It is believed by Jack Vromen that the antidote should come from an equally solid training in the history of economic thought and the methodology of economics. Students' openness and skills to compare and understand the evolution in economic thinking should be built into the curriculum.

In discussing the need to change the economics curriculum, almost always a plea for more history is made. Albert Jolink addresses the important role of historical conscience. According to Jolink the main problem with teaching economics nowadays is the assumption that 'content comes naturally'. When proceeding from simple to complex it turned out that not content was added, but specialization. Economics was taught more and more separated from any context; this 'decontextualization' resulted in artificial mathematical tricks to show the 'conditions for pigs to fly'. Teaching economics is desperately in need of what Jolink calls 'historical economics', which does not mean just lining up cases, but an approach with a theoretical framework of its own.

When teachers and directors of study discuss changes in the curriculum an important aspect concerns the possibilities that public agencies allow them to make fundamental changes in the content of the courses. In most countries there exists a department of the Ministry of Education, a committee or agency that sets the norms and standards of what an economics curriculum should be. In discussing the UK case Roberto Simonetti describes the freedom faculties have to state their own objectives and that it was, at least in theory, possible to include non-technical and pluralist approaches in the economics curriculum. The reviewers would not ask about the objectives, but about the effectiveness of the programmes given the objectives. The Quality Assurance Agency (QAA) allows for different aims and objectives and interdisciplinarity and innovation in the curriculum is possible. However, in practice the devil is in the detail and it seems unlikely, according to Simonetti, that pluralism is stimulated by the QAA. The minor importance in general of teaching compared to research, the higher status of research and teaching in orthodoxy, are factors that explain why teaching pluralistic economics remains the exception. Moreover, the skills that economists should master all work against a discursive, interdisciplinary approach and in favour of orthodoxy.

Daniel Underwood's is the first in a number of chapters in which the authors report on attempts to teaching a programme in a pluralistic or even interdisciplinary way. He underlines the importance of making students aware of the relation between values-visions-analysis and policy. Each paradigm rests upon an alternative set of premises indicative of the underlying value system leading to a unique explanation of the nature of the economic phenomena and what policy-makers should do about it. Reliance upon a singular analytical apparatus necessarily decreases the number of alternatives that can be explored and thus reduces the choice set from which judgement is derived. All theory is value laden and students should become aware of that by linking to the world they live in. The purpose of education in general and of teaching economics in particular should be the promotion of 'critical thinking'.

In discussing the Master of Business Telecom Program at the Delft University of Technology, Wolter Lemstra shows how bringing context into the analysis makes students aware of the complexity of real world problems. Such awareness is necessary for making the step to more content (instead of isolated specialization) and to multidisciplinary and interdisciplinary approaches. The case shows an approach in which the participants themselves are placed in a position to compare and contrast the material presented by the different lenses and compare that with their own knowledge and experiences. They are then able to make a first judgement about the relevancy and applicability of different theories in the specific context.

Rifka Weehuizen discusses the case of infonomics at the University of Maastricht, The Netherlands. The ideal envisioned future for infonomics was that in the end it could grow out into a real, autonomous thematic discipline by itself, fed by other disciplines, but with a body of knowledge and methodology of its own. This discipline would study changes in the basic patterns of human behaviour as the result of information and communication processing, and deal with how digital information and communication technology changes these patterns in all domains: in the economy (for example electronic markets), in law (information law, intellectual property rights), in the political domain (e-government, e-democracy), and in the social domain (new forms of community). Weehuizen discusses the problems that emerged in the case of infonomics showing that in practice it seems that the combination of multi- and interdisciplinarity, Problem Based Learning (PBL) and the use of the Internet, lead to a 'postmodern' attitude among students.

Wolfram Elsner discusses combining advanced mainstream micro and macro courses with evolutionary institutional economics at the University of Bremen, Germany. It is shown that such a combination is especially attractive to the Business Administration programme. Realizing a programme in which orthodoxy and heterodoxy are both present demands a major effort of the faculty; close cooperation with, especially, US departments of economics has proven to be very effective.

The chapter by Ruud Knaack and Henk Jager discusses the transition process in several East European countries and demonstrates how a more integrated theory could provide broader insights to students of economics. They demonstrate that changes in economic systems are the result of human interaction, not of human design and conclude from their theoretical analysis on economic systems in transition: 'a dynamic and innovative system will require a structural combination of variety and rigidity, of statics and change, of centralized guidance and decentralized autonomy' (Knaack and Jager, this volume: 216). They illustrate the dialectical relation between the institutional theory of economic stability and the institutional theory of economic change with the cases of Czech Republic, East and West Germany and Russia. Their chapter is an example of Reality Economics in an institutional context.

NOTES

[1] See Salanti and Screpanti (1997) for one of the first publications on pluralism in economics

[2] Different levels can be distinguished (Dow 1977): The concept of pluralism can be applied to the epistemological understanding of reality, to the methods used to theorize about that understanding of reality, to the methodology which sets the criteria for theory choice, and finally to the study of the methodologies themselves.

[3] I think economists do have a subject matter: "the study of the working of the economic system, a system in which we earn and spend our incomes" (Coase 1998: 73). In discussing the question of economic welfare, what increases the productivity of economic systems, how specialization leads to the question of coordination, Ronald Coase stresses the importance of institutions. The type and degree of specialization is largely influenced by the environment of actors. Exchange depends on the institutions of a country- the legal system (property rights and their enforcement), the political system, the education system, and the culture.

[4] Teece (2004: 11): "Too frequently, one equates rigor with mathematical modelling, but this is not so. More mathematical rigor often implies less institutional factual, and statistical rigor".

[5] With respect to the role of game theory and experimental economics in the following grateful use is made of the presentation of Geoffrey Hodgson at the annual conference of the Belgium Dutch Association for Institutional and Political economy (AIPE), November 2005 at the Delft University of Technology , The Netherlands.

[6] A recent overview of New Institutional Economics (NIE) is provided by Richter (2005). See also Rutherford (1994) and Ménard (2000). In this chapter we take Transaction Costs Economics (TCE) as developed in Williamson (1975, 1985) to be the core of NIE.

[7] Williamson distinguishes TCE as an ex post approach from agency theory as an ex ante approach. In the normative version of the latter rational actors can select ex ante the fittest governance structure in contrast to the bounded rational actors in TCE, who can only remedy failures out of which ex post the fitter results. Bounded rationality is also part of the positive version of agency theory.

[8] 'What I should like to emphasize are that 1) theories of organization that feature adaptations should not be described as "static" and 2) theories that rely on administration to accomplish cooperative adaptation (sometimes by fiat) are very definitely concerned with "management". The upshot is that transaction costs economics is very much an intertemporal, adaptive, managerial exercise – although this is not to say that more dynamic theories or more prominent provisions for management are unneeded' (Williamson, (1998: 33).

'Indeed, a still earlier zero level of analysis warrants remark: an evolutionary level in which the mechanisms of the mind take shape ... Our evolutionary psychologist and cognitive science colleagues are vital to the exercise' (Williamson, 2000: 600).

'Finally, I should call attention to technology. As compared with technological innovation, the study of organizational innovation has been comparatively neglected. The NIE has attempted to rectify that – the idea being that "truly among man's innovations, the use of organization to accomplish his ends is among the greatest and earliest" (...). We cannot fail, however, to be awed by the profound importance of technological innovation (...). 'Inasmuch as these two work in tandem, we need to find ways to treat technical and organizational innovation in a combined manner' (Williamson, 2000: 600).

[9] See on so-called shared mental maps Denzau and North (1994), who discuss evolutionary and revolutionary change of institutions.

REFERENCES

Aoki, M. (2001), *Towards a Comparative Institutional Analysis*, Cambridge, MA: MIT Press.
Becker W.E. (2000), 'Teaching Economics in the 21st Century', *Journal of Economic Perspectives*, **14**(1), Winter, 109-121.
Bush, P.D. and M.R. Tool (2001), 'Foundational Concepts for Institutionalist Policy Making' in P.D. Bush and Marc R. Tool (eds), *Institutional Economics and Policy Making*, Boston/Dordrecht: Kluwer Academic Publishers.
Coase, R. (1998), 'The New Institutional Economics', *AEA Papers and Proceedings*, May, 72-74.
Coase, R. (1999), Opening Address to the Annual Conference, International Society of new institutional economics, September 17, Washington, Ronald Coase institute: http://coase.org/coasespeech.htm.

Colander, D. (2000), 'New Millennium Economics: How Did It Get This Way, and What Way is It?' *Journal of Economic Perspectives*, **14**(1), Winter, 121-133.

Coriat, B. and G. Dosi (1998), 'The Institutional Embeddedness of Economic Change: An Appraisal of the "Evolutionary" and "Regulationist" Research Programme, in K. Nielsen and B. Johnson (eds), *Institutions and Economic Change: New Perspectives on Markets, Firms and Technology*, Cheltenham, UK and Lyme, USA: Edward Elgar.

Denzau, A.T. and D.C. North (1994), 'Shared Mental Models: Ideologies and Institutions', *Kyklos*, **47**(1), 3-31.

Dow, S. (1997), 'Methodological Pluralism and Pluralism of Method', in A. Salanti and E. Screpanti (eds), *Pluralism in Economics: New Perspectives in History and Methodology*, Cheltenham, UK and Lyme, USA: Edward Elgar.

Fiori, S. (2002), 'Alternative Visions of Change in Douglass North's New Institutionalism', *Journal of Economic Issues*, **36**(4), 1025-1043.

Fullbrook, E. (ed.) (2003), *The Crisis in Economics, the Post-Autistic Economics Movement: the first 600 days*, London: Routledge

Greif, A. (2000), 'Commitment, Coercion, and Markets: The Nature and Dynamics of Institutions Supporting Exchange', in C. Menard (ed.), *Institutions, Contracts and Organizations: Perspectives from New Institutional Economics*, Cheltenham, UK and Northampton, MA, USA: Edward Elgar, pp. 727-786.

Groenewegen, J., F. Kerstholt and A. Nagelkerke (1995), 'On Integrating New and Old Institutionalism: Douglass North Building Bridges', *Journal of Economic Issues*, June.

Groenewegen, J. and J. Vromen (1996), 'TCE and Beyond; A Case for Theoretical Pluralism', in J. Groenewegen (ed.), *Transaction Cost Economics and Beyond*, Boston: Kluwer Academic Publishers.

Groenewegen, J. and R. Kunneke (2005), 'Process and Outcome of Infrastructure Reform: An Evolutionary Perspective', in: Kunneke et al. (eds) *Institutional Reform, Regulation and Privatization*, Cheltenham, Edward Elgar.

Hodgson, G.M. (1993), *Economics and Evolution: Bringing Life Back into Economics*, Cambridge and Philadelphia: Polity Press and University of Pennsylvania Press.

Hodgson G.M (ed.) (2002), 'Introduction', *A Modern Reader in Institutional and Evolutionary Economics, Key Concepts*, Cheltenham, UK and Northampton, MA, USA: Edward Elgar, pp. xiii-xxix.

Kahneman, D. (1994), 'New Challenges to the Rationality Assumption', *Journal of Institutional and Theoretical Economics*, **150**(1), 18-36.

Lawson, T. (1994), *Economics and Reality*, London: Routledge

Mäki, U. (1997), 'The One World and The Many Theories', in A. Salanti and E. Screpanti (1997).

Mantzavinos, C., D.C. North and S. Shariq (2004), 'Learning, Institutions, and Economic Performance, Perspectives on Politics', **2**(1), 75-84.

Kirman A.P. (1989), 'The Intrinsic Limits of Modern Economic Theory: The Emperor has No Clothes', *Economic Journal*, **99**, 126-139.

Ménard, C. (ed.) (2000), *Institutions, Contracts and Organizations: Perspectives from New Institutional Economics*, Cheltenham, UK and Northampton, MA, USA: Edward Elgar.

North, D.C. (1990), *Institutions, Institutional Change and Economic Performances*, Cambridge: Cambridge University Press.

North, D.C. (2005), Understanding the Process of Economic Change, Oxfordshire: Princeton University Press.

Rutherford, M. (1994), *Institutions in Economics*, Cambridge: Cambridge University Press.

Salanti, A. and Screpanti, E. (eds) (1997), *Pluralism in Economics: New perspectives in History and Methodology*, Cheltenham, UK and Lyme, USA: Edward Elgar.

Schotter, A. (1981), *The Economic Theory of Social Institutions*, Cambridge: Cambridge University Press.

Smith, V. (1992), 'Rational Choice: The Contrast between Economics and Psychology', *Journal of Political Economy*, **99**(4), 877-896.

Solow, R. M. (2000), 'Towards a Macroeconomics of the Medium Run', *Journal of Economic Perspectives*, **14**(1), 151-159.

Streeten, P. (2002), 'What's Wrong With Contemporary Economics?', *Interdisciplinary Science Reviews*, **27**(1), 13-24.

Teece, D. (2004), 'Sustaining Creative Tensions in Management research: A Perspective from an Interdisciplinary Economist', Presentation at Lappeenranta University of Technology, May 18, mimeo.

Williamson, O.E. (1975), *Markets and Hierarchies: Analysis and Anti-Trust Implications: A Study in the Economics of Internal Organization*, New York: Free Press.

Williamson, O.E. (1985), *The Economic Institutions of Capitalism, Firms: Markets, and Relational Contracting*, London: Macmillan.

Williamson, O. (1998), 'Transaction Costs Economics: How it Works, Where is it Headed', *De Economist*, **146**(1), 23-58.

Williamson, O.E. (2000), 'The New Institutional Economics: Taking Stock, Looking Ahead', *Journal of Economic Literature*, **38**, September, 595-613.

2. Pluralism in Economics

Sheila C. Dow

2.1 INTRODUCTION

Modern economics operates within a wider cultural and intellectual context in which pluralism is widespread. This pluralism arose from a reaction in the last few decades against the measuring of cultural experience and intellectual ideas against some notion of an absolute norm, which tended to dominate in the middle of the twentieth century. Thus there is now a positive embracing of the pluralist society and a rejection of scientism.

Economics, like all disciplines, has been influenced by this development. But economics can be distinguished from the other social sciences by its conscious positioning as being closest to the physical sciences. Thus, while other social sciences develop theories of human nature and social structure, mainstream economics has captured human nature in a set of 'self-evident' axioms. These axioms in turn form the foundation of a system of classical logic from which propositions are deduced whose truth content can be determined by means of empirical testing. The origins of this approach can be found in physics (see Mirowski, 1989). Now that physics no longer conforms to logical positivism, the model of modern economics can more readily be found in pure mathematics (see Blaug, 1999). The methodological framework espoused by mainstream economics, therefore, is not apparently open to pluralism. Classical logic applied to the axioms and testing the ensuing propositions against 'the facts' are seen as definitive; there may still be arguments, but these can 'in principle' be resolved with sufficient technical advance in modelling and testing.

Nevertheless there are distinct signs of pluralism within mainstream economics. There is for a start a notable diversity of approach, such that mainstream economics can no longer readily be defined simply in terms of a general equilibrium system. For example, while game theory depicts deterministic axiom-based behaviour, it does not fit readily into a general equilibrium system. Further, the kind of inconsistency which general equilibrium theory was designed to resolve is now evident in mainstream economics; new growth theory for example incorporates an endogenous money supply function in contrast to the exogenous money supply function of New Classical macroeconomics.

This pluralism in mainstream economics can be supported by the postmodern argument that the methodological strictures of logical positivism cannot be sustained. Thus for example Phelps (1990) describes New Classical Economics as postmodern. Indeed McCloskey's (1983) argument for the end of prescriptive methodology was embraced by mainstream economists, who prefer not to engage in methodological debate. In a modern version of the earlier realism-of-assumptions debate, the implication that was drawn was that the structure of theory did not matter; all that mattered was empirical testing.

But in the meantime, other approaches to economics have been evolving, some with long pedigrees, employing methodologies quite consciously different from mainstream economics. Central to this choice was the view that 'the facts' themselves are theory-laden and our capacity to test theory is highly constrained. As a result, economics consists not only of a dominant mainstream which has been fragmenting, substantially cut adrift from methodological scrutiny, but also of a wide range of approaches, or schools of thought, or paradigms, each of which asks different questions, and answers them in different ways. A feature of some of these non-mainstream approaches is an openness to other social science disciplines, which extends the plurality. In sum, economics consists of a plurality of approaches.

This plurality poses particular problems for policy-makers. While methodologists have concluded that there is no one best way of choosing a theory, policy makers have to be decisive (even if the decision is not to act) and they need some basis for making such decisions. It is the first purpose of this chapter to consider pluralism in economics and how policy-makers can make reasoned choices between theories. We shall see that, in the absence of absolute criteria for theory choice, policy-makers need to be able to exercise judgement with respect to a wide range of sources of knowledge. This has direct implications for economics education. The most obvious implication is that economics education should develop students' knowledge and skills with respect to a wide range of sources and types of knowledge. The more difficult implication to address is that the foundations need to be laid for developing skills in exercising judgement. Considering the implications of pluralism for economics education is the second purpose of this chapter.

In order to lay the groundwork for these two analyses, we start by exploring the meaning of pluralism, distinguishing particularly between the different levels at which the term may be applied. We then discuss the reasons why pluralism can be justified in economics, by considering the nature of the economic system. This involves exploring the meaning and

significance of open and closed systems, in the real world, and in knowledge
and theory. We are then in a position to proceed to considering how policy-
makers can profit from this pluralism, and what this implies for the education
of future generations of academic economists and economic policy-makers.[1]

2.2   THE MEANING OF PLURALISM

Pluralism can be present at several levels, and these need to be distinguished
if we are to understand what is involved in theoretical pluralism. Pluralism in
general involves variety, a classification according to a plurality of
categories. It can be distinguished from monism, which involves unity rather
than plurality, or dualism which involves categorization by a duality.

Pluralism involves something more than plurality.[2] It involves some
element of judgement rather than pure description, such that pluralism can be
grouped along a spectrum, from weak pluralism to strong pluralism. Weak
pluralism simply involves an acknowledgement of plurality, a willingness to
contemplate 'otherness', without any judgement as to whether or not this
plurality is welcome. Pluralism becomes stronger the greater the degree of
advocacy for plurality; we consider arguments for this more clearly
normative pluralism in the next section.

But first we need to consider a further feature of pluralism, that it can be
applied to a variety of levels. We start here with theoretical pluralism. When
policy-makers face a variety of theories which provide different analyses of
real problems, suggest different solutions and predict different outcomes they
encounter pluralism at the level of theory. As long as the decision-maker has
a set of criteria for choosing the best theory to address a particular problem,
this variety is not problematic. It is variety where it is not clear which is the
best theory that is regarded as a problematic pluralism. It is a common joke
told against economists that we can never agree, and even that the same
economist may simultaneously put forward more than one view ('on the one
hand . . . on the other hand . . .').

Within economics itself, pluralism may also be understood in terms of
pluralism of method, whereby theories may draw on different types of model,
or more generally reasoning, and on different types of evidence. This is often
referred to also as eclecticism. The economist may be thought of as carrying
a toolbox out of which a range of tools can be produced. But without any
apparent criteria for deciding which are to be used for which purpose this
does not take us very far. This can be a source of regret, among those seeking
monism of method. Blanchard and Fischer (1989: 505) put it as follows:

Although it is widely adopted and almost as widely espoused, the eclectic position is not logically comfortable. It would be better for economists to have an all-purpose model, derived explicitly from microfoundations and embodying all relevant information, to analyse all issues in macroeconomics (or perhaps all issues in economics). We are not quite there yet. And if we ever were, we would in all likelihood have little understanding of the mechanisms at work behind the results of simulations. Thus we have no choice but to be eclectic.

For some, therefore, theoretical pluralism and pluralism of method are seen as problematic at a different, methodological, level. What is looked for is a methodology which provides a basis for deciding on the methods to be used and the criteria by which theories are to be judged. But a methodology which provides this guidance in turn may be one of many. There can also be methodological pluralism – more than one methodology. How then are we to choose between different sets of criteria? This pushes us back to the level of epistemology, but again there is scope for pluralism in that there may be different theories as to the best way to build up knowledge and therefore as to the best methodology. Theology might suggest a monist epistemology – all knowledge derives from divine revelation – while a pluralist epistemology might involve knowledge being derived from experience, imagination and reason, for example.

This categorization can be applied further at the level of reality. This can be called ontological pluralism. Indeed pluralism or monism in philosophy refers to whether reality consists of many substances (physical or spiritual) or only one. A monist ontology would involve all matter being reducible to one basic substance, like a subatomic particle, or all behaviour being reducible to a common basic element of human nature.

Starting again now from the level of ontology, we can see a logic connecting the presence or absence of pluralism at all levels. If reality derives from a unity in nature, then, as long as that unity were accessible, there would be one best way of constructing knowledge about it, so that science would have one best methodology which in turn would specify the best theories and methods to be used to derive and assess them. In other words monism in nature feeds through into monism at all other levels. The logic breaks down however if the monism in nature is not accessible. Then it becomes a matter for argument whether or not it is still possible to settle on one best epistemology, methodology, theory and method. The outcome may be monism or pluralism. Similarly, if nature is understood to be pluralist, it is a matter for argument whether the best knowledge system, methodology and so on should be pluralist or not. In other words, pluralism at the different levels may be something to be welcomed rather than regretted.

We will turn in the next section to consider the arguments for pluralism. In the process we will consider a further refinement of what is meant by pluralism which derives from Mearman (2005). When we refer to the different number of categories in monism, dualism and pluralism (one, two, many) there is further the issue of the status of those categories. They can be regarded as all-encompassing, mutually exclusive, with fixed meaning, or they can be regarded as existing along a spectrum, where the divisions are provisional in terms of meaning and 'location', and partial in that different divisions may apply on different occasions. Which understanding prevails depends on the system of thought within which pluralism is being considered. In order to treat all these matters, we need to understand the meaning and significance of open and closed systems.

2.3   OPEN AND CLOSED SYSTEMS – THE REASONS FOR PLURALISM

A guiding principle we will employ here is that the nature of the subject matter should determine the way in which we build knowledge about it. We therefore start now with the level of reality. There is a risk of circularity – what we can say about the nature of the subject matter depends on what we know about it. There are different alternative routes to ontology. One is theology, whereby knowledge comes from revelation. Another is philosophy, as in the transcendental realist argument (Bhaskar, 1975). My own preferred route is that of David Hume, which combined scepticism about the scope of reason with the Scottish tradition of common sense philosophy. According to Hume, our knowledge of existence comes from conventional belief built up over time in the form of socially-constructed knowledge, fed by generations of experience, and embedded in institutions and conventions (Dow, 2002).

As we argued above, monist subject matter justifies a monist knowledge way of building up knowledge. If economic behaviour and economic structures are understood to be such that they can all be derived from one common set of axioms, as in the axioms of rational individual behaviour, then it follows that knowledge should be built up as a deductive system from these axioms. The result was the general equilibrium framework, which became the conventional socially-constructed basis of knowledge in mainstream economics. But in the last decade or so, the confrontation of this framework with reality has not been satisfactory. In policy-making, the large general equilibrium macro models have proved unsatisfactory. Their primary rationale was that they were designed for prediction, but they failed to predict well. There is now open discussion in central banking circles about model uncertainty – uncertainty as to which is the best model (Goodhart, 1999). Similarly, within economic theory as well as policy, alternative types of theory have been developed, notably game theory, which seem to explain reality better.

If the economic system is monist, therefore, we have not identified yet what that system is. Indeed the general belief is that the economic system is pluralist. There is to start with the issue of how far the economic system can be separated off as a unity from other aspects of reality. For most economists there is some degree of acceptance that other disciplines address aspects of reality which cannot be separated entirely from economics. The Robbins (1932) definition of economics as being concerned with any circumstance of scarcity was an attempt nevertheless to define a clear disciplinary boundary. The Becker (1991) approach is to address this by extending the boundaries of that unity as far as possible, to the economics of the family for example. But the scarcity definition rules out situations of underemployment, where at least one factor is not scarce, and dynamic situations of evolution and growth where the boundaries of capacity change their nature and shift outwards. The scarcity definition therefore achieves a demarcation at the cost of severely narrowing scope.

The scarcity definition as an attempt to define a boundary is addressed to closing off economics to anything which falls outside the definition, whether that scope is wide or narrow; it can be used further to define the subject matter of economics as a closed system.[3] There is a close relationship between the pairs closed system/open system and monism/pluralism, which we will now explore. But we will also find that pluralism itself takes on a different meaning depending on whether it is applied within a closed system or an open system.

A closed system is one where all the relevant variables can be identified, where the boundaries of the system are knowable, so that variables can be classified as endogenous or exogenous, and where the relationships between variables are knowable and unchanging (so that all change in the system can be accounted for). The constituent parts of the system are of a common, fixed nature, with independent existence (as in atoms, or rational individuals). It is a system in reality which displays regularities between variables at the empirical level, and which can be represented theoretically by an epistemic system of covering laws. It is a monist system in reality which generates a monist system of knowledge, and thus a monist methodology: there is one best way of building up knowledge about the system. This is an axiomatic system of deductive logic, where the axioms refer to the smallest constituent element – in the case of general equilibrium economics, rational economic man.

An open system is one where not all the relevant variables can be identified, and where the external boundaries of the system are therefore not knowable. The system is subject to outside influences which cannot be accounted for in advance (where 'accounted for' includes knowledge that an outside influence, or relationship, is random). Further, within the system, there is scope for change in the relationships between variables which cannot be identified in advance, and indeed for change in the nature of the constituent variables themselves. Since the system in reality cannot be understood in terms of constituent parts of a fixed nature, it is pluralist.

The choice could nevertheless still be made to require that knowledge be a closed system, even though the subject matter is a pluralist open system. Thus, even if economists accept that the real social world is an open system, theory may be built up as a closed system, as in general equilibrium theory. But then how does theory correspond to reality? If it is built on axioms which are not a good representation of reality, what are we to make of the conclusions? If real factors are excluded, how do we include them when we come to draw policy conclusions? *Ceteris paribus* does not apply in reality. If the empirical evidence comes from an open-system reality, in what sense can it be used to test theory? One of the leading figures in the development of general equilibrium theory, Frank Hahn, has made precisely these arguments, but put a priority on a monist methodology: mathematical formalism within an axiomatic deductive system (see for example Hahn, 1973).

The clinging on to this monist methodology is in part an (understandable) unwillingness to embrace what is seen as the alternative, pure pluralism. At the epistemic level, pure pluralism implies a plurality of approaches to building up knowledge, which supports a plurality of methodologies and thus of theories. It is the extreme relativism which Blaug (1980) categorizes as the 'anything goes' approach. There is an infinite range of legitimate theories, without any (monist) absolute methodological criteria for choosing between them. If this were the only alternative, then indeed science in any meaningful sense would be impossible.

But this dualist, all-or-nothing view of knowledge is a reflection of epistemology itself being understood as a closed system, with only two categories which are mutually exclusive and all-encompassing, and of fixed meaning. Neither category is workable as a means of building knowledge about a reality which, as far as we can have access to it, is pluralist. In practice, since scientific practice addressed to real problems is driven by the nature of the real subject matter, a study of practice reveals that it is the middle ground between monism and pure pluralism which is the main focus.[4]

As a guide to knowledge systems, it is important to note that reality apparently is not pluralist in a pure sense. In the social world in particular, elements of (provisional) fixity have evolved in order for the system to function: these include institutions such as the firm, conventions such as price-setting, and habits of mind such as formation of expectations which are not continuously revised. Rather than complete diversity, we have pockets of commonality which promote effective communication and coordination. Individuals rarely operate as isolated atoms, but rather condition their behaviour by the common mores of society.

Therefore, just as the nature of social reality can be understood as a structured plurality, so can knowledge systems be understood as a structured plurality, allowing for a finite range of methodologies. Each methodology is validated by a scientific community which judges this methodology to be the best to address an open system reality (Dow, 2004a). That judgement in turn is based on that community's view as to the main features of the real social system. Thus in economics some will focus on methodological individualism, some on class, some on institutions, and so on.

In turn, an open-system methodology, to be operational, requires some closure (Chick and Dow, 2001, Loasby; 2003). Building a theory requires that some variables be taken as exogenous, and that there is sufficient stability in the underlying causal mechanisms for them to be drawn out. Theory inevitably abstracts, and abstraction is a form of closure. But closure within an open system is different from closure within a closed system. In the former, any closure is only partial and provisional, for the purposes of analysis, while in a closed system, closure of a subsystem is part of the overall set of predetermined relationships between atomistic variables. In a closed system, it is in principle possible to put together all the closed subsystems in a coherent whole. If the (monist) method of mathematical formalism is applied to all subsystems, then it is a technical question how they should be put together. In an open system, however, if the methodology is not monist but pluralist, then the methods selected for analysing different subsystems may be incommensurate, so that the parts cannot be combined using one method into a whole. Further, the closure is partial – the influence of exogenous variables cannot be assumed to be stochastic – and provisional – the form of closure may change as the subject matter evolves.

Since neither pure monism nor pure pluralism has proved to be an adequate guide to policy, most of economics occupies some of the middle ground between the two. In the next section we attempt a mapping out of the middle ground.

2.4   PLURALISM AND ECONOMICS

Conceptions of the economy as an open system are based on an understanding of human behaviour as being purposeful and creative (and thus not deterministic) and also as being social; social behaviour is in turn influenced by conventions and institutions which evolve over time in an indeterminist fashion. If we accept this conception of the real social world as an open system, that there is no basis for building economic knowledge in the form of laws, then there is scope for methodological pluralism, that is, a range of views as to the best way to build up economic knowledge. Pure methodological pluralism being unworkable given the real social nature of science, the range of methodologies is limited to a range of communities. These communities are identified with different paradigms – mainstream, Post Keynesian, institutionalist and so on – which take different views as to the essential nature of the economic process, and thus different views as to how best to build up knowledge about it (Dow, 1996).

To be operational, a pluralist approach requires some closure – focusing on some variables rather than others, taking different things as given and so on. Just as in the real economy, closure enables rather than constrains, but only if the closure is partial and provisional. It is closures which remain fixed in the face of evolutionary change which ultimately constrain, both in the economy and in knowledge (Hawkins, 2003). With this in mind, we now consider whether there is any difference in kind between the closures involved in mainstream economics and those involved in the various heterodox approaches to economics.

Having moved away from explicit espousal of the ideals of general equilibrium theory, mainstream economics gives the appearance of a moderate form of pluralism. The parts do not readily fit together to make a whole. There is in particular a bifurcation between theoretical and applied mainstream economics. Both theoretical and applied models, in turn, are often partial. Most mainstream economists, were such explicit methodological discussion more commonplace, would probably justify this situation in terms of the complexity of the subject matter, knowledge limitations and so on in a way which seems to accord with open systems thinking.

But the key ingredients of the monist methodology of logical positivism are still there. First, theory is built on the axioms of rational individual behaviour. Second, empirical work is presented as 'testing' theory.[5] The difficulties in putting the theorizing and testing together are seen as procedural and regrettable. The underlying conception of reality and knowledge therefore is a closed-system conception. If the building blocks of theory are (narrowly-defined) rational individuals and the conclusions of theory can be tested against objective 'facts', then the presumption is that the economy is a closed system waiting to be discovered.

Further, this closed-system conceptualization applies to pluralism itself. Within a closed system, pluralism involves many all-encompassing, mutually-exclusive categories with fixed meaning, where dualism involves two such categories and monism one. Theory is one category and empirical testing another. In principle, mathematical formalism should be able to represent all different categories in a commensurate manner, allowing their combination into a whole.

In contrast, the pluralism of heterodox economics is an explicit response to the openness of the real economic system. This system is understood to be such that covering laws are not there to be discovered. Rather there are underlying causal mechanisms (the system is not chaotic) which we experience only indirectly. Furthermore these mechanisms, as tendencies, are not always in operation, and, when they are in operation, can operate across each other. As the institutions and conventions of the economy evolve, so too do the ways in which the causal mechanisms operate. Finally, knowledge is seen as socially-constructed. This is important for the subject matter of economics, since knowledge is a key aspect of the economic process.

But social-constructedness is also important for our understanding of our own economic knowledge. Different paradigms understand the economy differently and have a different conception of what constitutes 'the facts'. Categories are not mutually exclusive, all-encompassing with fixed meanings. Within an open-systems mode of thought, pluralism itself involves partial, provisional closures.

The implications of this different foundation for pluralism, in an open-systems understanding of the economic system, are profound. Methodological pluralism itself is welcomed as providing a range of means of building up knowledge of a complex whole. Since the closures of this type of pluralism are partial and provisional, there is an openness to cross-fertilization of ideas across paradigms. This is increasingly evident in non-mainstream economics, with the emergence of umbrella institutions like ICAPE and AHE[6], and in the work of younger scholars which is increasingly addressed to the middle grounds between paradigms. Indeed, to employ the metaphor of biological evolution, variety is essential to the survival of a species in the face of unpredictable outside influences.

Second, methodological pluralism grounded in the inability of any one set of methodological principles to dominate as the best way to construct knowledge in turn justifies pluralism of method. Different paradigms, employing different methodological principles, will employ a different range of methods suited to those principles. This is not eclecticism in the sense of 'anything goes' regarding choice of method. It is a conscious choice of method derived from a particular paradigmatic understanding of the nature of the real world and the consequent choice of methodology. Thus, for example, Keynes could accept the use of formal mathematics and econometrics as contributing to analysis, if they could be justified by the subject matter; specifically the closures entailed by econometrics had to be mirroring something approximating a closure in the real world. This typifies an open-systems pluralism, in contrast to mainstream economics which presents itself as consisting solely of mathematical formalism and econometric testing.

Now that we have explored the reasons for pluralism and the different meanings of the term, we are in a position to turn explicitly to the needs of the policy-maker looking to economics for guidance.

2.5   PLURALISM AND POLICY-MAKING

Theoretical pluralism poses problems for policy-makers in that theoretical economics itself does not generally present one clearly preferable policy solution to particular problems. There may be different assumptions, different uses of evidence, different understandings of the evidence and different uses of language which make the different bodies of theory incommensurate. And methodological pluralism means that there is no one set of criteria agreed on by economists by which to decide which is the best theory.

Nor is it reasonable for policy-makers to consider all methodologies and all theoretical approaches when deciding on a policy measure. Policy-makers usually do not have the luxury of time to consider all the methodological options. Further, it is a tall order for anyone to simultaneously retain several different conceptualisations of reality, uses of language, and so on. Just as an academic economist belongs to a particular community within which there is a shared conceptualisation of the economy, use of language and so on in order to function, the same applies to policy-makers. Kuhn (1970) argued that normal science within paradigms is the process by which science progresses. This implies that policy-makers need to first of all decide on a particular understanding of the nature of the economic process, and only then on the methodology and theoretical approach which follows. This is how schools of thought within economics are defined. The decision then is taken at the level of ontology. Looking only at the level of theory, there is no clear basis on which to choose one theory over another.

But policy-makers face more immediate questions than academic economists about the congruity of theory with reality. The closure involved in defining paradigms for Kuhn was a provisional and partial closure. At the same time as most economists are engaged in normal science, some are engaged in extraordinary science, examining the ontological and epistemological foundations of the ruling paradigm. What sparks off attention to this activity, and potentially a scientific revolution, is the growing perception of a disjunction between the dominant paradigm and reality. The classic case in economics is the Great Depression, which challenged a ruling paradigm which did not address unemployment. Since the real world evolves, new problems emerge to which the ruling paradigm may not be best suited. Policy-makers need to be more alert than most to the possibility that their chosen paradigm no longer addresses the problems they now face. More than academic economists, therefore, policy-makers need to be aware of a range of paradigms and be ready to either adapt or shift paradigm if the nature of the real problems they face changes.

From this point of view, therefore, pluralism is helpful to the policy-maker. Since the real world, and thus the nature of the problems policy-makers face, changes over time, a single approach would be seriously inadequate. It is only if the real world retains its essential characteristics and these can be understood to operate within a closed system that one (closed-system) approach could be judged to be appropriate. If the real world is understood as an open system, therefore, pluralism is to be welcomed rather than thought of as a problem. The crucial point is to recognise the origins of theoretical approaches in methodological approaches and ultimately in conceptions of reality.

At the level of method, too, pluralism can be seen to be helpful to the policy-maker. A monist methodological approach involves one method, as in mathematical formalism (the method best suited in economics to a closed-system approach). An open system approach sees no one method as being sufficient and therefore advocates recourse to a range of methods. Knowledge can then be built up by approaching an issue from a variety of directions, employing different methods. By definition these methods are incommensurate (or they could be collapsed into one method). Thus for example questionnaire evidence is of a different sort than historical time-series evidence; they can't be put together in any formal way, but each does provide some knowledge. Different collections of methods will be suited to different methodological approaches.

Pluralism thus is helpful for policy-makers in addressing a changing economic system where there are different types of knowledge about it. But, while more helpful than a monist approach in dealing with reality understood as an open system, it poses particular challenges. The key challenge is in choosing a paradigm, deciding when it no longer addresses real problems as they emerge, and considering whether adapting the paradigm is sufficient, or whether a switch of paradigm is required. Since policy-makers operate within a political arena, too, there will be criticism from the perspective of other paradigms, so that there needs to be a continual awareness of how thought is progressing in other paradigms. The second challenge lies in putting knowledge together within the chosen paradigm. Different methods of building knowledge may appear to cut across each other for example. If there are underlying causal mechanisms, which we cannot directly access, but which themselves can cut across each other, then it is inevitable that empirical knowledge of different sorts will be confusing.

The faculty which policy-makers require to deal with these challenges is judgement. Rationality in the rational economic man sense is insufficient, since that requires information held with certainty and thus a closed system (all relevant variables known and so on). Judgement rather is the exercise of practical reason or as in the Keynesian literature, human logic or ordinary logic (see Mizuhara and Runde, 2003). This is the exercise of reason under uncertainty, where rational belief is built on a combination of direct knowledge, on the one hand, and on indirect, theoretical knowledge which draws on imagination and convention as well as reason, on the other hand. Monetary policy literature poses the issue of choice among a plurality of theories as 'model uncertainty'. By posing the issue in formalist (monist) terms, this literature seeks a formal solution. But Keynesian uncertainty, expressed in open-systems terms, indicates the need for practical reason which draws on a range of methods in order to arrive at an (uncertain) conclusion (Dow, 2004b). This implies that skills in judgement, for example in the exercise of practical reason, are essential for effective decision-making. We turn in the next section to considering what this implies for economics education.

2.6   PLURALISM AND EDUCATION

Economics education has increasingly become dominated by the monist methodology of mathematical formalism. Training has focused increasingly on building up technical expertise in formal modelling and empirical testing. This is most noticeable at the graduate level, and has been documented in various studies, notably Colander and Klamer's (1987) survey of graduate students and Krueger et al.'s (1991) study commissioned by the American Economic Association. This trend is an affirmation of the methodological preference for mathematical formalism, which students implicitly absorb and then tend to perpetuate. In addition, time being a scarce resource, the increase in attention to training in mathematical formalism squeezes out training in other skills and sources of knowledge, so that students are provided with less equipment with which either to assess the relative merits of mathematical formalism or to adopt an alternative methodology. But the surveys noted above reveal that students themselves are aware of the disjunction between theory and real world experience.

The first requirement, then, is that economics education include instruction on methodology, to increase awareness of what is involved in methodological choice. Students, like policy-makers, may still opt for mathematical formalism. But no methodology can be said to have the best (or indeed any) claim to truth, so that choice in favour of one approach requires awareness of the opportunity cost involved in rejecting other approaches. In fact, from a pluralist standpoint, methodological awareness is essential if policy-makers are to be able to respond to a changing real environment, assessing how far their chosen methodology is still preferable.

At what stage of an economics degree programme methodological instruction occurs is a matter for debate. The educational approach adopted in higher education during the Scottish Enlightenment, and continuing thereafter, was to teach all subjects historically, so that an awareness of knowledge systems developing and changing in the light of what was needed in order to address practical problems developed naturally. Further, early instruction in moral philosophy provided a grounding in epistemology. Ideally, I would suggest, methodological awareness should be developed in students naturally as a by-product of how economics is taught, drawing on a foundational level of education in philosophy and a historical approach.

The historical approach has particular importance for economics. As an open social system, any economy evolves over time, requiring theory and possibly methodology to change with it. Economic history and the history of economic thought provide an array of case studies by which to learn how, in new situations to arise in the future, theory might adapt to suit changing circumstances. For the monist mathematical formalist, economic history simply extends the data set for testing timeless theory. But by studying different cases of theory development and the building up of knowledge more generally, students can learn to develop their own judgement. In the process students also learn about a range of methods of acquiring knowledge other than published data sets.

The type of educational approach suggested here would ideally be general to all subjects. If all subjects were taught historically, with the knowledge that all students were trained in philosophy, then the question of drawing across disciplines for different types of knowledge would follow naturally. The increasing professionalization of academic fields puts up barriers to communication across fields. Within the social sciences, economics in addition puts up barriers by treating the economy as a closed system and thus, as we have seen, economics as a closed system of knowledge. Yet, if the economy is understood as an open system, then it follows naturally that economists would, as part of their pluralist approach, look to other disciplines for additional sources of knowledge about the economy.

Thus, while ideally a radical restructuring of modern education would seem to be called for, there is much that could be achieved in the meantime within the economics curriculum itself. But it has got to the stage that a pro-active effort is required to achieve this. Until recently, economics was taught by instructors who may well have adopted the methodology of mathematical formalism, but nevertheless had been educated much more broadly themselves. The teaching staff increasingly now have themselves mostly come through mathematical formalist programmes.

Many economics programmes are in fact much broader than a pure form of mathematical formalism. Many academic economists are applied economists who themselves have to grapple with the disjunction between formalist theory and reality. Students learn much from them about the exercise of judgement. But as long as the official discourse is that of mathematical formalism, and signals are given to students that technical skill is more important than methodological awareness, educational opportunities are being missed. Further the official rhetoric carries forward into policy-making circles, influencing how analysis is presented and understood, inhibiting the practice of pluralism.

2.7   CONCLUSION

We have considered theoretical pluralism as a problem faced by policy-makers, and concluded that it may in fact be something to be welcomed. To pursue this question further, it was necessary to put theoretical pluralism in the context of the methodologies within which the theories were developed, and the understanding of the nature of the reality being studied. In particular, it was argued that pure pluralism (an infinite plurality) is unworkable. When we talk of a workable pluralism, we are talking of a structured form, whereby there is a limited range of approaches, each approach is conditioned by the underlying understanding of the nature of the economy, and each approach is therefore open to change.

If the real world is understood as a closed system, then it follows that one best way of identifying the laws which govern that system can be identified. This monist methodology provides the criteria by which the policy-maker can choose the best theory.

However if the real world is understood as an open system which evolves internally as well as in its external relations, then no one best way of theorizing about it can be established; the logical consequence is methodological pluralism. It is then welcome to have a range of approaches available for the policy-maker to choose among. But it is also therefore important for policy-makers to be methodologically aware. This does not mean that they should constantly actively function simultaneously within the different paradigms. Rather it means that there should be awareness of the limitations of any one approach, awareness of the nature of alternatives, and sensitivity to the point at which the chosen methodology and theories no longer shed light on a changing reality. Progress in knowledge (by some criteria) requires adoption of one or other paradigm, even if the eventual outcome is to change to another one or create a new one. Further, just as the partial, provisional closure of paradigms facilitates the building up of knowledge, theorizing itself requires some closure of a partial and provisional sort to be useful. But it is this modified form of closure, rather than the fixed application of the *ceteris paribus* clause which allows theory to be applied to a reality where *ceteris paribus* does not in general hold, and certainly not in any fixed way.

We then discussed the implications for economics education of this embracing by policy-makers of pluralism. Technical skill has come to dominate economics education, particularly at the graduate level, at the expense of education in other skills. Of primary importance is the teaching of methodological awareness. This need not take the form of separate specialist courses. Indeed it is all the more effective for economics to be taught in such a way that methodological awareness is absorbed naturally. This would follow from a historical approach to teaching which encourages the idea that economic theories and evidence may change to suit the practical requirements of different contexts, and that different economists may quite legitimately offer different accounts of the same circumstances, and different policy solutions. By studying the development of theories to address particular contexts and the application of different methods, students will build up the skill of judgement which is central to the role of the policy-maker.

To conclude, if there has been a single theme in the chapter it has been the following: far from being a source of weakness, the kind of modified pluralism presented here (with partial, provisional closures) is a source of strength. To exploit this strength requires an openness of mind to the different possibilities for economic analysis and training beyond the technical skills of mathematical formalism.

NOTES

[1] See Salanti and Screpanti (1997) for a diversity of treatments on the subject of pluralism.
[2] See in particular Mäki's (1997).
[3] We are referring here to the modern use of the criterion rather than Robbins's (1932) original exposition.
[4] For McCloskey (1983), a monist mathematical formalism provides the framework for the official rhetoric of economics, while a more pluralist approach characterises the unofficial rhetoric.
[5] Two characteristics which reveal closed-system thinking are the tendency to derive policy conclusions directly from a model (with simplifying assumptions) without explicit justification, and also the reference to theory testing; see Lawson (1997) for a detailed critique of the use of econometrics for testing theory.
[6] The International Confederation of Associations for Pluralism in Economics, and the Association of Heterodox Economists, respectively.

REFERENCES

Becker, G.S. (1991), *The Economics of the Family*, Cambridge, MA: Harvard University Press.
Bhaskar, R. (1975), *A Realist Theory of Science*, Leeds: Leeds Books.
Blanchard, O. and I. Fischer (1989), *Lectures in Macroeconomics*, Cambridge, MA: MIT Press.
Blaug, M. (1980), *The Methodology of Economics: Or How Economists Explain*, Cambridge: Cambridge University Press.
Blaug, M. (1999), 'The Formalist Revolution or What has Happened to Orthodox Economics after World War II', in R.E. Backhouse and J. Creedy (eds), *From Classical Economics to the Theory of the Firm: Essays in Honour of D.P. O'Brien*, Cheltenham, UK and Northampton, MA, USA: Edward Elgar, pp. 257-80.
Chick, V. and S.C. Dow (2001), 'Formalism, Logic and Reality: A Keynesian Analysis', *Cambridge Journal of Economics*, **25**(6), 705-22.
Colander, D. and A. Klamer (1987), 'The Making of an Economist', *Journal of Economic Perspectives*, **1**, 95-113.
Dow, S.C. (1996), *The Methodology of Macroeconomic Thought: A Methodological Approach*, Cheltenham, UK and Brookfield, USA: Edward Elgar.
Dow, S.C. (2002), 'Historical Reference: Hume and Critical Realism', *Cambridge Journal of Economics*, **26**(6), 683-96.
Dow, S.C. (2004a) 'Structured Pluralism', *Journal of EconomicMethodology*, **11** (3): 275-90.

Dow, S.C. (2004b), 'Uncertainty and Monetary Policy', Oxford Economic Papers, **56**: 539-61.

Goodhart, C.A.E. (1999), 'Central Bankers and Uncertainty', *Bank of England Quarterly Bulletin*, February, 102-16.

Hahn, F.H. (1973), *On the Notion of Equilibrium in Economics*, Cambridge: Cambridge University Press.

Hawkins, P. (2003), *The Open Economy and its Financial Constraints*, Cheltenham: Edward Elgar.

Krueger, A.O. et al. (1991), 'Report of the Commission on Graduate Education in Economics', *Journal of Economic Literature*, **29**, 1035-53.

Kuhn, T.S. (1970), 'Reflections on my Critics', in I. Lakatos and A. Musgrave (eds), *Criticism and the Growth of Knowledge*, Cambridge: Cambridge University Press.

Lawson, T. (1997), *Economics and Reality*, London: Routledge.

Loasby, B.J. (2003), 'Closed Models and Open Systems', *Journal of Economic Methodology*, **10**(3), 285-306.

Mäki, U. (1997) 'The One World and the Many Theories', in Salanti and Screpanti (eds).

McCloskey, D.N. (1983), 'The Rhetoric of Economics', *Journal of Economic Literature*, **21**, 434-61.

Mearman, A. (2005), 'Sheila Dow's concept of dualism: clarification, criticism and development', *Cambridge Journal of Economics*, **29**, 619-34.

Mirowski, P. (1989), *More Heat then Light: Economics as Social Physics. Physics as Nature's Economics*, Cambridge: Cambridge University Press.

Mizuhara, S. and Runde, J. (2003), *The Philosophy of Keynes's Economics: Probability, Uncertainty and Convention*, London: Routledge.

Phelps, E.S. (1990), *Seven Schools of Macroeconomic Thought*, Oxford: Oxford University Press.

Robbins, L. (1932), *An Essay on the Nature and Significance of Economic Science*, London: Macmillan.

Salanti, A. and E. Screpanti (eds) (1997), *Pluralism in Economics*, Cheltenham, UK and Lyme, USA: Edward Elgar.

3. Pluralism in Economics: A Public Good or a Public Bad?

Hendrik P. van Dalen

> John, I can't make a damn thing out of this tax problem. I listen to one side and they seem right, and then – God! – I talk to the other side, and they seem just as right. I know somewhere there is a book, that will give me the truth, but hell, I couldn't read the book. I know somewhere there is an economist who knows the truth, but I don't know where to find him and haven't the sense to know and trust him when I find him. God, what a job!
> (Warren G. Harding, US president (1920-1924) in a conversation with his assistant, cited in Morison, 1965: 920)

3.1 INTRODUCTION

Economists are often portrayed as a quarrelsome lot. Paul Krugman (1994) stamps his feet about the stupidity of 'madmen in authority' like Laura Tyson and Robert Reich; Joe Stiglitz (2002) denounces the 'one-size-fits-all' attitude of IMF-advisers in East Asia, Latin America and Russia; and Ronald Coase (1998: 577) also acknowledges, as a sadder and wiser sage, that 'I find it difficult to ignore the role of stupidity in human affairs.' Policy-makers, in turn, who want to have sound economic advice, throw their hands in the air, despairing the inconclusiveness of the state of economic knowledge. President Harding had a hard time figuring out who knew the truth among his economic advisers and many a president today would mumble the same words. Why can't these economists decide what is the right thing to do? Surely, there must be some theory that survives all tests imaginable. The problem that outsiders, and even some insiders, are confronted with when they enter a conversation in economics is the idea of pluralism: the fact that there are many organizing principles about one and the same phenomenon. And pluralism magnifies the decision problem, not only does one need to deal with theoretically derived trade-offs, but who is going to tell the difference between one theory and another? It would be most convenient if theories had to pass some Darwinian acid test, so in the end there would only be one superior theory. Alas, that is not the way the world works.

Nowadays the number of theories, methodologies and specializations is almost without bound. The editors of the *Journal of Economic Literature* (*JEL*) have to think of new *JEL* codes for new categories each year. The big issue is: is the pluralist state of economics good or bad? Without giving the entire content of the chapter away I will evaluate the pros and cons of pluralism for economics, with the eye of an academic and that of a policy-maker. By and large, a pluralist approach is a beneficial state of affairs as long as different strands of thought are connected. This connection refers to both schools of thought within a science (pluralism) and between sciences (interdisciplinarity). To establish a connection the maxim 'Don't specialize without intellectual trade' is the most simple but effective guideline one can think of in situations of diversity. In that respect, things look brighter than they did some twenty or thirty years ago. The present state of economics impresses me as a state of diversity with a common language binding the different strands of economics, the common language being good old 'price theory'. In the 'ordinary business of life' present-day economists make use of stories in which ideas like externalities, transaction costs, asymmetric information, fairness and reciprocity abound. The world of general equilibrium, modelled so neatly in the work of Arrow and Debreu, is slowly but gradually moving into the background as more and more economists realize that talking about real life economies is a very tough assignment if you are not going to deal with problems of information, knowledge creation and institutions, elements which in the end make economies 'tick'. Thanks to the efforts of 'giants' like Ronald Coase, Douglass North and Oliver Williamson on whose shoulders we stand, the horizon of economists has widened and their efforts reveal that with simple price theory you can transcend the narrowly defined resource allocation questions that general equilibrium theory poses, and you can move on to understand a wider class of phenomena.

After a short evaluation of the pros and cons of pluralism (in sections 3.2 and 3.3) the next question is how to educate future academics, policy-makers and advisers to deal with a pluralist economic science. Are the standard economics textbooks well suited to deal with the present state of economics or is an entirely new type of text or approach necessary? I venture that these two options are both necessary: keep the core of economics, but improve the way students learn and practise economics. Even though I have no special affinity with the finer points of pedagogy, the present state of economics and the diversity of methodologies employed offer in my opinion a rich menu of stories to improve the present day 'chalk-and-talk' teachings of economics.

3.2 IS PLURALISM A PUBLIC GOOD? AN ACADEMIC ECONOMIST'S PERSPECTIVE

Why do we need N theories about business cycles? Why couldn't we be satisfied with just $N-1$ theories? Or let's act the naive optimist, why not decide on one theory being the best? Although there are a number of definitions of pluralism this essential dilemma will be my point of departure. Pluralism is all about the multiplicity of organizing principles (Dow, 2001) or to put it slightly differently, it revolves around different theories about one and the same phenomenon. Now one may well ask whether society at large, and not only the society of scientists – benefits from such pluralist sciences. Why pay for all these engineers with white collars when all they produce is brooha? In other words, is the diversity of theories or organizing principles a beneficial character trait of science?

3.2.1 Competition

The easy way out of this question is to murmur the cliché 'it depends'. It depends on what you mean by pluralism. If by pluralism is meant the idea that two people talk about exactly the same phenomenon but the two use different concepts in dealing with their subject and as a result of this 'language problem' or semantics cannot exchange ideas, then obviously pluralism is 'bad'. So far I am not talking about substance, only about exchange and competition. Part of the idea of academia is that each and every participant engages in the ongoing conversation in the community of academics and when this is prevented by a language problem the academic ideal of 'community' is smothered. But there is more to this problem, because when each participant restricts his attention to his own set of rules and talks to himself in the safe surroundings of his room there can be no competition. Even worse, there is also no check on the validity of opinions uttered, as scientists are not only producers and demanders, they are also gatekeepers of the academic conversation. Under such Babylonian circumstances pluralism is tantamount to excessive duplication.

    The trouble starts, of course, when you *do* start to think about the substance of ideas. Who has the arrogance or knowledge to deem one theory better than another? In all honesty, no one possesses such knowledge although it is part of the game to advertise with the arrogance of young Turks that you do know. As Robert Lucas once told graduates on their first day in 'grad school': 'We here at Chicago believe that what we do matters and is more important than events in Washington (cited in Klamer and Colander, 1990: 129). Schools of thought have a function as they make clear that they differ and in order to differ each and every graduate student learns to utter the words of professor X or Z. Of course, what you end up with can be a pluralistic approach to the subject in which everyone seems to be inventing the wheel in an imperfect manner, or in which each and every school seems to be in conversation, but in actual fact the only thing they share is an agreement to disagree. The capital debate between the two Cambridges in the 1960s, lingering on in the 1970s, was perhaps the ultimate example of what Solow (1971: 10) called a 'violent, unproductive, and confused controversy', that nevertheless filled the journals of that time.

The key to making pluralism work is the actual exchange of ideas. As McCloskey (2000: 149) cries out loud: don't specialize without intellectual trade! The exchange of ideas is by definition a social phenomenon and this fact impinges directly on questions of theory choice and development in science. And although the noun 'choice' suggests that the neoclassical view is most suited to give an answer to questions of 'theory choice', neoclassical theory remains largely silent on this subject. The reason for this can be traced to the absence of transaction costs in the seamless world of neoclassical theory. The invisible hand of truth would direct us in the right direction. Of course, the question remains whether the metaphor of the invisible hand is an aptly chosen one. Can the market for ideas be mimicked by the world of Arrow and Debreu? I dare say it cannot and the reason why can perhaps best be phrased by citing Coase who criticizes neoclassical economics:

> Exchange takes place without any specification of its institutional setting. We have consumers without humanity, firms without organization, and even exchange without markets. (1988: 3)

And the same applies to science: we have science without conversation. Trading involves costs and the same applies to economic science; at certain moments in time economists have gone too far in their specialization drive, even reaching the point of adverse specialization. The way we model science or research is essentially an intellectual exchange of ideas without talk or a 'conversation'. The 'invisible hand' view of science revolves very much around deriving rational choices of individual optimizers and aggregate states of the economy that satisfy some (aggregate) consistency condition. Perhaps this approach may yield a few extra credit points in the tenure system, but it does not adequately capture what's going on in science. Science is about social interaction and choice, and this 'fact' implies that apersonal models of choice will not do. An economist who throughout his career has paid close attention to social interaction is Thomas Schelling (1978). His claim is that the equilibrium analysis of markets is a large and important special case: 'Equilibrium is simply a result. It is what is there after something has settled down, if something ever does settle down' (1978: 26). To understand all social phenomena with this simple model would therefore be something of a miracle and Schelling makes the point that interactive behaviour − 'What people do affects what other people do' (p. 27) − is the key to understanding truly social behaviour. Micromotives induce macrobehaviour. Gradually this point has been catching on and is nowadays known as the complexity approach to economics (see Arthur et al., 1997; and Durlauf, 2001), an approach which stresses the interaction among individuals and tries to incorporate empirical insights from sociology, economics and anthropology. Interaction based theories are, however, not sufficient to understand science, one also has to explain how institutions − the rules by which the game of science is played − come about and change. In that respect, one can learn a lot from what sociologists of science teach us and slowly but surely one can say the same about the economists of science, who are making worthwhile contributions (see for overviews Sent, 1999; Gans, 2000; and Klamer and van Dalen, 2002).

3.2.2 Specialization

One of the institutions that helps scientists cope with the problem of exchange is the clustering in groups and discursive entities (Klamer and van Dalen, 2002). Scientists cluster in universities, set up barriers to entry, organize professional associations in order to organize conferences and issue journals, constitute schools, subscribe to research programmes, develop specialized research communities which will organize specialized conferences and issue specialized journals, and form networks of like-minded souls. The reason clustering is such an often sought strategy can be traced to economies of scale and scope but when it comes down to issues of communication these reasons offer no firm grounds and other avenues have to be searched. A well-known theorem in signalling is that communication is optimal when sender and receiver have an identical 'make-up'. It helps explain why innovations in science are geographically localized and not evenly dispersed throughout the world, and it also helps explain why professors of economics departments try to select staff who they can talk to. In order to make an intense conversation possible face-to-face communication with like-minded colleagues appears to be essential. The

University of Chicago is perhaps one of the most outstanding examples in economics (van Dalen, 1999) but the importance of geographic proximity runs throughout the history of other sciences as well (Zuckerman, 1977).

But, of course, science is no different from other areas of society and many of the benefits flow from the structure of science. Is science a close-knit society or is every man and every cluster an island? The model in which we learn from others and conform to opinions of neighbouring colleagues or neighbouring disciplines is clearly a realistic one as the oeuvre of the bibliometrician Eugene Garfield (1998) shows when he models the entire world of science as a chain-like system. The basic feature of these models of learning is that people learn not only from their own experience, but as most experiments are time consuming people also learn from the experience of their peers. The central insight of the learning literature is that the interaction structure of individuals or groups of individuals matters a lot (see Bala and Goyal, 1998). The 'learning from neighbours' models is not only a plausible model at the micro-level, it is particularly powerful in its explanatory power at the macro-level. For instance, in theory it does not take much effort to start an informational cascade when individuals learn by observing others (Bikhchandani et al., 1998). The role of opinion leaders or leading journals is critical in bringing about fads and conformity. It is in this respect that the 'Matthew effect' in science (Merton, 1968) becomes dysfunctional if the ideas that are accepted are not entirely foolproof. Under such circumstances one can arrive at the case that behaviour of a star, let's say Robert Barro running numerous economic growth regressions, is imitated because Barro makes it legitimate to do such simplistic research (and perhaps because it is so simplistic, it is easy and inexpensive to copy such behaviour).

There are two responses possible in putting fad-prone scientists in perspective, a theoretical and an empirical one. The theoretical answer can be found in some detail in Brock and Durlauf (1999) who claim that the role of social factors in science is far more complex than is often recognized. They demonstrate that, under some plausible interaction conditions, social factors may not hinder the development of science but increase the degree of consensus around a superior idea. This finding may seem counterintuitive, but it makes perfect sense. Once the consensus of the community focuses its attention on the superior theory, this consensus will speed up its rapid acceptance. Of course, one can still claim that judging theories to be superior to others – a key assumption made by Brock and Durlauf – is a questionable assumption and a speedy convergence to only one theory may just as well be seen as a bad thing.

The diversity of science which is central in Callon's (1994) argument for defending science as a public good becomes a relevant issue at this point.

Diversity circumvents science, and in the end also society, from becoming stale or as Callon puts it: 'without this source of diversity, the market – with its natural propensity to transform science into a commodity – would be ever doomed to convergence and irreversibility' (p. 418). What Callon does not deal with is the question of the optimal amount of diversity. Diversity as such is no great quality if each and every scientist has a different idea and operates as a lone wolf. Perhaps one of the reasons European economics departments until quite recently have been such a stale territory for economists may be pin-pointed to this quality of 'isolated' diversity (see Coats, 2000). A complete consensus of opinion (which is behind the worry about 'Americanization' of science) may also not be wholesome as it would destroy original insights outside the false state of consensus.

The empirical response to the possibility of fads and ending up in a 'bad' state is that the evidence is mostly anecdotal and is not thoroughly scrutinized. *A priori* one would expect this reputation effect in bringing about cascades to reflect the property of increasing returns to the scale of an individual's reputation. The higher the reputation, the easier it becomes to bring about fads. In examining the elements which might make a scientific research article influential, van Dalen and Henkens (2005) show that the characteristics of a journal (the reputation of the journal and its editors) overwhelms the reputation of an individual in getting ideas accepted. So the reputation of journals outranks by far the reputation of the author, a message that also comes across in a refined network-analysis by Baldi (1998) who demonstrates that the reputation of the author of an article does not affect the reception of published ideas, whereas writing in a widely disseminated journal generates a distinct attention bonus.

3.2.3 Creativity

Science does not revolve solely about being connected and competing for the applause of peers, it is of course also about the ability to innovate. And in understanding science one simply has to deal with the aspect of creativity. The equilibrium approach surely has its merits but in matters of creativity the tacit 'principle of plenitude' ('every conceivable entity already exists'; see for a discussion Romer, 1994) becomes a straitjacket in thinking about science. One could arrive at the rather bold conclusion of the head of the patent office who recommended at the turn of the nineteenth century to abolish the patent system because everything had already been invented.

Triggering new ideas

The key to creativity is the ability to play with a subject, by some termed as 'blue sky' research (Portes, 1997). The more original work is the work that dares to move outside the boundaries of economics and invades the turf of political science, public administration, sociology, anthropology and psychology. By demonstrating that your theory also applies outside the 'sample', you have shown to have mastered your subject and as a by-product you make ideas or at least you make other people think again. This is the way to proceed when talking about interdisciplinary research. Interdisciplinarity is a difficult principle and much lip service is paid to supporting such research, but the efforts by research foundations and 'think tanks' in supporting interdisciplinary research reflect the efforts of a man bringing a horse to water, without being able to make it drink. Interdisciplinary research or policy groups are often a bunch of people put together in the hope that diversity will spontaneously spark creativity. Of course, this is bound to fail and in fact most of the time scientists from different stripes of life that are living under the same roof are essentially ships that pass each other in the night. To give researchers the chance to play their role as specialist, as well as enable them to exploit their comparative advantage, they need to connect. So they too are in need of a standard language or some common ground, sharing basic propositions or puzzles. It's no good for economists to try to mimic sociologists or anthropologists in their use of methods (and the reverse applies also to sociologists who try to mimic economists). However, it is a good thing to surpass the existing boundaries. By acting the imperialist, the conversation may flourish and make an intellectual exchange possible, even though languages may diverge. To give a recent example of such a beneficial conversation, Akerlof and Kranton (2002) started to re-explore the economics of education by focusing on the role identity can play in schools, and along the way they incorporated elements of sociology, psychology and anthropology. However, this meeting of different minds poses a language problem which can be resolved by plain pedestrian prose but it can also be resolved by such trespassers or intermediaries in science as Akerlof, Schelling and Hirschman.

Facing the real world

But there is a different source of creativity and that is the world outside your window. The inspiration should be to look outside and try to make sense of what's going on in the real world. Economics has on that count been too much inwardly directed, too much in search of questions posed by its own models. In that respect economics can take a more realist turn by moving inside the 'pin factory' and trying to understand the management and technology of work, production and exchange. Of course, the true historian would say that there is nothing new under the sun. Ronald Coase visited American plants in the 1930s, he studied the monopoly case of the BBC and the FCC in the 1950s; Alfred Chandler tried to make sense of American entrepreneurs; Joe Stiglitz found inspiration for his work on moral hazard in the case of sharecropping in India, and his years at the CEA and the World Bank were also an inspiration to attack the governance structure of globalization; and recently we have seen initiatives by people like Truman Bewley (1999), Ed Lazear (2000a), and Alan Blinder et al. (1998) on American business life, Diego Gambetta (1993) about the Sicilian Mafia, William Easterly (2001) about the reality of development economics, James Wilson (1989) about the inner workings of bureaucracy, and my own work together with Arjo Klamer (van Dalen and Klamer, 1996, 1997) in discovering what makes economists tick, in science and in bureaucracies. Without intending to be offensive, economists should perhaps learn some investigative journalism: to note, watch and detect what's going on in the real world. There are excellent examples of this research methodology: George Lowenstein (2001) about the rise and fall of the Long-Term Capital Management group, and Dava Sobel (1996) about the priority race in discovering the instrument to measure longitude. In reviewing endogenous growth theory Robert Solow suggested that 'it would be a good idea for economists who are interested in endogenous technology and growth theory to do a little observational work on industrial research laboratories' (cited in Clement, 2002). One reason why this has not been done very much is that 'the kind of person who's good at observing things like this is not necessarily the kind of person who's good at making models'. I will return to this failure later on.

The same realist attitude would also serve the methodology side of economics well. Methodologists are often given the evil eye by practitioners. Irving Fisher could not suppress his disdain for methodologists in his presidential address to the American Statistical Association when he said: 'I have usually felt that the man who essays to tell the rest of us how to solve knotty problems would be more convincing if first he proved out his alleged method by solving a few himself. Apparently those would-be authorities who are telling others how to get results do not get any important results themselves.' (Fisher, 1933, p. 1) In the age of Irving Fisher, Milton Friedman and Paul Samuelson, the economist and the methodologist was one and the same person. But with the ongoing specialization and professionalization in economics (and every other science for that matter), methodologists and economists have drifted apart. Methodologists expound in a jargon that seems to be almost incomprehensible for the ordinary practitioner. In that respect, there is also a lesson to learn here as I think that methodologists shouldn't drift too far away from their intended audience: economists. And I think the best methodologists of today, like Mark Blaug, Kevin Hoover and Deirdre McCloskey, have their roots in economics and are credible and informative in conversation. The rhetoric of economics (McCloskey, 1983) is indeed Reality Economics of a different kind, namely Reality Methodology, but one economists cannot do without. Linking the actual practice of how economists talk and persuade, and pinpointing the pitfalls of that practice may one of the biggest contributions a methodologist can make. Because it is human to err, having professional gatekeepers – methodologists who know how knotty problems can be – is part of the institution called 'academia'. The market for ideas can only function properly with the appropriate checks and balances, and having arbitrators (read: methodologists) who can communicate with the suppliers of ideas is an essential ingredient in the functioning of this particular market.

3.3 IS PLURALISM A PUBLIC GOOD? – A POLICY MAKER'S PERSPECTIVE

Still, academic economists expect policy-makers to make their decisions based on the best available information, information that the academics themselves provide. Obviously, if you think pluralism is beneficial in the ivory tower, it surely must be in the 'emergency room' in Washington DC, Whitehall or even in The Hague. You cannot afford to make large mistakes in matters of national or international welfare. So the initial answer to the question 'Is pluralism a public good?' is 'yes'. Stimulating competition in the market for policy ideas is a necessity. The real world is far too complex to be trusted to one gigantic (monopolist) adviser with only one *Weltanschauung.*

Still, policy-makers are generally economists who were trained in an era in which it was preached that economics is *Wertfrei*, advice should preferably be given by committees or task forces of 'wise men' and politics should be left to politicians. And just like Warren Harding the thought that crosses the mind about economic advisers is still: 'I know somewhere there is an economist who knows the truth.' This model of economic advice has a certain 'Jim 'll-fix-it' ring to it, the fairytale figure of the benign philosopher-king who knows all and fixes all. Needless to say, this model of policy-making denies the existence of pluralism and if it ever has worked it has only worked by sheer luck. So the first thing that has to be taught is that pluralism exists and that economic policy-making under such circumstances differs markedly from the traditional infinitely lived social planner's model. Given the present-day desire among policy-makers for 'road maps', 'blueprints' and 'action plans', bringing this subtle message across will be hard enough.

But let's suppose that policy-makers have survived the shock that economists don't know the truth, what's to be done next? Policy-makers everywhere are pragmatic; they need simple rules because in the end they also have to convince their principal, ministers and their ultimate principal: Everyman. At this point the world of academia should carry some responsibility in making economics an asset. But the largest part of the responsibility should rest on the applied economist. What we sometimes forget is that every theory can and ought to be simple. Frank Knight used to say that economics is so simple he was surprised why not everybody is a great economist. And of course, if you ask many a highbrow economist about their key contributions it always seems to be the case that their theorems turn out to be simple maxims. But economics has become so specialized and technical that it is virtually impossible to cover all territories as an economist. The need for being a Renaissance economist is not necessary as long as the key message is brought across in plain English. The responsibility for a proper functioning of the market of ideas should rest to some degree with the suppliers of ideas.

But, as mentioned earlier, the largest part of the responsibility should rest with the users of ideas. The trick with policy work is not so much about reciting the entire *Palgrave Dictionary* by heart, it is having a keen eye for what's relevant, and the gift to apply ideas is perhaps just as scarce a commodity as the gift to produce novel ideas. One can linger on at length about this key ingredient and try to devise 'blueprints' but in the end putting theory into action is a tacit skill. As Sutton (2000) points out there is more to observing reality than the idea that it is the representation of a true equilibrium model plus some 'random noise', or what he calls 'Marshallian tendencies'.

Alfred Marshall used the metaphor of tides in expounding his view on economics, apparently with some authority as most economists of the twentieth century were (and still are) persuaded by this image. Tides are influenced by two forces: the gravitational pull of the moon and the sun, which can be predicted rather accurately, and by meteorological forces which are inherently difficult to predict. Luckily the primary forces – the gravitational forces – are far more important and by focusing on their own 'primary forces' economists can still arrive at a theory that works satisfactorily, although subject to some error. Marshall was aware of the limitations of economic science and asserted that economists can only capture tendencies, as economic laws are bound to be less precise than for example the laws of physics. In that respect we should not be surprised to see that the standard paradigm in economics does work in some places (auctions, option pricing) but, as economists with a reflective bent have discovered, it does not work in most places. Real business cycle theorists are, in that respect, betting on the wrong horse. What's more, policy-makers do not need – to mix up some phrases of Ronald Coase and Deirdre McCloskey – 'social blackboard engineering': social engineers who look at the economy as a mechanism with the eye of a pure mathematician. The last thing a policy maker needs is a logical but senseless policy, or at least a policy that does not take account of the fine intricacies of real life economic transactions. The end result of such a 'one size fits all' attitude is havoc, or at least badly designed policies based on badly informed policy advice. The number of 'reasonable' models is simply infinite and making a choice between models has to be supplemented by a skill or tacit knowledge which Keynes once summed up neatly in correspondence with Roy Harrod: 'Economics is a science of thinking in terms of models joined with the art of choosing models which are relevant to the contemporary world.' (4 July 1938, see Moggridge, 1973, p. 296)

Yes, but ...
So pluralism is also needed in policy circles, but this time there is an extra proviso to be made, as there is more at stake in applying ideas than there is in producing ideas. If someone publishes an article on an esoteric subject, which by chance will never trickle down to an audience with a good set of brains, no harm is done. But what if ideas are abused for political reasons or vested interests? Poverty amidst plenty, fraud, rent-seeking, starvation, crime – you name it, economists can deliver it if their advice is not well applied or delivered. The application of economics to economies in transition in Eastern Europe and Russia is a case in point. And at this point I would even suggest, just like Ronald Coase (1974), that government involvement in regulating the market for ideas has to be far larger than regulating the market for, let's say, cars or petrol. There are essentially two reasons why a multiplicity of views in matters of policy is necessary (and perhaps much of what I bring forward applies equally to the world of academics) and needs to be 'regulated': one is to prevent folly in a dogmatic policy environment and the other boils down to safeguarding diversity in the social sciences. The first reason is about designing institutions for policy debates that minimize blunders in decision-making, the other is about designing institutions that stimulate a biodiversity of views.

- *Institutions for minimizing 'Marches of Folly'*. Knowledge is not merely information, it is also interpretation. As a consequence of this simple observation pluralism is going to be a natural state, unless dogmatism rules; in other words the 'madmen in authority' only allow one view and one interpretation. This is an extremely dangerous development that is akin to situations one would expect in command economies. But as numerous policy watchers have observed in the recent past the 'Washington Consensus' has dominated every policy debate not only in Washington, but perhaps in every OECD country. From time to time, free societies seem equally likely to create circumstances or institutions that produce dogmatism. Interpretation of 'facts' and information is no longer free and is being governed by rules and preconceptions. The consequences of such an intellectual deadlock can be seen in *The March of Folly* (1984), the book by historian Barbara Tuchman, which describes how governments pursue policies contrary to their own interests, despite the availability of feasible alternatives. To have an open and imaginative mind is a valuable good. The selling of spectrum rights took almost 67 years from time of invention to application. Ronald Coase remembers how his ideas were classified as a joke, and the history of economic thought provides us with similar errors in judgement. The path-breaking ideas on adverse selection by George Akerlof were initially discarded as 'trivial stuff' which the editors of the *American Economic Review* were not in the habit of publishing. Friedman's ideas on flexible exchange rates were put away as ridiculous and not realistic.

  Of course, regulation of the market of ideas smacks of censorship. But in reality it is about how to structure debates when people have different world views. Just as competition among different government departments can be a good way to produce information (Tirole, 1994), so can a policy debate profit from competition in advice or points of view. Dewatripont and Tirole (1999) give hints to how such a debate might be framed. The only way out of this situation seems to be to organize competition among advisers instead of trusting committees of wise men or by merging government departments into one gigantic bureaucracy. However, competition is not sufficient as this competition for the president's ear has to be supplemented by gatekeepers – scientists and journalists – who can tell when the public is taken for a ride by the 'cons' among us.

- *Institutions for protecting biodiversity of views*. Having a conversation or debate in matters of policy is only going to be a worthwhile act if a diversity of views exists. Economics may perhaps be seen as the 'Queen of the Social Sciences' by its own practitioners; in policy circles, economists are still the barbarians who dare to speak of costs and benefits and privatizing social security or the national art gallery. Economists are not listened to outside the safe circle of economists and in persuading our 'significant others' economists will fare better if they listen to what politicians or bureaucrats see as the key problem, how they are worried by transition problems, income distribution, and the excessive use of incentives. Politicians have to simultaneously deal with uncertain and biased policy advice and the other way round, policy advisers also have to deal with biased politicians. A diversity of views is only going to last if the receiver of the economist's message can interpret and apply it. The penultimate question is, of course, how to create such minds. History seems to prove that keeping an open mind is not a widespread character trait in policy circles. As Stiglitz (2002, chapter 9) observes, policy-makers from the IMF have substituted economics by ideology. The 'Washington Consensus' (Williamson, 1994) seems to have played a far too dominant role in privatization, fiscal policy and matters of regulation. Again just as in the case of academic economics, having a common language will certainly help but will not be a sufficient condition for attaining an open mind. Innovating the education of economists, which will be dealt with in the next section, might help in attaining that goal.

3.4 IMPLICATIONS FOR TEACHING AND CURRICULA

Pluralism in academia and among policy-makers is a desirable characteristic of the economic debate. The trouble with economics is that diversity of views is at risk as the standard view – whether it be Keynesian in the 1960s and 1970s or neoclassical in the 1980s and 1990s – crowds out alternative views. This 'crowding out' effect seems to be reinforced by the 'rules of the game' or the incentive structure inside science which favours received views. This is also the reason why Frey and Eichenberger (1997) claim that the more interesting developments in economics develop and occur outside the walls of the 'economics department'. The network externalities tied to the reigning standard view of the day make the life of dissenting economists difficult, but then again being a dissenting economist right now may make for a Nobel Prize winner of the distant future.

How can a modern-day curriculum deal with the desirable aspect of pluralism? Intellectual exchange inside and outside academia will flourish if we at least share a language. And the most sensible thing to do is to share the language of neoclassical economics or good old price theory. As Coase (1999) stressed in a lecture, 'We will not replace price theory (supply and demand and all that) but will put it in a setting that will make it vastly more useful.'

The use of price theory makes sense, not only from an economic point of view because it minimizes the switching costs for those who have a 'foreign' language (Lazear, 2000b), but primarily because neoclassical economics deep down embodies the meta-language which economists share: equilibrium, rationality and efficiency. But at the same time the story does not end there, because mastering the grammar of a language does not imply that you can make conversation from 'day one'. There is more to economics than blackboard economics and practitioners seem to understand intuitively. The economists profession churns out more and more theorists who seem to lack a reality check on the ordinary business of life. In that respect the following quotation by Stephen Roche who heads the global economics division at Morgan Stanley is a telling one (cited in Cassidy, 1996): 'We insist on at least a three-to-four year cleansing experience to neutralize the brainwashing that takes place in these graduate programs.'

Economics has gone astray, at least that is the impression you get if you read the gatekeepers of science. Economists toil for the only coin worth having: the applause of their peers. Although this mechanism has its merits, it can easily lead economists to believe that the only principal they work for is the scientific community or their colleague down the hall. But this is just as wrongheaded as the politician who believes that the party head office is the principal, and the bureaucrat who looks up to the permanent secretary or the minister as his ultimate principal. The ultimate principal in both economics and politics is the citizen, or as Klein (2001) describes the citizen: the Everyman. In communicating with the Everyman a common language is needed. Just like armchair scientists, practitioners – economic policy makers and advisers – need to share a language in order to make the entire sequence of reasonings clear to the outside world or the Everyman.

Summing up, I acknowledge the need for standards in conversations and debates, in other words a common language. Now what does this imply for teaching economics? As anyone with a fair understanding of economics can predict, standards have the danger of 'locking in', creating path dependence. And this is exactly what can and perhaps will happen with designing textbooks and curricula. Paul Samuelson's textbook (1948) presented a clear break with the post-world war textbooks and since that time, textbooks have been more or less variations on the theme set by Samuelson. There are exceptions, but by and large most textbook writers follow suit in mimicking

Samuelson or his modern day equivalent Greg Mankiw (2001). So one of the challenges ahead lies in designing a standard curriculum that offers a language for all economic specializations, that at the same time should be a lively standard that can evolve as time goes by, and insight and experience grows. In thinking this through, the following six maxims offer a starting point for such a standard:

- *Teach the art of economic policy.* Economics is not merely an approach or a language, as Gary Becker (1975) is wont to say. As Coase (1998) once criticized the economic approach of Becker and others: 'We study the circulation of the blood without the body.' Studying economics by studying the grammatical rules isn't going to yield much insight. Economics is about the world outside the ivory tower. And in teaching, as well as in research, I am more and more persuaded to see the art of economics revolving around the interaction between Questions-Theory-Data (Leamer, 1996). Asking the right questions about the data of the real world and in turn choosing models that shed light on these data and questions is a trick that does not come easy, but it is marriage of principles that produces the best of economics. With due respect for the contributions of people like Gerard Debreu or Frank Hahn, their style of work should not set the standard for the teaching practices of economists. The art of economic policy is all about mingling normative and positive economics (Colander, 1994) and about discovering the rhetoric of economics. In that respect philosophy and methodology should be essential elements of an economics curriculum.
- *Teach economics by learning from the past.* Economists sometimes perceive their job as that of an engineer and perhaps that is why the outside world also perceives economists as just as reliable as engineers. The image is however a false one. The age of diminished expectations, as dubbed so adequately by Paul Krugman (1994), is riddled with disappointments of social engineering. The ultimate question is, of course, why applying economics to real world problems seems to fail so miserably. One option is to learn from past economists, their thought processes, their controversies, and the way in which economic circumstances influenced their outlook and advice: the debates about sticking to the gold standard in the nineteenth century and, following WWI, the best way to tackle the depressions, the restructuring of Europe after WWII, the establishment of the EMU and the enlargement of the European Union, the East Asian Crisis, and so forth. What this implies for the economics curriculum is that the

history of economic thought and economic history can (and perhaps should) be taught in tandem.

- *Teach economics by crossing disciplinary boundaries.* In practice this would amount to, for lack of a better phrase, economic imperialism. Acting the imperialist does not imply that economists should force other disciplines to yield to the Almighty Economist's methodology. The argument to push forward an imperialist attitude in teaching and practising economics hinges on four grounds. First of all, economics is a social science in the respect that the view you offer students should transcend the narrow view of traditional economics in which the family plays a minor role, politics is out of the question and values are given once and for all. Second, the element of play should enter the curriculum, as audiences are more apt to listen and learn when you can surprise and entertain. A third reason boils down to my claim that when you can play with your subject you have mastered it. And last but certainly not least economics by imperialism helps to get a conversation going between disciplines. The prime contribution of economists like Lazear, Becker and Greif is that they stimulated controversies across disciplines. Lazear opened the eyes of personnel officers, Becker infuriates demographers and sociologists, and Greif shows how the insights of game theory and agency theory can help to understand and reinterpret economic history.

- *Merge business economics with general economics.* The issues which are dealt with in business administration, public administration and economics are becoming indistinguishable. The jargon may differ as well as the level of technical sophistication but essentially all sub-disciplines are dealing with the same subjects. Furthermore, the techniques of neoclassical economics are used in territories where you might not expect them. The techniques of modern finance are used frequently in law and economics, marketing research techniques are used in labour market econometrics, and agency theory essentially laid the foundation for looking into questions of central bank independence and the efficiency of corporate governance principles. One could go on and on with the examples of economic theory which are used in different contexts. The message is clear: delineating economics' along lines of business and general economies is an artificial distinction and no longer serves a purpose.

- *Practice Reality Economics.* Economists, taking their cue from Milton Friedman's influential essay on positive economics, are not very enthused about asking their economic agents what goes on inside their black box. One should judge an agent by his actions and not by his words is the tacit message economists bring across. Preferences do not have to be stated, they will reveal themselves by the deeds of agents. The funny thing is that the cornerstone of every economist – the benefits of the division of labour – was explained by way of recounting the organisation of a pin factory. Adam Smith, or should I say his teacher Francis Hutcheson who had already used the example of the pin factory, discovered the use of reality economics. Economists do not visit the pin factories of today and yet it is there that we can really get a feel for what 'productivity' and 'technical progress' really mean, how these are brought about and how they are destroyed. The main benefit of growth accounting is that it shows how large our ignorance is, and reality economics is one way of getting nearer to the truth of the 'wealth of nations' than endless growth regressions and accounting exercises. Reality economics can improve this stalemate by asking people, listening and watching them, and finally interpreting what people do (with theory in the back of your mind). Reality economics or 'learning by asking', as Alan Blinder et al. practice in their book *Asking about Prices* (1998), seems to be going through a revival. Ed Lazear (2000) discovered from a visit to the *Safelite Auto Glass Company* how a switch from time-rates to piece-rates of pay stimulated productivity. Truman Bewley (1999) discovered by interviewing business people, labour leaders, business consultants and counsellors of unemployed why wages are more sticky than theory would predict or subscribe. Of course, there have always been economists of name and fame who have practised this art. Alfred Chandler and Ronald Coase are perhaps economists that can serve as role models. The basic idea of reality economics, as I would like to dub this style of economics, is that it not only offers a source of inspiration but also a reality check on blue sky theorizing. And for the policy economist, reality economics offers not only interesting reading, it is even necessary as I discover more and more. Economists who have to get their hands dirty know that 'blackboard economics' is not sufficient to persuade their audience. Still they muddle through, mumbling what the Washington Consensus of the day is and this in my opinion can improve. Economic policy should move beyond macroeconomic statistics, which in the end can cover up any policy failure an economist or policy adviser wants to hide. Instead they should practise reality economics because they will discover that markets cannot function without institutions, privatizing the public sector has its limits and technical progress is not something which you discover only in a laboratory but anywhere in society. By confronting theory with practice in the most direct manner possible you can make economists and policy-makers think twice, and 'thinking twice' is perhaps the closest one can come to creating 'an open mind'.

- *Teach basic principles of economics (especially in the under graduate stage) in a Socratic manner.* I think it is essential for undergraduates to develop an intuition for economics by answering the age-old dilemmas of economics themselves. That is in my opinion the only way to get acquainted with the meta-language of economics and at the same time see its possibilities and limitations. Economic theory taught as a painstaking exercise of solving a hundred constrained maximization problems is not going to get the message of economics across. This is not an easy task but it can be enhanced by using experiments and games (see for example Bergstrom and Miller, 1997; and Holt, 1999). Recently, a Dutch commission led by Coen Teulings (see report of the Committee Teulings, 2002) came up with a similar suggestion for the future Dutch high school economics curriculum. Of course, undergraduates in economics should extend their knowledge of basic economic principles. But in three years time – which is the standard for becoming a bachelor in economics – one cannot hope to learn economics in a very profound manner. The master stage of the economics curriculum is better suited to dealing with the deeper questions of economics. By applying the meta-language of economics in different territories one can see how many miles a theory generates and what the pitfalls are of applying a particular theory.

3.5   CONCLUSION

> To a person of analytical ability, perceptive enough to realize that mathematical equipment was a powerful sword in economics, the world of economics was his oyster in 1935. The terrain was strewn with beautiful theorems begging to be picked up and arranged in unified order. (Paul Samuelson, 1972: 160)

Economics was a 'cinch' for those who had mastered mathematics and applied it to economic problems. Like Paul Samuelson, who was reminiscing over the state of economics in the 1930s, the new generation of economists could not help it. In a way the mathematical turn in economics was also a necessary step as it helped to focus on the essentials of a problem. On that account there is nothing wrong with mathematics. The real problem with economics starts when people really believe that with a beautiful mind you can solve all the problems in the world. Economic policy is a never a 'cinch', or to rephrase this: economic theory is a necessary element of applying economics but it is never sufficient. Still, when you listen closely to what Paul Krugman or Tom Sargent have to say you will notice that they have fallen victim to what Coase calls the vice of 'blackboard economics' (see also McCloskey, 1997): something is true just because you write (and prove) it on a blackboard. Paul Samuelson is a giant just like Adam Smith is a giant, but in retrospect he exemplifies the professionalization of economics that has taken place. The 'business of ordinary life' has, on the one hand, produced specialists who are out of touch with reality, and on the other hand, specialists who are in touch with reality but throw their hands up in despair in light of what's to be done. Again there are the usual exceptions to the rule, but by and large the two-handed economist has become a one-armed economist, so much in demand by President Truman, who could not stand the endless 'on the one hand ... and on the other hand' of his chairman of the Council of Economic Advisers, Edwin Nourse. The present situation amounts to a division of labour on the market for economists that has become counterproductive. The golden triangle of Questions-Theory-Data is split up among the 'specialists': theorists, measurers and 'journalists'. Theorists practise blackboard economics, econometricians think that data tell the whole story (or worse, let the data decide) and 'journalists' or 'travelling salesmen' ask perhaps the right questions but cannot back up their story by a frame of mind and the data to support it.

Economics may therefore appear to be an easy subject, but putting theory into action is an entirely different matter. Besides knowing your way around economic theory and statistics, you need the eye of a biologist, the sharpness of a spin doctor, the brashness of an investigative journalist, the ability to make an argument 'sing' like a poet, the gift of the gab of an orator, the stubbornness of a lone wolf and last but not least the common sense of the man in the street. Of course, we can't all be this utopian economist, even though some economists score good points on a number of dimensions. The best we can do is to change our habits. Every conversation in economics that values pluralism as a public good is in need of a standard language. However, at the same time this standard should be a language that adapts and evolves as experience grows. Price theory offers such a language (so, first of all, teach the basics of economics); it can evolve by confronting theory with reality (by teaching and practising Reality Economics), present ideas with lessons from the past (by practising and linking history of economic thought with economic history), and the insights from economics with that of other disciplines (by practising Imperialist Economics). By confronting theory with reality not only can economics become a more interesting subject for insiders and outsiders, it will also make the users of economics think twice, which is synonymous for 'having an open mind'. In short, changing course will perhaps not bring the truth Warren Harding was after any closer, but it certainly will prevent the economist from making big mistakes and make economics the social science it deserves to be. 'God, what a job!'

REFERENCES

Akerlof, G.A. and R.E. Kranton (2002), 'Identity and Schooling: Some Lessons for the Economics of Education', *Journal of Economic Literature*, **40**, 1167-1201.
Arthur, W.B., S. Durlauf and D.A. Lane (1997), *The Economy as an Evolving Complex System II*, Reading, MA: Addison-Wesley.
Bala, V. and S. Goyal (1998), 'Learning from Neighbours', *Review of Economics Studies*, **65**, 595-621.
Baldi, S. (1998), 'Normative Versus Social Constructivist Processes in the Allocation of Citations: A Network-Analytic Model', *American Sociological Review*, **63**, 829-846.
Becker, G.S. (1975), *The Economic Approach to Human Behavior*, Chicago: University of Chicago Press.
Bergstrom, T.C. and J.H. Miller (1997), *Experiments with Economic Principles*, New York: McGraw-Hill.
Bewley, T.F. (1999), *Why Wages Don't Fall During a Recession*, Cambridge: MA Harvard University Press.
Bikhchandani, S., D. Hirshleifer and I. Welch (1998), 'Learning from the Behavior of Others: Conformity, Fads and Informational Cascades', *Journal of Economic Perspectives*, **12**, 151-170.
Blinder, A.S., E.R.D. Canetti, D.E. Lebow and J.B. Rudd (1998), *Asking about Prices: A New Approach to Understanding Price Stickiness*, New York: Russell Sage Foundation.
Brock, W.A. and S.N. Durlauf (1999), 'A Formal Model of Theory Choice in Science', *Economic Theory*, **14**, 113-130.
Callon, M. (1994), 'Is Science a Public Good?', *Science, Technology & Human Values*, **19**, 395-424.
Cassidy, J. (1996), 'The Decline of Economics', *New Yorker*, 2 December: 50-60.
Clement, D. (2002), Interview with Robert Solow, *The Region, Federal Reserve Bank of Minneapolis*, September 2002.
Committee Teulings (2002), *'Economie moet je doen'* ['Putting Economics into Practice'], Zoetermeer: Ministry of Education, Culture and Science, www.ocw.nl
Coase, R.H. (1974), 'The Markets for Goods and the Markets for Ideas', *American Economic Review, Papers and Proceedings*, **64**, 384-391.
Coase, R.H. (1988), *The Firm, The Market and The Law*, Chicago: University of Chicago Press.

Coase, R.H. (1998), 'Comment on Thomas W. Hazlett: Assigning Property Rights to Radio Spectrum Users: Why Did FCC License Auctions Take 67 Years?', *Journal of Law and Economics*, XLI, 577-580.

Coase, R.H. (1999), 'The Task of the Society, Opening Address to the Annual Conference', *International Society of New Institutional Economics*, 17 September.

Coats, A.W. (ed.) (2000), *The Development of Economics in Western Europe since 1945*, London: Routledge.

Colander, D. (1994), 'Vision, Judgement, and Disagreement among Economists', *Journal of Economic Methodology*, 1, 43-56.

Dewatripont, M. and J. Tirole (1999), 'Advocates', *Journal of Political Economy*, 107, 1-39.

Dow, S.C. (2001), 'Methodology in a Pluralist Environment', *Journal of Economic Methodology*, 8, 33-40.

Durlauf, S.N. (2001), 'A Framework for the Study of Individual Behavior and Social Interactions', *Social Methodology*, 31, 47-88.

Easterly, W. (2001), *The Elusive Quest for Growth – Economists' Adventures in the Tropics*, Cambridge, MA: MIT Press.

Fisher, I. (1933), Statistics in the Service of Economics, *Journal of the American Statistical Association*, 28, 1-13.

Frey, B.S. and R. Eichenberger (1997), 'Economists: First Semester, High Flyers and UFOs', in P.A.G. van Bergeijk et al. (eds), *Economic Science and Practice*, Cheltenham, UK and Lyme, USA: Edward Elgar, pp. 15-48.

Gambetta, D. (1993), *The Sicilian Mafia – The Business of Private Protection*, Cambridge, MA: Harvard University Press.

Gans, J.S. (ed.) (2000), *Publishing Economics – Analyses of the Academic Journal Market in Economics*, Cheltenham, UK and Northampton, MA, USA: Edward Elgar.

Gans, J.S. and G.B. Shepherd (1994), 'How are the Mighty Fallen: Rejected Classic Articles by Leading Economists', *Journal of Economic Perspectives*, 8, 165-179.

Garfield, E. (1998), 'Mapping the World of Science', paper at the 150 anniversary meeting of the AAAS, Philadelphia.

Goyal, S. (1999), '*Networks, Learning and Equilibrium*', inaugural lecture, Erasmus University, Rotterdam.

Holt, C.A. (1999), 'Teaching Economics with Classroom Experiments', *Southern Economic Journal*, 65, 603-610.

Klamer, A. and D. Colander (1990), *The Making of an Economist*, Boulder: Westview Press.

Klamer, A. and H.P. van Dalen (2002), 'Attention and the Art of Scientific Publishing', *Journal of Economic Methodology*, 8, 289-315.

Klein, D.B. (2001), 'A Plea to Economists Who Favor Liberty: Assist the Everyman', *Eastern Economic Journal*, 27, 185-202.

Krugman, P. (1994), *Peddling Prosperity – Economic Sense and Nonsense in the Age of Diminished Expectations*, New York: W.W. Norton.

Lazear, E.P. (2000a), 'Performance Pay and Productivity', *American Economic Review*, 90, 1346-1361.

Lazear, E.P. (2000b), 'Diversity and Immigration', in G.J. Borjas (ed.), *Issues in the Economics of Immigration*, Chicago: University of Chicago Press, pp. 117-142.

Leamer, E. (1996), 'Questions, Theory, Data', in S.G. Medema and W.J. Samuels (eds), *Foundations of Research in Economics: How Do Economists Do Economics?*, Cheltenham, UK and Brookfield, USA: Edward Elgar, pp. 175-190.

Lipsey, R.G. (2001), 'Successes and Failures in the Transformation of Economics', *Journal of Economic Methodology*, **8**, 169-201.

Lowenstein, R. (2001), *When Genius Failed – The Rise and Fall of Long-Term Capital Management*, London: Fourth Estate.

Mankiw, N.G. (2001), *Principles in Economics*, Forth Worth: Harcourt College Publishers.

McCloskey, D.N. (1983), 'The Rhetoric of Economics', *Journal of Economic Literature*, **21**, 481-517.

McCloskey, D.N. (1997), *The Vices of Economists, the Virtues of the Bourgeosie*, Amsterdam: Amsterdam University Press.

McCloskey, D.N. (2000), *How to be Human though an Economist*, Ann Arbor: University of Michigan Press.

Merton, R.K. (1968), 'The Matthew Effect in Science', *Science*, **159**, 56-63.

Moggridge, D. (ed.) (1973), *The Collected Writings of John Maynard Keynes, Volume XIV – The General Theory and After, Part II Defence and Development*, London: MacMillan, pp. 295-297.

Morison, S.E. (1965) *The Oxford History of the American People*, New York: Oxford University Press.

Portes, R. (1997), 'Users and Abusers of Economic Research', in P.A.G. van Bergeijk et al. (eds), *Economic Science and Practice*, Cheltenham, UK and Lyme, USA: Edward Elgar, pp. 49-59.

Romer, P.M. (1994), 'New Goods, Old Theory, and the Welfare Costs of Trade Restrictions', *Journal of Development Economics*, **43**, 5-38.

Samuelson, P.A. (1948), *Economics – An Introductory Analysis*, New York: McGraw-Hill.

Samuelson, P.A. (1972), 'Economics in a Golden Age: A Personal Memoir', in G. Holton (ed.), *The Twentieth Century Sciences: Studies in the Biography of Ideas*, New York: W.W. Norton, pp. 155-170.

Schelling, T.C. (1978), *Micromotives and Macrobehavior*, New York: W.W. Norton.

Sent, E.M. (1999), 'Economics of Science: Survey and Suggestions', *Journal of Economic Methodology*, **6**, 95-124.

Sobel, D. (1996), *Longitude*, London: Fourth Estate.

Solow, R.M. (1971), *Capital Theory and the Rate of Return*, Amsterdam: North-Holland.

Stiglitz, J.E. (2002), *Globalization and its Discontents*, New York: W.W. Norton.

Sutton, J. (2000) *Marshall's Tendencies – What Can Economists Know?*, Cambridge MA: MIT Press.

Tirole, J. (1994), 'The Internal Organization of Government', *Oxford Economic Papers*, **46**, 1-29.

Tuchman, B.W. (1984), *The March of Folly – From Troy to Vietnam*, New York: Ballantine.

Van Dalen, H.P. (1999), 'The Golden Age of Nobel Economists', *The American Economist*, **43**, 19-35.

Van Dalen, H.P. and K. Henkens (2005), 'Signals in Science - On the Importance of Signaling in Gaining Attention in Science', *Scientometrics*, **64**, 209-233.

Van Dalen, H.P., and A. Klamer (1996), *Telgen van Tinbergen – Het verhaal van de Nederlandse economen*, Amsterdam: Balans.

Van Dalen, H.P. and A. Klamer (1997), 'Blood is Thicker than Water – Economists and the Tinbergen Legacy', in P.A.G. van Bergeijk et al. (eds), *Economic Science and Practice*, Cheltenham, UK and Lyme, USA: Edward Elgar, pp. 60-91.

Williamson, J. (1994), 'In Search of a Manual for Technopols', in: J. Williamson (ed.), *The Political Economy of Policy Reform*, Washington DC: Institute for International Economics, pp. 11-28.

Wilson, J.Q. (1989), *Bureaucracy – What Government Agencies Do and Why They Do It*, New York: Basic Books.

Zuckerman, H. (1977), *The Scientific Elite – Nobel Laureates in the United States*, New York: Free Press.

4. In Praise of Moderate Plurality

Jack Vromen

4.1 INTRODUCTION

This chapter is in two parts. One part, the first part, is scholarly. The second part is somewhat less scholarly. The first part is definitely on firmer ground than the second part. It discusses what I take to be significant new theoretical developments at the fringes and frontiers of economic theorizing, developments that make drawing a hard and fast dividing line between mainstream (or orthodox) economic theorizing and heterodox economic theorizing a far more problematic affair than many protagonists of pluralism in economics want us to believe. In the second part of this chapter I join the ongoing discussion of how an ideal or desirable curriculum in economics might look like (see, for example, Fullbrook, 2003). Among other things I argue that what I call an excessively pluralistic curriculum might do more harm than good. I believe that economics students are entitled to a solid disciplinary training in prevailing economic theory and this leaves little room for heterodox schools and traditions in economics. I also argue for the inclusion of history of economic thought in the curriculum because it provides a healthy if not indispensable antidote against what can be called the opposite danger of excessive pluralism: excessive disciplining of economics students. Excessively disciplined economics students might come to believe that how things currently are in economics is 'natural', normal and optimal. Contrary to what several historians of economic thought seem to believe, however, I argue that by themselves useful historical arguments to the effect that things could have been different in economics from the way they are now do not establish that the current situation in economics cannot be optimal. Discussions on whether or not the current situation is optimal are best left to a normatively significant methodology of economics. Thus in contra-distinction to protagonists of pluralism and post-autistic economics, I will unashamedly plead for inclusion of my own field in the curriculum. When everything seems to be up for grabs at the moment, I do not feel inhibited to put my own cards on the table.

4.2 CURRENT PLEAS FOR PLURALISM IN ECONOMICS

'Taking on "Rational Man": Dissident economists fight for a niche in the discipline', in the *Chronicle of Higher Education'* (24 January 2003), contains all the elements that are characteristic of debates about pluralism in economics. It gives voice to dissident or heterodox economists who are trying to safeguard or establish their own place in the sun. They accuse 'orthodox' or mainstream economists of 'aggressively excluding pluralism'. In the report there are also spokesmen of the 'orthodoxy' lamenting that the dissidents are attacking a straw man. They argue that several alleged shortcomings are in fact already repaired in current economic theorizing. There is another element in the report in the *Chronicle* that is typical of ongoing discussions of pluralism in economics: 'pluralism' itself is ill defined. No attempt is made to clarify what 'pluralism' means.[1] This would not be so much of a problem if proponents and opponents of pluralism in economics had roughly the same understanding of 'pluralism'. This does not seem to be the case, however. Upon closer inspection, 'pluralism' turns out to mean different things to different people. Even proponents of pluralism in economics differ in their understanding of it. In the reading of some, it means that orthodox economists should be more open-minded to dissenting views expressed by heterodox economists.[2] Orthodox economists are called upon here not to dismiss dissenting views out of hand, and heterodox economists are called upon not to give up in their attempts to speak to orthodox economists. There is still the sense of one conversation, or one audience or community in which *all* economists of all stripes and persuasions partake. Others advocate 'parallel conversations': heterodox economists are advised to address each other, rather than orthodox economists. It seems that these proponents of pluralism have given up on what the first group of proponents is still fighting against: their marginalization in the economics profession and their expulsion from the profession's conversation.

In fact, there are more things on which there are not only disagreements between orthodox and heterodox economists, but also internally within the camps of orthodox and heterodox economists. Some orthodox economists simply ignore or neglect heterodox economists. Other orthodox economists acknowledge the existence of heterodox economists, but justify the exclusion of heterodox economics from the curricula on the ground that doing otherwise would harm the interest of students. If students are not well trained in orthodox economics, so the argument goes, they will have fewer chances to publish in leading journals. And publication in leading journals provides the key to promotion and tenure. Still other orthodox economists do not doubt that some heterodox economists have interesting things to say. Only they do not believe that what these heterodox economists are saying belongs to economics proper.[3] Yet other orthodox economists are more self-critical. They agree, for example, that developments within orthodox economic theorizing is too much driven by theory and mathematics, and not enough by empirical studies, relevance for policy matters and regard for history. These more self-critical orthodox economists are themselves internally divided, it seems. There are some, such as Kenneth Arrow (Monaghan, 2003), who argue that this is already changing for the good in orthodox economics. Others, like Edward Leamer (Monaghan, 2003), hold that a more drastic reorientation in the value system of orthodox economics is needed.

Heterodox economists seem to be internally divided even more severely. It is not just that there are heterodox economists of very different stripes and persuasions. Also their understanding of orthodox economics and their diagnosis of its shortcomings seem to be very different. Some heterodox economists argue that what is wrong with orthodox economics is not so much that it treats certain phenomena in a wrong way, but that important and interesting phenomena such as poverty, (in)equality and (un)employment are considered to be outside the scope of economics. When it comes to identifying the essential and distinguishing features of orthodox economics, some heterodox economists focus on 'substantive' assumptions and presuppositions. Some focus on the rationality assumption for example, whereas others believe that selfishness or equilibrium are more central to orthodox economics. Others see orthodox economics' inbuilt tendency to favour markets and capitalism as one of its defining characteristics. Then there are those, like Tony Lawson, who argue that orthodox economics is engaged in closed world deductivist modelling. Yet, in line with critiques offered by economists as different as Ronald Coase, Deirdre McCloskey and Mark Blaug, others point at orthodox economics' excessive emphasis on formal modelling and blame orthodox economists for practising 'blackboard economics', dealing with imaginary (rather than real) worlds. Still others, such as Philip Mirowski, do not so much object to orthodox economics' preoccupation with formal modelling as to its use of obsolete modelling methods. Finally there are heterodox economists who agree that orthodox economics has been changing for the better over the last few decades, but who lament that so little of this can be found back in the curricula.

This should suffice to demonstrate the heterogeneity in the views of heterodox economists about the central tenets of orthodox economics and its shortcomings. Note that some of the complaints made by heterodox economists are compatible with each other, but that others are not. Arguing that orthodox economics is (too much) tied to the notions of rationality and equilibrium and arguing that orthodox economics is (too much) committed to formal modelling do not exclude each other, for example. But arguing that orthodox economics has emptied rationality from any empirical content (rendering it vacuous, or making it tautological) is incompatible with arguing that orthodox economics is committed to cherishing selfishness as being rational. Likewise, arguing that formal modelling in economics is wrong or inappropriate is incompatible with arguing that orthodox economists use obsolete modelling techniques that should be replaced by more up-to-date ones. Either one argues that any kind of formal modelling (or an excessive emphasis on it) in economics is wrong after which it does not make sense any more to point out that the particular modelling techniques used are obsolete. Or one argues that there is nothing wrong with formal modelling per se, but that there is something wrong with the particular modelling techniques that orthodox economists deploy (because economists use obsolete methods, for example). But one cannot have it both ways.

So, whatever 'pluralism' means and whatever the reasons given for its desirability, there certainly seems to be a plurality in the complaints levelled against orthodox economists! In the next section I will deal with a few of them. I will argue that current 'orthodox' theory is more heterogeneous and more subject to internal changes than some heterodox economists want us to believe. Indeed, so many things seem to be changing nowadays that in some cases it is hard if not impossible to tell whether the economic theory or model in question belongs to orthodox or heterodox economics. If we nevertheless insist on drawing a hard and fast dividing line between orthodox and heterodox economics, I will argue, the key differences are to be sought in terms of favoured ways of theorizing and modelling rather than in terms of substantive assumptions made about economic reality. This is not to deny that there can be profound substantive differences between different schools or traditions in economic thought. For example, most heterodox economists reject methodological individualism, the doctrine that only individuals and their properties may be referred to in explanations of social phenomena, that they believe orthodox economics is committed to.[4] But I do maintain that the new generation of economists publishing in top journals seems to cling more tenaciously to prevalent formal standards for modelling than to certain substantive assumptions in or results of their modelling. They seem to be more willing to deviate from 'standard' assumptions than from established standards.

4.3   THE BLURRING BOUNDARIES BETWEEN ORTHODOX AND HETERODOX ECONOMICS

Some heterodox economists object to 'orthodox' (or the mainstream's) alleged commitment to assumptions of perfect individual rationality, self-interest and equilibrium. With the exception of self-interest, this indeed coincides with how for example Gary Becker (1976) characterizes the economic approach. And perhaps one could argue that a vast number of papers in orthodox economics still cling to all three of them. However, the notions have undergone slow but significant shifts in meaning. 'Rationality' no longer refers to informed and flawless conscious means-ends deliberations on the part of economic agents, as it was in the times of Robbins (1932). 'Rationality' has been effectively transformed into formal consistency-requirements imposed on overt behaviour (no matter how behaviour is arrived at – via conscious deliberations, for example, or through habit, custom, instinct, programmatic instruction, or whatever). As far as 'equilibrium' is concerned, the focus has shifted from market-clearing prices to the consistency of mutual expectations and on the absence of a good reason to deviate unilaterally from some situation. 'Self-interest', finally, is also cut loose from its original connotations with material gain. If *homo economicus* is understood in the classical Millian sense of a creature that is exclusively concerned with improving its own wealth, then this mythical figure left the scene a long time ago. Robbins (1932) already indicated that economic subjects might well prefer immaterial goods to material ones. In short, although a superficial look at contemporary economic theorizing might suggest otherwise, the landscape has changed considerably. Unfortunately, it seems that quite a few heterodox economists have missed these semantic changes.[5]

Research nowadays done at the frontiers of economic theorizing and modelling increasingly dispenses with any one of the three ingredients of 'the economic approach'. If one looks at recent issues of top economic journals, it cannot escape one's attention that many theoretical papers assume bounded instead of perfect rationality. Furthermore, sometimes a heterogeneity of individuals with different degrees of rationality is assumed and analysed (the 'representative agent' has been abandoned). What is more, models of asymmetric rationality were widely investigated way before Akerlof got his Nobel Prize for it. A similar historical narrative can be told about 'equilibrium'. For quite some time the issues that preoccupied theoretical (mathematical) micro-economists were the existence, uniqueness, stability and optimality of (market) equilibria. But this exclusive focus has withered away too. Instead of equilibria, notions such as stationary points and attractors sometimes take centre stage. Dynamic out-of-equilibrium processes are now explicitly modelled, without the assumption that such processes necessarily lead to some equilibrium. Much effort is spent on solving the equilibrium-selection problem, for example: if there are multiple equilibria, which one (if any) will be reached? In some situations the trajectory followed is shown to be highly sensitive to historical accidents and contingencies at the beginning of the process. And only under certain conditions and in the ultra long run can lock-in effects be avoided. Path dependence and lock-in effects are nowadays surely not taken seriously and studied only by heterodox economists! Partly pushed by experimental findings an increasing number of economists have been suggesting that next to self-interest, fairness, altruism and (strong) reciprocity (to mention just a few) should also be allowed as terms in utility functions (see, for example, Rabin, 1993 and Fehr and Gächter, 2002).

I could easily go on here. More examples could be given of significant new developments in economic theorizing. After a few decades in which the general equilibrium theory framework was more or less mandatory for applied work, for example, there seems to me more space now for developing special-purpose models that are tailor-made to study particular problems at hand. At the same time, the resistance amongst economists against non-standard, non-axiomatic (Bourbaki)-type mathematical modelling seems to be decreasing. Let it suffice though, to conclude that current economic research at the frontiers of the discipline can no longer be characterized in the standard terms of self-interested and fully informed (perfectly) rational individual behaviour and aggregate (comparative) static equilibrium analysis. At least some of the standard criticisms of orthodox economics levelled by heterodox economists have been rendered obsolete by developments within 'orthodox' economics. If heterodox economists want to insist that there still is a gap between orthodox and heterodox economics because orthodox economists unlike themselves cling to notions of (individual) rationality, self-interest and equilibrium, then it seems that they ignore several interesting new developments in orthodox economics.

The apparent ease with which economists give up what have long been taken to be cornerstones of their discipline is remarkable. It also raises the issue whether a lasting, invariant identity of orthodox economics can be pinpointed at all! Perhaps a more enduring trait of orthodox economics is, as Robert Sugden (2001) has argued, a commitment to a particular type of theorizing and modelling and a disregard of empirical research and empirical data in a broader sense.

What seems to be revealed is an endemic unwillingness on the part of economic theorists of decision-making to face up to empirical questions. It seems that the most persistent feature of the theory is not any unifying explanatory principle, but a commitment to an a priori mode of enquiry. It is as if, when a line of research runs into a fundamental problem that can be solved only by empirical research, that line has to be closed down – as if it is better to conserve the formal structure of a theory and to give it a new interpretation than to conserve the questions that are asked and to look for new ways of answering them. The result is a slash and burn approach to social science – an approach which uses a priori methods to derive quick results in whatever is the current field of investigation, then moves on as soon as real empirical work becomes necessary. (2001: 128)

So what Sugden is suggesting here is that economists are willing to give up any alleged fundamental or foundational principle of their theory, as long as this keeps them away from a serious engagement in empirical research (which they want to avoid at any cost). This implies that the methodology of a priorism, with its indulgence in arm-chair theorising, is still an apt characterization of present-day research at the frontiers of economic theorizing.

Sugden is by no means the only one to observe that 'orthodox' economists have a tenacious preference for this sort of theorizing. Orthodox economists seem to cherish theoretical virtues such as analytical tractability, rigour, precision, generality, parsimony, simplicity and elegance. Other theoretical virtues such as realism, plausibility, relevance, comprehensiveness and the like are held in much lower esteem, it seems. Some orthodox economists seem to acknowledge that there may exist a trade-off between the virtues in the former category and those of the latter (Mayer, 1993). It seems that they are ready to accept a sacrifice in the latter category if that is the price they have to pay for securing the virtues in the former category.

But even this may be changing. In experimental game theory and behavioural economics, for example, it seems that empirical research is taken much more seriously. Experimental results here are consequential for economic theorizing not only in the negative sense of strongly suggesting that there is something wrong with some behavioural assumptions standardly made by orthodox economists (like the assumption that individuals always prefer personal material gains over other options). Robust experimental findings, as well as insights from adjacent disciplines such as (cognitive) psychology and evolutionary theory, here have a heuristic function in guiding the search for alternative behavioural assumptions. Partly based on abundant evidence about actual play in bargaining games, Gintis (2000) and Fehr and Gächter (2002) have postulated the existence of strong reciprocity in human beings, for example. A person is a strong reciprocator if she is willing to sacrifice resources to be kind to those who are being kind, and to punish those who are being unkind. A strong reciprocator forgoes benefits when confronted with like-minded persons and incurs costs by punishing other-minded persons ('cheats'). A strong reciprocator does all this also in situations that do not bring present or future material rewards for the reciprocator. So her behaviour cannot be 'rationalized' by referring to her enlightened self-interest, or to reputation advantages that she reaps by behaving so.

Is this still orthodox economics? Well, who cares? It is a fact that the economists mentioned succeed in getting their work published in prestigious mainstream journals and in getting tenure at top-ranked universities. And it is also a fact that these economists do not eschew using 'orthodox' modelling techniques. But, as said, they also conduct and draw on experimental work and they also look beyond the borders of their own discipline for relevant work and insights in other disciplines. Furthermore, they sometimes reach conclusions that go both against assumptions that orthodox economists have routinely made for quite some time and against doctrines that many orthodox economists have endorsed. This clearly shows that 'orthodox' modelling techniques have no inbuilt pro-market or pro-capitalism bias. The economists in question seem to have a pragmatic take on these techniques. They regard the techniques merely as a language in which you have to express yourself if you want to be heard by the economics community.[6]

All in all it can be concluded that, even though things may not be moving quickly and drastically, the boundary lines between orthodox and heterodox economics have increasingly become blurred. Part of the criticism of orthodox economics by heterodox economists has ceased to hit orthodox economics, for the simple reason that orthodox economics has been a moving target. It can even be argued that orthodox economics is changing in a direction that should be agreeable to many heterodox economists. Apart from the recent developments already mentioned, there is more attention to conventions, values, emotions and commitments, and group-level influences (Frank, 1988; Ben-Ner and Putterman, 1998; Young, 1998; Nesse, 2001; Durlauf and Young 2001) and how these affect individual human behaviour, for example. Of course, some heterodox economists may feel that the way in which these phenomena are treated here does not do justice to their real nature. In particular they may believe that orthodox economics' continuing overemphasis on theoretical virtues like analytical rigour, tractability and precision and consistency with methodological individualism stands in the way of really coming to grips with these phenomena. And they may object that these are changes on the margins and fringes of orthodox economics only. Surely it cannot be denied that the new developments spoken of here still meet resistance within orthodox economics. But it cannot be denied either that the heterogeneity of voices and approaches in economics that can be found in leading journals is growing. The times in which orthodox economics could rightfully be looked upon as a monolithic bloc are gone.

4.4   CONTRA EXCESSIVE PLURALISM: THE BLESSINGS OF A SOLID DISCIPLINARY TRAINING

In their petition (Open letter) the French students suggested that the complexity of the objects economics deals with warrants a pluralism in approaches. This is not further explicated.[7] Presumably the idea is that there are many aspects, facets, sides and dimensions to the phenomena economics studies, and that each single approach addresses or covers one or a few of these only. The further presumption seems to be that the different approaches do at most partly overlap in this respect. If so, then putting together several approaches (pluralism) implies that more aspects, facets, and so on are covered than by any one approach. Thus pluralism does more justice to the complexity of the phenomena studied than exclusive attention paid to any one approach only. There are several problems with this suggestion. One is that the undeniable fact that there are many aspects and facets to economic phenomena does not rule out the possibility that focusing on only a few of them provides the key to understanding them. Underlying complex phenomena there may be relatively simple (generative) principles. It may of course be the case that mainstream economics fails to highlight these principles. But if there are indeed such essential underlying principles, the thing to do, it seems, is not to have as many complementary approaches as possible, ideally covering all aspects and facets, but to try to develop a theory that better captures these principles. Another problem with this kind of plea for pluralism is that it seems to confuse two meanings of 'comprehensive'. A more comprehensive picture, in the sense of a picture that includes more aspects and facets, is not necessarily more comprehensive in the insightful sense. A combination of several approaches may be bewildering rather than illuminating. As many have observed, understanding is often a matter of grasping general patterns and principles in seemingly unrelated phenomena.

Although I fully agree with the French students that narrow-mindedness is a real danger (more on that below), the question is whether having a curriculum that gives voice to as many different approaches as possible would provide a satisfactory answer to this danger. One gets the impression that the ideal curriculum would be one in which all the existing schools and traditions in economic thought get an equal share of attention. Curricula should not display any bias (in terms of attention paid to any of these) in favour of any of these schools and traditions. I call this 'excessive pluralism'. I call it excessive, because the by itself legitimate plea for including dissident voices into the curriculum is inflated here into the much more radical (and in my eyes illegitimate) plea for giving all voices equal attention. The question is whether excessive pluralism does not harbour an even greater danger than a one-sided mainstream economics oriented curriculum. That danger is that students remain outsiders to all the approaches taught. Time-wise there are of course severe limits to what can be taught properly and profoundly in a curriculum. If the time available is to be spread evenly over the various schools and traditions, the danger is that in the end students will not really have become familiarized with any of these. They will not have made any of these their own. They will not have learned how to think new, unprecedented situations through along the lines of any particular school or tradition, for example. They will not really have got into any of these. Internalizing any of these takes a lot of time, effort, and practice.

I am afraid that if the French students' wishes ever were to come true, the situation resulting would be similar to the one in business and management studies and other 'hybrid' sciences that are often advertised as providing an interdisciplinary programme. With all due respect for these hybrid disciplines, the problem or danger is that students touch on a variety of disciplines and approaches, but do not 'internalize' any particular discipline or approach thoroughly. Moreover, in these hybrid disciplines the crucial and notoriously difficult synthesis of the various approaches and disciplines to obtain real interdisciplinarity instead of multidisciplinarity is often left to the students. What results is bewilderment, disorientation and cynicism rather than the promised overarching rich and broad picture on their subject matter.

I believe it is better that students get a solid training in a particular school, tradition, and approach than that they only touch upon, in a rather facile way, various schools and approaches. And it seems obvious to me that this particular school, tradition, and approach should be the one that is dominating the discipline.[8] Regardless of one's personal stance towards the dominating school, students are entitled to become acquainted with it. They should not be denied this. All economics students, not just those who plan to pursue a career outside academia after their undergraduate studies, need to be introduced properly to the prevailing state of the art in economics.

In their training, students should in my opinion become accustomed to disciplined, systematic thinking.[9] It is only possible to make sense of what is going on around one if one is able to reason systematically, that is if one knows how to make use of some analytical, conceptual or theoretical framework. Only then can one think things through. Students should also get an idea of what disciplined thinking is. It is possible to argue that clear reasoning is disciplined thinking. Or it is possible to argue that disciplined thinking is a necessary, though perhaps not sufficient condition for clear thinking. And there is no better way to learn what disciplined thinking is than by acquiring the ability to practise it oneself. This holds true also if there are doubts about the validity, credibility and reliability of some specific discipline. It is better to have a cranked discipline than to have no discipline at all.

Having said all this, I am well aware that there are also dangers to systematic disciplined thinking. Systematic disciplined thinking runs the risk of collapsing into dogmatic thinking. One can easily become blinded to the possible limits, weaknesses shortcomings, blind spots, faults and so on of the discipline's framework and specific way of thinking. So immersed can one be in his discipline's framework and specific way of thinking that he forgets that it is a framework and a way of thinking that he is exercising. The framework and way of thinking is taken for reality itself, or is reified as Marxist economists and philosophers used to say in the 1970s. Then even the possibility eludes one that there might be other frameworks and ways of thinking, let alone that there might be better frameworks and ways of thinking. The following section is meant to illustrate that this is not just a mere 'contrived' possibility in the case of economics training.

4.5   CONTRA EXCESSIVE DISCIPLINING

Surely not all students entering economics programmes start out with the conviction that people are opportunistic egoists who cannot be trusted in co-operative enterprises and that the more parsimonious, analytically tractable and rigorous a theory the better. Surely there are at least some who entertain the more or less common views that there are many different people around, some of whom can and some of whom cannot be trusted in cooperative endeavours, and that a good theory is one that helps improve current practice or that gets its subject matter roughly or exactly right. Yet it cannot be denied that at the end of their training many of them, especially those who choose to pursue a career in academia, seem to have come to share orthodox economics' convictions and 'tastes'. Now how can this be? Orthodox economics' preferred answer of course is that economics students are smart people who quickly learn what the real world is like and how economics should be best practised. A more cynical answer would be that economics students are smart in a somewhat different sense: they quickly figure out the rules of the game in economics. They adapt to the social environment of economics as a profession they are in. They know how to make headway in a world ruled by certain convictions and standards. But this cynical view suggests that the impact of 'living among the Econ' is superficial and transient only. It would only alter the students' expectations of how to be a successful member of the tribe, something that can easily be changed again once the tribe is abandoned.

There is some evidence, however, that exposure to economics training in the formative years has a more enduring and pervasive effect. The evidence suggests that undergoing economics education in these years can leave traces not only in how economics students come to see how things in economic reality and in economics as a discipline and profession actually are, but also in how they come to value these things. On the basis of a few experimental studies done with economics students in various stages of their education and with other students, Frank et al. (1993) concluded that studying economics significantly reduces the willingness to cooperate in social dilemmas. Not only does this have negative social welfare consequences, the authors also noted, tongue in cheek, that contrary to the high expectations of many economics students, studying economics is not particularly conducive to the students' own personal wealth. After all, by failing to cooperate in social dilemmas, students forgo the personal benefits associated with cooperation. Their study provoked some hilarious responses. In the Netherlands, for example, a well-known economics professor pleaded in a respected newspaper for a cut in the budget for economics programmes in Dutch universities for the reason that Frank et al.'s study showed that studying economics had adverse welfare consequences.

Yezer et al. (1996) object that the result reported in Frank et al. (1993) that economics training makes students less likely to cooperate in social dilemmas need not be due to economic training having the effect of making students less inclined to give charitably. Yezer et al. suggest that the result may also be due to economics training making students more knowledgeable of the actual behaviour of people in social dilemmas. It may be the case that at the start of their economics training students cooperate more because they have too optimistic false expectations about the readiness of others to cooperate. The economics training then let the students adjust their expectations to actual cooperation rates. On the basis of these more informed expectations, during their economics training students become subsequently less willing to cooperate. Yezer et al. argue that if this is true, this should speak in favour of the economics training rather than against it: 'If students in economics courses learn that the world is in actuality less cooperative than they initially and incorrectly perceived it to be, then the teaching that produces this result should be viewed in a positive light' (Yezer et al. 1996: 178).

It seems Yezer et al. have a point here. If indeed actual people (drawn from the general population) in the real world defect more often in social dilemmas than students initially thought, then learning effects brought about by economics training alone may explain why they themselves become less inclined to cooperate in later stages of their training.[10] In their response, Frank et al. (1996) seem to agree with Yezer et al. that the behaviour of economics students changes during their training because their expectations change. Frank et al. stress the self-fulfilling nature of expectations in social dilemmas. If individuals distrust each other they are not going to cooperate. But they do cooperate if they trust each other. Note, however, that for this to be true individuals cannot have the sorts of preferences or inclinations that economists normally assume.[11] For if individuals are always inclined to reap opportunities to improve their own position, then it does not make a difference whether they expect others to cooperate. If they are so inclined, then in social dilemmas they always choose not to cooperate regardless of whether they expect others to cooperate or not. By contrast, Frank et al. assume that people are in principle willing to cooperate (and thus to forgo possible personal benefits) if others do so as well. It is in virtue of this conditional disposition to cooperate that people cooperate if they trust on it that others do so as well.

Thus Frank et al deviate from the standard assumption that mainstream economists make about preferences and motives. They deviate from mainstream economics' assumptions in an even more fundamental way. The standard assumption in mainstream economics is that the individuals' preferences and motives do not change in the periods under study. What makes Frank particularly interesting, I submit, is that he allows for the possibility that the inclinations and dispositions of individuals change under cultural influences. What people pursue and aspire to is sensitive and responds to what in the prevailing culture counts as admirable, appealing behaviour and what counts as pitiable if not despicable behaviour. Frank (1988) gives a telling story of a boy of eleven who is taught a lesson in scepticism by his nine year old sister. The humiliation the boy feels could not have been greater... Nobody wants to be looked upon by others as naive. Consider a social environment in which people who believe in the goodness or nobler inclinations of people are ridiculed, in which people who do not serve their own interests well are regarded as fools, suckers or losers, and in which people who care about the well-being of others are called softies.[12] In such an environment it is not just that people who do believe in the goodness or nobler inclinations of people are discouraged to express their beliefs. They are also discouraged to display their own nobler inclinations. 'By encouraging us to expect the worst in others, it brings out the worst in us: dreading the role of the chump, we are often loath to heed our nobler instincts' (Frank, 1988: xi).

If Frank is right, then the impact of going through an economics programme can be much more pervasive than an adjustment of expectations. It can also alter the repertoire of actively practised behavioural dispositions. Frank is convinced that people do have a disposition to cooperate, but this disposition can dwindle if it is incessantly hammered into individuals that cooperation is for chumps and dumb heads. More generally speaking, social and cultural circumstances can be such that dispositions that are not actively encouraged and promoted are not exercised regularly and, because of that, disappear eventually. Studying economics can even alter the identity, self-image, aspirations and mind-sets of students. If Frank is right, 'positive' and 'normative' views are not neatly separable here. The way in which students come to look at how people actually are and behave has consequences for what they themselves aspire to be.

Robert Frank is not the only economist working on the fringes of orthodox economics arguing that people tend to clothe what they perceive as the actual situation with attributes of 'naturalness' and 'normality' and even with desirability. There are more of them. One of them is Timur Kuran. Kuran (1995) gives an interesting account of how it could be that some given situation that is self-reproducing and that participants perceive as 'obviously' or 'self-evidently' good or right might nevertheless be bad in the sense of not reflecting the participants' true private preferences. The starting point of Kuran's account is his notion of 'preference falsification'. Preference falsification occurs if someone deliberately does not express his true private preferences to others, for example out of fear to meet social disapproval. Social pressure prevents people to speak openly and truthfully on matters. If the norm for women in some country is that they cover their heads in public settings, for example, then this puts severe pressures to conform on those women who wish to remain unveiled. Women who nevertheless decide to remain unveiled run the risk of losing respect, of being expelled or worse. Knowing this, many will yield to the social pressure and conform to the norm.

The intended outcome of preference falsification, concealment of one's true motivations and dispositions to others (so as to avoid social disapproval), may indeed not be too hard to achieve. But Kuran points out that preference falsification also can have unintended consequences that are harmful to all. A relatively stable public opinion (having behavioural consequences) may come about that does not reflect true private preferences.

> At any given equilibrium, public opinion may differ from private opinion. In fact, the equilibrium may owe its existence and stability largely to preference falsification on the part of people unsympathetic to the policies it makes possible. Such disgruntled people, even if they form a huge majority, will refrain from dissenting because of social pressures – pressures that they themselves sustain through acts of preference falsification. One socially significant consequence of preference falsification is thus widespread public support for policies that would be rejected in a vote taken by secret ballot. (Kuran, 1995: 18)

The individuals do society at large a disservice, because they withhold relevant information from the process of forming public opinion. Massive schizophrenia may be the result: individuals partake in the continuation of public opinion, although no one really believes it is true. Up to this point individuals may still recognize that public opinion is a big lie. But in a subsequent second step it may happen that participants become blinded to the disadvantages of the prevailing situation. Precisely because of the fact that dissident ideas are not voiced, people tend to forget the shortcomings of the prevailing situation.

> The status quo, once sustained because people were afraid to challenge it, will thus come to persist because no one understands its flaws or can imagine a better alternative. Preference falsification will have brought intellectual narrowness and ossification. When that point is reached, current preference falsification ceases to be a source of political stability. From then on, people support the status quo genuinely, because past preference falsification has removed their inclination to want something different. (Kuran, 1995: 19)

Is Kuran's analysis orthodox or heterodox? I don't know. I also don't care. Perhaps one could argue that Kuran's analysis combines both orthodox and heterodox elements. The heterodox element would be the importance attached to the shaping of individual choices by social outcomes. What Kuran has to tell about this resembles what sociologists traditionally have called socialization and internalization. And the orthodox element would relate more to the type of analysis Kuran favours. Kuran wants to make sense of social patterns as simply as possible, using as few primitive concepts as possible (Kuran, 1995: 21). But such a characterization of Kuran's analysis would not be terribly illuminating, I am afraid. The more important thing to notice, of course, is that Kuran presents an interesting and plausible account of why situations that we never wanted to have in the first place may nevertheless come about and obtain such an aura of naturalness and normality that we really can no longer think of any alternative.

Although Kuran speaks mostly of paradoxical societal phenomena, it is tempting to apply his analysis to what happens to economics students when disciplined thinking turns into dogmatic thinking. Is it very far fetched to think that similar processes to the one Kuran writes about can explain at least partly why economics students during their economics training seem to start identifying themselves completely with the profession's standards and presuppositions? I do not think so. On the contrary: this seems to be pretty close to what is actually happening with at least some economics students. At first they may feel a bit like guests at a party who do not want to spoil the evening by announcing that they find the taste of the host despicable. Instead they keep quiet or even flatter the host with his or her good taste. At that stage they are still painfully aware that they do not express what they are really thinking. But later on they have become so accustomed to the profession's tastes and standards that they can think no longer of promising alternatives.[13] What is more, they start defending their profession's standards against criticism voiced by outsiders.[14]

What Frank and Kuran tell us about the pervasive influence of social and cultural circumstances, not only on what individuals believe and how they think, but also on what they value, cherish and aspire, is of course miles apart from the picture of the autonomous agent that economists have traditionally drawn. From that traditional perspective it is incomprehensible and inconceivable that something of the sort that Frank and Kuran are describing could happen. Why would an economics student passively undergo all of this, if he does not like it? He could simply quit the programme and find another program or training that would suit his tastes better.[15] And perhaps the stories that Frank and Kuran tell are indeed a bit exaggerated. And yet, I submit, it seems that they indicate what could happen if the disciplining in mainstream economics is excessive. If the disciplining is not counterbalanced by courses that help students in putting mainstream economics 'in perspective', there is a danger that they develop into dogmatic uncritical devotees. The danger is not only that they become blinded to possible weaknesses, limits, blind spots and the like of mainstream economics. The danger is not just either that they take mainstream economics for economic reality itself and that they fail to appreciate that mainstream economics represents or exemplifies a certain approach to economic reality. The danger goes even further in that they come to conceive of the existing state of affairs, both in economic reality and in economic theory, as a natural and normal situation. 'Natural' in the sense that things as they are now were bound to be this way. There is really nothing we can do, or could have done about it. And 'normal' not only in the sense that it is prevalent, but also in the sense that it is how things should or ought to be. Things are as they are for good reasons. So there is no reason to try to do something about it.

4.6   PRO HISTORY OF ECONOMIC THOUGHT

No respectable economics programme can do without a decent course in the history of economic thought. A course in the history of economic thought can serve several purposes. One is that it challenges the mostly implicit belief, entertained, it seems, by many novices, that the ideas and theories of the 'old folks' are by definition obsolete or are, at best, imperfect forerunners of the much more sophisticated and refined current economic theories. Time and again the history of economic thought has shown that new original and trend-setting new ideas in economics have been derived from, or at least have been inspired by reading the classics in economics. The history of economic thought has proven to harbour an enormous richness in ideas. This richness should not be denied to economics students, if only to prevent them from reinventing the wheel. There is so much they can draw on when doing research at the frontiers of their discipline. So even if we are primarily concerned with advancing economics as a discipline, a convincing case can be made that a decent course in the history of economic thought should be part of the curriculum.

It can also be argued that the history of economic thought is indispensable in demystifying the notion that things as they are now in economic theory were pre-ordained to become like this. A lot of research currently done in the history of economic thought, it seems, is aimed at pointing out that things (in economics) could have been different. It is possible that economics, as we currently know it, would never have come about if in the past other possible paths or avenues had been taken. This, I shall argue, provides a healthy antidote against the belief that the prevailing state of the art in economics is natural, in the sense that things were bound to become as they are now. But sometimes historians of economic thought seem to believe that pointing out that the course that economics actually took is not inevitable suffices to demonstrate that arguments that economics currently is in an optimal shape are unwarranted. This, I want to argue, is not sufficient. Historical studies cannot possibly provide demonstrations of this sort.

Arguments to the effect that 'It could have been otherwise' assume that there were paths or avenues of research and theorizing in the past that were not actually chosen or pursued, but that could in principle have been chosen. The image that suggests itself here is one of a branching tree with several decision nodes. It can be argued that the very fact that the path that economics actually took critically depended on choices made by economists (and possibly others) in the past already establishes that it was not necessary or self-evident that economics became what it is now.[16] But it seems something more is required. If we all now thought that economists in the past took the right decision (given what they could know at the time they made their decisions) with an eye to the advancement of economics as a discipline at every possible decision node, then pointing out that they could have made different decisions does not seem to make much sense. Of course economics would have been different from what it is now if instead of actually making excellent decisions economists in the past made foolish or stupid decisions, but this does not seem to yield a particularly interesting or revealing insight. So it seems it is not enough to point out the mere existence of different choice options or paths in the past. What is needed, it seems, is some reasonable doubt that at critical episodes economists in the past made the choices that best served the advancement of economics as a discipline. There must be some evidence or ground for believing that they could as well have made, or even could better have made different decisions. It is possible, for example, that at critical episodes crucial economists made choices with an eye on their own personal glory and reputation, whereas a different choice would perhaps have been better for economics as a discipline.[17]

But we have to be careful here. 'Things could have been otherwise' need not necessarily relate to choices that economists in the past could have made, but did not make. It could also relate to choices economists in the past could not possibly make but would perhaps have made differently if they had been given the opportunity. One can think here for example of funding. Perhaps economists in the past would have chosen different paths or avenues if there had been funding for that. If we continue to think of 'Things could have been different' in terms of a branching tree, the tree would contain branches that economists, given the prevailing circumstances (and funding regime, for example) could not have chosen. So it seems we have to make a distinction here between the circumstances, conditions and opportunities under which economists had to make decisions (and about which they had little say) and the actual decisions they made given the prevailing circumstances, conditions and opportunities. 'Things could have been different in economics' either if circumstances, conditions and opportunities had been different, or if given the actually prevailing circumstances, conditions and opportunities economists in the past had made different decisions.

Arguing that 'Things could have been different' is to engage in counterfactual reasoning. How would economics have evolved if America's military industry had had no stake in it? How would game theory have evolved if the majority of game theorists had not embarked on Nash's programme? No matter how interesting such counterfactual reasoning can be, there is also the question how reliable or credible their results can be. One issue here is how many degrees of freedom we allow ourselves. Sometimes it is argued that in the past economists did not pursue promising research avenues because suitable modelling techniques were not yet available (Nelson and Winter, 1982; Velupillai, 2000). An issue that this raises is what would have happened if at that time suitable modelling techniques had been available. Or alternatively we could ask ourselves what would have happened if economists had decided to endure a temporary period of impasse rather than to embark collectively on an avenue for which there were suitable modelling techniques readily available. In the first counterfactual scenario we contemplate what difference a difference in circumstances or opportunities would have made, and in the second scenario we contemplate what difference a difference in the psychological make-up of economists would have made. What counterfactual scenario makes more sense and delivers more significant answers? Or, to give another example, do we just tinker with the idea that not the military industry but some other agency would have taken care of the funding, or do we also contemplate the possibility that completely different economists than the ones who actually have been the main suspects would have played key roles in the development of economics (Mirowski, 2002)? When engaging in such counterfactual reasoning it seems wise to keep in mind that there is much that we do not and cannot know. Perhaps we could make a convincing case that the path taken would have been different, but would the eventual outcome have been different also? Paths taken need not always be irreversible.

But all this does not diminish my belief that the history of economic thought can do a splendid job in deconstructing the myth that the present state of the art in economics is natural or necessary or inevitable. We have seen that an exercise in pointing out that 'Things could have been different' does not make sense only if all possible opportunities were always available to economists and if economists always made the uniquely right decisions. One need not be overly suspicious of the motives of individual economists or a strong believer in conspiracies to believe that these two conditions are not met in reality. In fact, it suffices to acknowledge that it sometimes is impossible to identify what would have been the right decisions in certain decision nodes. There is so much that economists then could not have known or could not have anticipated that their decisions were definitely ones under pervasive uncertainty.

As said, arguments to the effect that 'Things could have been different' are also sometimes taken to effectively undermine the claim that the present state of the art in economics is optimal. It is true that arguments that things, as they actually are, are natural and optimal often come in a package. In creationist narratives, for example, the creator meant things to be the way they actually are. And to the extent that the creator is believed to be benevolent next to omnipotent, the 'argument from design' also implies optimality of the prevailing status quo. Nowadays, 'pop' evolutionary arguments seem to have replaced such creationist narratives (Kitcher, 1985). Applied to the state of the art in economics the argument runs roughly as follows: if the present state of the art in economic theory were not optimal, it would never have materialized in the first place. Here too we see a blending of images of 'naturalness' and 'optimality'. The general idea is that a natural selection force, holding sway in the market for ideas in economic science, guarantees optimal results in terms of theories. Even if we grant that there is such a force operating in economic science, it is now well understood that unique, let alone optimal results obtain only under very specific circumstances.

As a matter of fact, one way to show this is to take 'mainstream' economic theory, and more specifically evolutionary game theory, to task. Evolutionary game theory points out that in some games systematic 'evolutionary' forces see to it that no matter where the process starts and no matter what contingencies obtain in the early stages of the process the process will always tend to move in the direction of a unique attractor. Evolutionary game theory also points out that only for a subset of such games the unique attractor is optimal. In the well-known Prisoner's Dilemma, for example, the unique attractor is not optimal.[18] In another set of games, there is path dependence. What path is taken, and also what outcome eventually obtains, depends here crucially on where the process starts and what happens in the early stages of the process. Contingencies and 'accidents' play a crucial role here. If certain contingencies and accidents obtain, the process can get locked into a suboptimal equilibrium. Note, however, that this need not be the case. If there is path dependence, optimal outcomes may result if the right sort of contingencies and accidents obtain. These insights can be summarized and generalized as follows. If systematic 'natural' forces are decisive so that, in a sense, 'Things could not have been different', optimality is not guaranteed. Vice versa, if contingencies can be decisive, so that, in a sense, 'Things could have been different' (if other contingencies had occurred), optimality can result. In short, there is no necessary or logical connection between inevitability and optimality.

Those historians of economic thought who think that successful attempts to undermine claims of necessity and inevitability *ipso facto* also undermine claims of optimality make the same mistake as protagonists of pop evolutionary arguments. They confuse naturalness or inevitability with optimality. Worse, they could even be accused of committing something like the 'naturalistic fallacy'. They implicitly seem to assume that if, contrary to what they are actually arguing, 'Things could *not* have been otherwise' in economics, everything in economics would be fine as it is. But it is a fallacy to draw normative conclusions from factual statements about necessity and inevitability. If something is necessary or inevitable, it does not follow that that something is desirable or good or optimal or whatever. Normative conclusions can only be drawn in a valid way if some of the premises are normative. And, indeed, it can be argued that historians of economic thought who want to draw (or at least suggest) normative conclusions from their demonstration that 'Things could have been otherwise',[19] implicitly smuggle in normative premises. Surely, if the funding regime was based on the interests of the military industry, what has come out must be suspect? Or, surely, if crucial economists at critical moments let their own interests prevail over that of their discipline, there must be something amiss with their decisions? One can also put this as follows. Historians suggesting, on the basis of their demonstration that 'Things could have been different', that economics presently is in a sorry state, implicitly believe that the selection mechanism that actually operated in economics is not the right one. Economists who 'selected' theories or paths or avenues for the reason that it served their own interests, for example, are taken to have made their decisions on the wrong grounds.

Note, however, that the advancement of economics as a discipline need not be impaired by economists making decisions on the wrong grounds. As, in particular, Hull (1988) and Kitcher (1993) have pointed out, just as there can be invisible hand processes in economic markets, there can be invisible hand processes in the market for scientific ideas, leading to optimal results even if individual scientists behave selfishly. And recall also that evolutionary game theory points out that even if we believed that economists in the past made their decisions on the right sort of grounds and that the selection mechanism operating is the right one, optimal results are not guaranteed. So again the situation is more complicated that it may at first seem. But let us abstract from such subtleties. My main point here is that if historians want to draw normative conclusions in a cogent and sound way, then they have to insert normative beliefs or normative standards somewhere in their arguments. The belief that military funding is not the best funding regime conceivable is such a normative belief. Likewise, the belief that economists should not let their concerns for their personal career prevail over their concern for the advancement of economics as a discipline is a normative belief. Similarly, the belief that economics as it is now is in a deplorable state, because it pursues the wrong kind of theoretical virtues, is a normative belief. There is nothing wrong per se with such beliefs. It is just that historians should not pretend that they logically follow from arguments to the effect that 'Things could have been different' in economics. Normative beliefs and standards cannot be derived from any historical account. Normative beliefs should stand on their own feet. They should be argued for in their own right.

4.7   PRO A NORMATIVELY SIGNIFICANT METHODOLOGY OF ECONOMICS

Economics students ought to have a solid disciplinary training in mainstream economics, I have argued. But excessive disciplinary training runs the risk of turning students into dogmatists who are blinded to possible shortcomings, weaknesses and blind spots in mainstream economics. Dogmatists tend to view mainstream economics as if it is somehow 'natural' and optimal. By pointing out that 'Things might have been different' in economics, the history of economic thought is a healthy, if not indispensable antidote to the belief that mainstream economics is 'natural'. But by itself pointing out that 'Things might have been different' does not touch on the issue whether or not the present state of economics is optimal. In order to tackle that issue we need to have reasonable and informed normative beliefs and standards. In this section I shall argue that here lies a challenging task for economic methodology (or methodology of economics). Ideally economic methodology helps students in developing a critical perspective, enabling them to form an informed and reasonable opinion about the strengths and weaknesses of mainstream economics.

Do not get me wrong here. I am not suggesting that students are unable to develop informed and reasonable opinions about the merits and demerits of their own discipline unless they have gone through a substantive course on economic methodology. Nor am I suggesting that a course in economic methodology is the only, or even the ideal way to equip students with the intellectual resources and skills needed to form such informed and reasonable opinions. In principle students could acquire such resources and skills also in core courses in the curriculum, such as Micro and Macro. This arguably could even be seen as a natural setting for a critical reflection on the principles and core ideas and notions taught in such courses. But then there should be time reserved for this in such courses on a structural and systematic (and not just an ad hoc) basis and for various rather obvious reasons it is unlikely that this can and will be done in such courses. For one reason, teachers believe that students already (that is, without having to spend time and energy on critical reflection) do not have time enough to master the minimal principles, ideas notions and techniques. For another, many teachers of such courses believe there is no need for critical reflection anyway and that confronting students with critical reflection will only confuse rather than enlighten them. So if we take the idea of equipping students with intellectual skills and resources needed for critical reflection on their own discipline seriously, it does not seem to be a promising avenue to leave this to teachers of core courses.

In order for economic methodology to be suitable for equipping students with the needed skills and resources, I believe that the field of economic methodology itself needs a bit of reorientation. Crudely put, over the last two decades or so the field of economic methodology has been transformed from a normative into a positive endeavour.[20] Economic methodology arguably started out as an exercise in theory appraisal and theory assessment (Blaug, 1980; Boland, 1982). The standards and criteria invoked in this exercise were taken to define scientific theorizing and theories (as demarcated from pseudo-scientific endeavours) throughout. For several reasons such standards thereafter rapidly fell into disrepute. One reason was that it soon turned out that almost all of economics would have to be rejected if economics were held to the strict Popperian standard of falsifiability. Another related reason was that philosophy rapidly lost credibility and authority as a supplier of impeccable standards for theory appraisal. As McCloskey (1985) put it, 'If you are so smart, why aren't you rich': if methodologists knew so much better than practising scientists how science ought to be undertaken, why then did they not come up with better theories than the ones practising scientists advanced? As a result of reasoning like this economic methodology turned into a positive endeavour. Rather than prescribing how to do science, economic methodologists now engaged in attempts to understand better the workaday reasons, arguments and criteria that practising economists actually deploy when promoting their favourite theories and models. There was much to be said in favour of this. And much good has come out of it. Furthermore, this job is not finished yet. There is still much to learn about ongoing practices in economics. Arguably, this job will never be finished. And yet, it also seems that something has got lost in this otherwise fruitful transformation. An economic methodology that eschews making any normative judgement runs the danger of deteriorating into a rather sterile and futile enterprise in which no one except economic methodologists themselves are interested.

To cut a long and complex story short, some economic methodologists seem to have drawn the conclusion that with giving up the pretence that philosophy harbours prefabricated standards, the universal validity of which is believed to be beyond doubt, making normative appraisals of economic theories and models is no longer a genuine feasible option. As if one would only be justified in making normative appraisals if one possessed impeccable standards or if one had superior knowledge of the subject matter! If this were true, if one would only be justified to appraise and assess economic theories and models if either of these two conditions were met, then arguably no one would ever be justified to assess economic theories and models. Impeccable standards simply do not exist and it would be outrageous for methodologists to claim to know more about economic processes and phenomena than economists. It is one thing (and a good thing too!) for methodologists to be more modest in their appraisals of economic theories and models. It is quite another thing (and not quite as good) for them to draw the conclusion that appraisals cannot legitimately be made at all.

To say that impeccable standards for theory appraisal do not exist is not to say that there are no sensible and reasonable standards. In fact, I venture that there is quite some agreement among practising scientists, of various disciplines, and philosophers of science as to what general virtues 'good', successful empirical scientific theories and models have. They may have different shapes and elaborations in different disciplines and different disciplines may put different emphases, but these virtues include empirical adequacy and empirical support, generality, consistency and coherence, both internally and with other well-established theories (which also relates to their plausibility and credibility), explanatory power, unifying power, precision and exactness, simplicity, elegance and parsimony. It is not just (some) economic methodologists and practising economists who believe that the virtues and values cherished by mainstream economics are rather lopsided. Virtues such as unifying power, precision, simplicity and parsimony are stressed at the expense of other virtues such as empirical adequacy, plausibility (and 'realism') and explanatory power. This squares with the impression that physicists got when exposed to leading economists

(Anderson et al. 1988). And the well-known biologist Edward O. Wilson (1999) arrived at a similar judgement.

Note that what is suggested here is that it is high time for economists to reconnect with other disciplines in a double sense. Not only should economics catch up with other virtues that are cherished in other disciplines and that it has itself treated rather niggardly for quite some time. Economics should also try to be consistent with well-established theories in other disciplines. This means effectively that economics is called upon to put an end to its self-chosen living in 'splendid isolation'. To forestall misunderstanding, I hasten to add that economics is not asked here to imitate the methods of other disciplines slavishly, nor that it should be rebuilt entirely on the basis of a metaphor. Nor is economics asked to yield to idiosyncratic reconstructions of what is going on in other disciplines by philosophers or methodologists. No form of (a renewed) physics, philosophy, biology or whatever imperialism is implied here. Instead, what is pleaded for is that economists re-start conversation with practitioners of other disciplines.

Of course, economic methodology cannot achieve this on its own. Fortunately, however, there are already developments at the fringes of mainstream economics that go in the same direction. An increasing number of economists have started looking at other disciplines to see whether there are things to be learnt that can help improve economic theorizing. The disciplines consulted range from other social sciences, such as sociology and psychology, to natural sciences, such as physics (mainly in a search for new modelling techniques) and (evolutionary) biology, and hybrid sciences, such as neuroscience.[21] Although it is too early to tell whether or not the harvest from this will be rich, I believe that opening economics up to ideas, notions, ways of arguing, reasoning and modelling developed elsewhere is refreshing at any rate. Economics as a discipline and as a profession has been 'autistic' in this respect for way too long. As I see it, a normatively significant economic methodology encourages and helps economists in bridging the gaps with other disciplines.

Back to teaching now: what are the consequences of forgoing teaching economic methodology to economics students? Paraphrasing Kant, it is tempting to argue that teaching economic methodology should awaken economics students from their dogmatic slumber. Or, better still, it should help prevent economics students from getting into a dogmatic slumber in the first place. Like the history of economic thought, it should help economics students in putting the things that they are being taught in other courses in perspective. A course (or courses) in the history of economic thought should help avoid students getting the impression that the way things are (and evolved historically) in standard economic theory is 'natural' in the sense that things could not have been different. A course (or courses) in economic methodology should help avoid students developing the intellectual reflex that 'of course' the way things are in standard economic theory is optimal.

Note that I am not arguing that a course in economic methodology should help foster the idea in economics students that 'of course' the way things are in standard economic theory is not optimal. Whether or not things in standard economic theory are optimal remains to be seen. Or, to be a bit more precise, although it is obvious that not all things in standard economic theory are optimal, it is not obvious at all that all things in standard economic theory are not optimal. It is as yet an open issue whether or not standard economic theory is optimal for addressing certain issues and optimal for serving several purposes under certain circumstances (see Groenewegen and Vromen, 1996). Anyway, the idea is, as said before, that a course in economic methodology should help economics students in acquiring the intellectual resources and skills that they need to form informed and reasonable opinions of their own about this. Teaching a course on economic methodology should help avoid narrow-mindedness. It should help avoid economics students coming to believe that economics is the only thing, or the only significant thing in the world, or that standard economic theory presents the only possible sensible perspective on things. Getting an idea of how practitioners of other disciplines look upon economics as a discipline can be conducive to this effect. Economics students will profit from this also if they do not pursue an academic career. In a non-academic working environment it can facilitate their encounters with people who did not go through an economics training.

4.8   CONCLUSIONS

I am well aware that the foregoing discussion is quite sketchy and that it is in need of careful elaboration and qualification. I might have given the impression that I believe that what is needed now are normative assessments rather than positive analyses. This is not at all what I actually believe. I believe that many more careful positive analyses of the present state of the art in economics, of the ways in which arrived at this state, of new developments in it, of its place in the overall intellectual landscape and of its (in)consistencies with other disciplines are badly needed in their own right and as indispensable inputs to our normative assessments. One of the things that I wanted to show in this chapter is that some of the new theories that appear at the fringes of economics can usefully be deployed to analyse what actually goes on in economics training and what might go wrong here. I am convinced that much more can and should be done in this direction.

A reoriented, normatively significant economic methodology appears here as part of a broader movement that seeks to reconnect economics with adjacent disciplines. In this view, economic methodology not only tries to articulate standards for theory appraisal that are uncontroversial throughout most, if not all disciplines. Economic methodology also encourages practising economists and economics students alike to look beyond the boundaries of their own discipline. Practising economists and economics students are encouraged to have a look both at the (mostly implicit) 'procedural' workaday standards in other disciplines and at 'substantive' ideas, notions, theories and ways of theorizing (and modelling) advanced in these disciplines. This arguably is (or should at any rate be) in line with what a post-autistic movement in economics worth that name stands for. A genuine post-autistic movement in economics is not only interested in what other-minded economists believe, but also in what non-economists believe, cherish and value.[22]

NOTES

Part of this chapter was written when enjoying the Ludwich M. Lachmann Fellowship at the London School of Economics.

[1] For interesting attempts in this direction, see Salanti and Screpanti (1997). See also Mäki (in this volume).

[2] Some also argue that orthodox economics should be more open to other social sciences, or to history. At any rate, it seems clear that 'pluralism' expresses a normative endorsement of plurality so that (contra Van Dalen, 2003) it cannot simply be equated with plurality.

[3] The Nobel Laureate in economics, Herbert A. Simon, has long been a famous case in point. Many 'orthodox' economists refused to take Simon seriously as an economist. Instead, they treated Simon as a psychologist.

[4] It remains to be seen, however, to what extent the theories and models of 'orthodox' economists really live up to methodological individualism's demands.

[5] A typical reaction of heterodox economists to this, I noticed, is that they tend to view such changes not as real or significant changes in orthodox theorizing, but as defences of an essentially unchanged theoretical 'corpus', or as 'cover ups' to conceal that nothing really has changed.

[6] This is how Gintis puts it (personal communication, 20 January 2003). Gintis calls himself a iconoclast and observes he is disliked because of this by orthodox and heterodox economists alike.

[7] In the petition a 'pluralism of approaches in economics' is pleaded for. In the 'core curriculum' that the PAE (Post-Autistic Economics movement) later proposed, one of the three groups of subjects is the history of economic theories. Here the suggestion is that different schools and traditions in economics should be given equal weight. Interestingly, microeconomics and game theory are not part of this. They are presented as options only. See Fullbrook (2003) for details.

[8] Perhaps a case could be made that some universities could specialize in one or a few heterodox schools and that such a specialization is in the interest of prospective students. But it remains to be seen whether students who just left high school are capable of making a reasoned and informed choice between such universities.

[9] Unfortunately it is to some extent inevitable that courses lag behind the frontiers of economic research.

[10] Note, however, that this explanation has its own problems: if people in general actually cooperate less than economics 'freshmen' initially believe, then economics 'freshmen' must be exceptionally naive. All other people apparently know that people do not actually cooperate that often without going through an economics training!

[11] I abstract here from possible reputation effects and from possibilities of individuals to punish non-cooperation by others. If notions like these are factored in, it may be personally advantageous for individuals to cooperate if others also do so.

[12] It is possible, of course, that what is ridiculed is not display of 'nobler instincts' per se, but only the pathetic and self-righteous way in which these instincts are displayed.

[13] Kuran here gives a possible explanation of the phenomenon reported by the 27 PhD students from Cambridge: that the situation in which dissenting approaches are not voiced or heard by the mainstream approach is self-enforcing (see Fullbrook, 2003: 37).

[14] Cognitive dissonance, as first investigated by Leon Festinger, may also help explain why economics students, after having gone through an intensive economics training (especially if they had to work hard to master the material), even if they are confronted with quite convincing counter-evidence, do not readily give up on what they have learned.

[15] Note, however, that it cannot be called a healthy situation if disagreeing students feel that their dissenting 'voice' will not be heard and that therefore there is no other possibility for expressing their disagreement than to choose the 'exit'-option.

[16] Unless, of course, it is maintained that all the choices actually made were themselves completely predetermined somehow. But I will henceforth assume that this is not the case.

[17] Note, however, that pointing this out is a complicated matter. It is for example not enough to show that crucial economists at critical episodes had dubious reasons to go one way rather than the other. It may still be the case that the advancement of

economics as a discipline was served well by this. See below for a further discussion of this point.

[18] This holds for the original version of the PD. In other versions of the PD, in which the game is repeated infinitely and in which individuals care sufficiently for future pay-offs, there are many different equilibria.

[19] Typically such historians are shrewd enough not to draw explicit normative conclusions, but to leave it with suggestions and insinuations to the same effect.

[20] For a detailed and accurate overview, see Hands (2001). Of course, before economic methodology established itself in the 1980s as a field in its own right, many practising economists already reflected on the peculiarities, strengths and weaknesses of their own discipline. Prominent examples are Robbins (1932), Hutchison (1938) and Friedman (1953).

[21] For my own attempts in this direction, see Vromen (2002, 2003 and 2004a and b).

[22] Orléan makes a similar argument ('In teaching, humility is called pluralism, confrontation with fact and other social sciences.'; Orléan, 2003: 117).

REFERENCES

Anderson, P.W., K.J. Arrow and D. Pines (eds) (1988), *The Economy as an Evolving Complex*, Reading, MA.: Addison-Wesley.

Becker, G. (1976), *The Economic Approach of Human Behavior*, Chicago: University of Chicago Press.

Ben-Ner, A. and L. Putterman (eds) (1998), *Values, Economics, and Organization*, New York: Cambridge University Press.

Blaug, M. (1980), *The Methodology of Economics, Or How Economists Explain*, Cambridge: Cambridge University Press.

Boland, L. (1982), *The Foundations of Economic Method*, George Allen and Unwin, London.

Durlauf, S.N. and H. Peyton Young (2001), *Social Dynamics*, Cambridge, MA.: MIT Press.

Fehr, E. and S. Gächter (2002), 'Cooperation and Punishment in Public Goods Experiments', *Nature*, **415**, 137-140.

Frank, R. (1988), *Passions within Reason: The Strategic Role of the Emotions*, New York: W.W. Norton.

Frank, R.H., T. Gilovich and D. Regan (1993), 'Does Studying Economics Inhibit Cooperation?', *Journal of Economic Perspectives*, 159-171.

Frank, R.H., T. Gilovich and D. Regan (1996), 'Do Economists Make Bad Citizens?', *Journal of Economic Perspectives*, 187-192.

Friedman, M. (1953), 'The Methodology of Positive Economics', *Essays on Positive Economics*, Chicago: University of Chicago Press.

Fullbrook, E. (ed.) (2003), *The Crisis in Economics: The Post-Autistic Economics Movement: The First 600 Days*, London: Routledge.

Gintis, H. (2000), *Game Theory Evolving*, Princeton: Princeton University Press.

Groenewegen, J. and J. Vromen (1996), 'A Case for Theoretical Pluralism', in J. Groenewegen (ed.), *Transaction Cost Economics and Beyond*, Boston: Kluwer Academic Publishers, 365-380.

Hands, D.W. (2001), *Reflection without Rules: Economic Methodology and Contemporary Science Theory*, Cambridge: Cambridge University Press.

Hull, D.L. (1988), *Science as a Process: An Evolutionary Account of the Social and Conceptual Development of Science*, Chicago: University of Chicago Press.

Hutchison, T.W. (1938), *The Significance and Basic Postulates of Economic Theory*, London: Macmillan.

Kitcher, P. (1985), *Vaulting Ambition: Sociobiology and the Quest for Human Nature*, Cambridge, MA.: MIT Press.

Kitcher, P. (1993), *The Advancement of Science: Science without Legend, Objectivity without Illusions*, New York: Oxford University Press.

Kuran, T. (1995), *Private Truths, Public Lies: The Social Consequences of Preference Falsification*, Cambridge, MA.: Harvard University Press.

Mayer, T. (1993), *Truth and Precision in Economics*, Cheltenham, UK: Edward Elgar.

McCloskey, D. (1985), 'The Rhetoric of Economics', *Journal of Economic Literature*, **21**, 434-461.

Mirowski, P. (2002), *Machine Dreams: Economics becomes a Cyborg Science*, Cambridge: Cambridge University Press.

Monaghan, P. (2003), 'Taking On "Rational Man": Dissident Economists Fight for a Niche in the Discipline', *The Chronicle of Higher Education,* January 24.

Nelson, R. and S. Winter (1982), *An Evolutionary Theory of Economic Change*, Cambridge, MA.: Harvard University Press.

Nesse, R. (ed.) (2001), *Evolution and the Capacity for Commitment*, New York: Russell Sage.

Orléan, A. (2003), 'Humility in Economics', in E. Fullbrook (ed.), pp.116-117.

Rabin, M. (1993), 'Incorporating Fairness into Game Theory and Economics', *American Economic Review*, **83**, 1281-1302.

Robbins, L. (1932), *An Essay on the Nature and Significance of Economic Science*, London: Macmillan.

Salanti, A. and E. Screpanti (eds) (1997), *Pluralism in Economics: New Perspectives in History and Methodology*, Cheltenham, UK and Lyme, USA: Edward Elgar.

Sugden, R. (2001), 'The Evolutionary Turn in Game Theory', *Journal of Economic Methodology,* **8**(1), 113-130.

Velupillai, K. (2000), *Computable Economics*, Oxford: Oxford University Press.

Vromen, J. (2002), 'Stone Age Minds and Group Selection – What Difference Do They Make?', *Constitutional Political Economy*, **13**(2), 173-195.

Vromen, J. (2003), 'Cognitive Science Meets Evolutionary Theory – What Implications Does Evolutionary Psychology Have For Economic Theorising?', in S. Rizzello (ed.) *Cognitive Developments in Economics*, London: Routledge.

Vromen, J. (2004a), 'Taking Evolution Seriously: What Difference Does it Make for Economics?' in J. Davis, A. Marciano and J. Runde (eds), *The Elgar Companion to Economics and Philosophy*, Cheltenham, UK: Edward Elgar, 102-131.

Vromen, J. (2004b), 'What Can Be Learnt From "Serious Biology and Psychology"?'
    in K. Nielsen and S. Iaonnides (eds), *Economics and Social Sciences:
    Boundaries, Interaction and Intergration*, Cheltenham, UK: Edward Elgar.
Wilson, E.O. (1999), *Consilience: The Unity of Knowledge*, New York: Vintage
    Books.
Yezer, A.M., R.S. Goldfarb and P.J. Poppen (1996), 'Does Studying Economics
    Discourage Cooperation? Watch What We Do, Not How We Say or How We
    Play', *Journal of Economic Perspectives*, **10**(1), 177-186.
Young, H. Peyton (1998), *Individual Strategy and Social Structure*, Princeton:
    Princeton University Press.

5. Preaching to the Econ-verted: Why History also Matters

Albert Jolink

5.1 WHEN HISTORY STARTED MATTERING

It is now one of those apocryphal stories in economics that have changed the course of the discipline: in the mid-1980s, Paul A. David had been invited to convince the participants at the American Economic Association meeting of the need to study economic history. Realizing that the average economist could hardly care less about the importance of history, David took the sexier turn by illustrating how certain historical trajectories could end up in complete inefficiency: the story of the QWERTY keyboard was born. The term that floated around during the next decades was that 'history mattered'. Although it was not always entirely clear what 'history' was, nor what it mattered for, the image of the mistakes made in the past resulted in the Great Curse due to our Forefathers' Sins: non-Pareto Outcomes. The Matter of History could, in fact, rise in importance because it was allowed to piggyback ride on another term which could arouse some economists' imagination: path-dependence. For some, the term 'path-dependence' was synonymous with 'history matters', or at least the two were closely associated for example (David, 2001). For others, path-dependence involved historical incidents as path-breaking events, hence making history matter. The symbiosis of history and path-dependence, as fellow travellers in late twentieth-century economics, gradually weakened towards the turn of the millennium, as the marriage of 'path-dependence' with sophisticated wizardry made history the unwanted bedfellow. The obvious, that history mattered, gradually evolved in the hands of the hard-boiled economist into 'history matters, but not much'.

But if history matters at all, it can at least show that one will never step into the same river twice. The events in history can happen, but they cannot 'un-happen'. Some twenty years after Paul David's rhetorical bombshell fell on the AEA participants, the event has not gone away and indeed, the wave of QWERTY stories has accumulated, trickling-down into educational caves.

95

Examples of cases in which history matters have been towed from a multiplicity of directions into the academic agora. VHS, Windows, Java, why Los Angeles has smog but no real public transit, and so on, have all become cases to illustrate positive feedback effects, lock-in, or inefficient market outcomes in the classroom. These very same cases have also been taken to illustrate the opposite, rejecting the historical account of historical grounds. In either case, at least one common denominator remained: history matters.

In this chapter I will, once again, make the statement that history matters for teaching economics. For some, this may be another case of stating the obvious and little, I am afraid, can be done about it; others, I trust, may be converted to economics teaching with more historical matter.

5.2 ECONOMICS WITHOUT CONTEXT = ECONOMICS WITHOUT CONTENT

It has been argued that a course in economics is easy to teach – but not to take. The difficulty for our undergraduates, and this applies a fortiori to MBA students, is their preconceived and sometimes innate notions of what economics is. The economics illiterates of our classroom usually do not enter our classroom as tabula rasa, waiting for our blackboard notes to gratify them. Instead, the tickertape of real life experiences is voiced as economic practice when confronted with the economic theoretical heritage of yesteryear.

The difficulty here lies not in the truth of truths of practice or of theory, but in the interface in their confrontation. Students may well claim, and often have claimed, that 'this is not how it is in real life', when the correspondence between their real life and their conceptual world is less than perfect. Similarly, our tutors may have taken this correspondence all too lightly, under the presupposition that complexity only follows after simplicity. With an interface that only allows for a one-directional transmission in the conversation, as some classroom settings are pre-arranged, the confrontation of economic experience and economic concepts is bound to end in economic precepts.

The interface in economic courses at universities world-wide over the last decades has, almost without exception, been a set of mathematical equations, referred to as a model. First year economics students are processed through a transition stage of mastering mathematical skills and their minds are prepared to observe economic entities cast as shadows in Plato's cave. This transition process is both painful and gratifying, as real life experiences are left behind, but new insights allow for a clearer vision of the road that lies ahead. But let there be no misunderstanding: the mathematization of economics has served the discipline well, and has allowed for more coherence and greater transparency within the field. The interface in economic courses has served as a powerful initiation rite, selecting brains rather than status or gender. It has created a new community with a language of its own, habits of its own, and its own history.

But the interface has been subject to wear and tear. Five years ago, students had grudgingly taken up the initiative to revolt against what they refer to as autistic economics. The main complaint of the students, then, was the inability of the teachings offered to connect to the understanding of real life economics. Opposition was not to the use of mathematics per se, but rather the introvert side-effects of the use of mathematics. The student initiatives blinked around the globe, and what started as a French revolution has now developed into a much larger movement claiming a broadening of the interface. Now, the movement has become a network, and the network has been expanded to allow for any opposition to a monoculture within economics.

Perhaps one of the main problems with the present state of economics teaching is the extreme reliance on the assumption that 'content comes naturally'. In our economics teaching the transfer of knowledge, of any kind, is presumed to add to the existing (previously transferred) accumulated knowledge. In part, and perhaps a small part, this is plausible as we often proceed from simple to complex or, for that matter, from module to module, hence adding to the credibility that content has been added. But content has not been added; specialization has been added. The economics curriculum, in general, is designed to specialize into particular theoretical domains within economics. By definition, specialization implies a narrowing down of the topic, reducing the broadness of the context, and replacing the nature of the content. Only in this narrowing context can we make sense of the domain in economics which we can (analytically) distinguish from other domains in economics. This has admittedly very little to do with real life or real problems. Instead, the content is more about theoretical (Lakatosian) research programmes translated into teaching programmes.

The resulting outcome of the economics teaching of the last thirty years is, at least, a retreat from context, finding a safe haven in the intricacies of game theory or non-linear dynamics. Economics teaching has reached a fair degree of streamlining, making a continuous flow of students to one of the specializations one of its major goals. This de-contextualization of the economics curriculum has not only led to subtle criticism by student populations ('Could you give us an example of what you are saying?') but has also led to open disagreement with practitioners and professionals contesting the employability of the economics graduates. The de-contextualization of the economic curriculum has eroded the content of economics teaching to the point of becoming vacuous, from a practical point of view. This raises the question 'why do we teach our students economics?', a question we will leave unanswered in this chapter.

5.3   CONTENT IS CONVEYED IN HISTORICAL PROCESSES

Some twenty years after the emergence of path-dependence, it is striking how little of it has pervaded the economics curriculum. Over the years, economics teaching has bowed to our Prisoner's Dilemmas, has saluted the zero-intelligent economic agents, and has paid tribute to the innovations of liberalization. But our students remain as innocent as they were twenty years ago regarding the (ir)relevance of path-dependent processes. To some extent, this is hardly surprising as (economic) processes in general do not occupy the bulk of the economics curriculum, nor are the majority of economic explanations in terms of procedural outcomes. And admittedly, with equilibrium at centre stage, there may be very little reason to emphasize path-dependent processes, with or without inefficient outcomes. With an emphasis on static situations, also the issue of content and context becomes somewhat over-exaggerated as content and context overlap (almost) completely. The mere distinction between content and context appears artificial with the focus on equilibrium.

Despite the relative absence of the concept of path-dependence in the economics curriculum, related concepts such as 'lock-in', 'irreversibility', or 'positive feedbacks' have washed ashore during the first waves of historical descriptions of the developments of typewriter keyboards, clock faces, video-systems or any other type of standardization process. The relevance of these related concepts for economic theory were conveyed in, and through, the descriptions of the historical processes. Although alternative historical stories of the same phenomenon (for example QWERTY vs. the Fable of the Keys) filled the journals, proving both the arguments in favour as well as those against, at the end of the day the concepts of 'lock-in' *cum suis* only proved their value by themselves becoming locked into economic theory.

What may be perceived as striking here is the alliance which history and economics have concocted in the interim, in particular the role of history in this alliance. Taking this alliance at face value, history has been the purveyor of content-laden examples of historical processes. In the case of path-dependence, lock-in and other exotics, the point can be easily made that economics has integrated, adapted and adopted the content of the processes of QWERTY and the like into its core. But taking a slightly more extended horizon makes the case that many other content elements have been slipped into economics through the description of historical processes. Without lining up the usual suspects of the history of economic thought, the case can easily be configured in which content in economics is conveyed in historical processes.

5.4   HISTORICAL PROCESSES = CONTEXT

As economists slaved through the hardships of the twentieth century, their successors in the twenty-first century have given up on the practical consequences of their economic deliberations. As Mark Blaug argued, 'Modern economics is sick. Economics has increasingly become an intellectual game played for its own sake and not for its practical consequences for understanding the economic world. Economists have converted the subject into a sort of social mathematics in which analytical rigor is everything and practical relevance is nothing' (1998, p. 12-13). But the illness of economics lies only in part in the mathematical inclination of the teaching staff and the ability of the researchers to line up yet another set of equations. The illness of economics lies also in part in an intrinsic weakness of economics, as a discipline, to withstand (political) ideologies, and its inability to let ideology prevail over science. But the main illness of economics is perhaps its yearning for universality at the expense of contextual sense-making. Economics has evolved from the storytelling of Adam Smith to striving for economic universality in the twenty-first century, be it through statistical averaging, through modelling 'as-if', or through the economization of reality by describing all social phenomena as economic phenomena.

The problem with universality in economics is that its applicability in practice becomes severely limited or, alternatively, overly misplaced. The critique of the students in the Post-Autistic Movement of the mid-1990s was largely directed towards this mismatch between the universal claims of economics and the practical correspondence. But in an era in which storytelling is synonymous with some lower version of fortune-telling, economists see no other options than either to renounce all practical claims or to reshape the world to their own ideals.

But the questions of our students in the classroom for more examples illustrate the need to add proper context to the content. The incomprehensible content without context in our economic teachings is taken by us for an illusionary purity, where intelligibility should have prevailed. The demands by the students seem to be more than reasonable; economics should not only explain itself but also explain the world we live in. If economics has any pretension to be a science, then it should at least deal with the explanation of real issues.

What may be striking again, in this respect, is that these concepts, their relations and their extent, were motivated by the historical processes in which they were pressed to our attention. These very same historical processes also supplied the contextual settings and, to some degree, offered the environment in which we could add sense to these concepts. In other words, path-dependence makes sense when we are confronted with the description of the historical process of the VHS-Betamax video battle. Similarly other concepts and elements of content have a context in a description of a historical process. Hence, if content is conveyed in historical process then historical processes convey the context as well.

5.5   ECONOMICS WITH CONTENT = HISTORICAL ECONOMICS

In the late 1990s, Paul A. David et al. (e.g. (David, 1985) and (Arthur, 1989)) took up the formidable challenge of recovering a conceptualization of change in economics, in terms of a process that is historical. This quest for the historical grail in economics led to a multi-tracked trajectory, meeting resistance on almost every path. A major opposition resulted from conceptual misunderstandings, which could have been anticipated though perhaps not to this extent. As in any attempt at reformation, some scholars in the field objected on the grounds that the conceptual importance was highly overrated, whereas others objected on the grounds that its implications had not been integrated far enough. The emphasis on the concept of path-dependence was in part to emphasize that the complement of historical economics lies not in the lining up of particular (historical) cases but in the theoretical framework that was offered:

> Examination of particular cases may serve to illustrate the phenomenon of path dependence, to exemplify one or another methodology of studying historical economics, and to identify and explore unresolved problems. The writing of a piece of economic history in this way may also be good fun, and, when it is well done it typically manages both to provide entertainment and to satisfy particular points of curiosity. To

> do it well, however, we must begin with some grasp of the
> conceptual issues and the theoretical framework that endows
> observations with meaning and import. (David, 2001, p.17)

With the emphasis on 'conceptual issues' and 'theoretical framework', economics with content is far less superficial than simply telling stories. Economics with content is explaining how change and evolution is more adequate than statics in approaching real practice. Although this should hardly come as a surprise, this observation has not been the guideline for economics teaching, let alone for the design of the economics curricula.

At the same time, staying away from historical economics and confining economics teaching to trodden paths will keep the Achilles heel of economics teaching in place, allowing for future cohorts of students asking for yet another 'example of what you are saying'. Despite the intellectual investments in a long tradition of economics teaching, and the path-dependent process thereof, the time has come to reassess the balance between content and context, between equilibrium and process, between mathematical skills training and evaluating real problems, in teaching economics.

5.6   TEACHING ECONOMICS = LEARNING ABOUT ECONOMICS

The economics profession has, just like other professions, changed and evolved. Ideologies have come and gone, new technologies have presented themselves and have been superseded, and new fields in economics have become outdated and been replaced by still newer fields. As a tribute to what is worth passing on, our economics textbooks have recorded the encoded knowledge and have served generations of students to level up to their professors, or have at least intended to. Although these economics textbooks have lagged behind by definition, they have leapfrogged forward to include the latest and the newest. As in nature, the capacity of textbooks to adapt has determined their success to survive in classrooms. Indeed, some economic textbooks have lived to see their eighth edition whereas other textbooks have reached a state of oblivion after a few years.

Our economics teaching, on the other hand, has changed very little. In the recent past, the design of the economics curricula was based on the requirements of the final term, and the final term was limited by the total amount of college years. The teaching of economics resulted in a transmission of a watered-down version of the state of research made digestible through the textbooks available. As the research frontier slowly moved beyond the horizon, and as textbooks caught up along this trajectory, the economics profession slowly (for some) started to realize that time would not allow for students to meet the demands of the latest state of affairs. In practice, more mathematics and more modelling were introduced to bridge some of the lacunae, mostly at the expense of introductory and/or historical courses in the curriculum. But even these measures have not remedied the tension that was becoming visible in economics teaching between the expectations of the students and the ambitions of the economics profession, as we have seen above.

One of the problems, among the many outlined by David Colander (2004), is that our teaching practice is focused on logico-scientific teaching, and the common belief is that this is the one best way. But not only are there other ways to teach economics, the logico-scientific way may not even be the best. Indeed, if the goal is to teach our students to see, explain, explore, and solve economic problems, the logico-scientific approach is only a limited instrument that excludes rather than includes economic issues, excluding those issues that do not rhyme with the paradigm.

The other problem is that of the decontextualization of economics teaching and the incongruence with the claims on real practice in economic policy recommendations. Students question this and their teachers do not answer. Instead, the teaching of abstractions without context illustrates on the one hand the barrenness of the state of affairs of the discipline, and on the other the degree of freedom in portraying and advising reality. Teaching economics without context is like teaching what the conditions are for pigs to fly or, in other words, making fantasy (sound) logical.

But as any pedagogical source will argue, the craft of teaching is about learning and about learning processes. Although it may be quite tempting to convince ourselves through our teaching of others, or it may be gratifying to transform our annoyance for teaching into the powers of conversion, at the end of the day the reward for our teaching lies in the observation of budding knowledge. To achieve this, economics teachers will need to bridge the gap between the seemingly intransigent state of economic science and the realistic experiences and expectations of economic students. As we have argued above, one way of achieving this is to connect content to context, form to sense, and to make logic of experience. What is required in our economic curricula is more rather than less history, more historical process rather than more abstract statics, and more attention to practice and less attention to paradigm. Teaching economics should make it clear that pigs do not fly and that pigeons do, and that there are eons of difference between the two.

REFERENCES

Arthur, W.B. (1989), 'Competing Technologies, Increasing Returns and Lock-in by Historical Events,' *Economic Journal,* **99**, 106-131.

Blaug, M. (1998). 'Disturbing Currents in Modern Economics', *Challenge,* **41**(3), 11-34.

Colander, D. (2004), 'The Art of Teaching Economics', *International Review of Economics Education,* **2**(1), 63-76.

David, P.A. (1985), 'Clio and the Economics of QWERTY', *American Economic Review,* **75**(2), 332-37.

David, P.A. (2001), 'Path Dependence, Its Critics and the Quest for "Historical Economics"', in P. Garrouste and S. Ionnides (eds), *Evolution and Path Dependence in Economic Ideas: Past and Present,* Cheltenham, England: Edward Elgar.

6. The Impact of the Economics Benchmarking Statement on Pluralism in Economics Teaching in the UK

Roberto Simonetti

6.1 INTRODUCTION

This chapter illustrates developments in the monitoring of teaching quality in the UK and analyses the possible impact of such developments on the economics curriculum in British universities. In particular, the chapter investigates whether the introduction of a 'benchmarking statement' for the subject of economics is likely to lead to less emphasis on pluralism and interdisciplinarity in the economics curriculum. Subject benchmark statements were introduced in the UK in 2001 by the Quality Assurance Agency (QAA), the agency responsible for monitoring the quality of the provision of higher education. They are defined as a description of the 'nature and characteristics of programmes' in a subject, and articulate the learning outcomes (that is, the knowledge and skills that students are expected to attain at the end of their studies) associated with the programmes in a subject. They are going to be used as tools to evaluate the appropriateness of the standards (in terms of knowledge and skills) set by the higher education (HE) institutions.

To what extent the subject of economics is open to pluralism and interdisciplinary approaches is a question already addressed in the literature. Previous studies argued that the subject was becoming more and more dominated by the neoclassical orthodoxy, and was increasingly relying on mathematical and statistical techniques of analysis and highly abstract models at the expense of a detailed analysis of historical processes and real world institutions (Lee and Harley, 1998). It is certainly undeniable that there is a feeling in many British universities that the subject is dominated by a strong orthodoxy that does not leave much intellectual space for heterodox approaches. Evidence of this feeling is the creation of the Heterodox Economic Association, whose creation is in itself evidence of the existence of a fairly closed orthodoxy.

Most of the debate has focused on whether research in economics is open enough, often focusing on the specific issue of whether it is necessary to carry out research within the mainstream (or orthodox) paradigm in order to publish in the more prestigious economics journals, and why it is so. Little attention has been devoted to the analysis of what kind of economics is taught in British universities, possibly because it has always been assumed that decisions about the content of the economics curriculum is, and should be, taken by universities or, more specifically, economics departments.

However, the introduction of the Economics Benchmarking Statement, against which the curriculum of economics departments will be assessed in the future, has raised the possibility that intellectual freedom in teaching economics is under threat. Given that status in the profession is largely dependent on research rather than teaching, it is possible to envisage a situation where the orthodox approach to economics is adopted as a benchmark because of the higher status of the research in this area therefore making it more difficult to justify teaching a pluralist curriculum.

In this chapter, I argue that whilst it is possible to envisage how the Economics Benchmarking Statement might lead to a more uniform and less pluralistic curriculum, especially in single honours (single subject) economics degrees, there are also reasons to believe that in practice its negative impact on pluralism in economics teaching is likely to be limited, especially in degrees where economics is taught in an interdisciplinary setting (joint honours or combined degrees).

The chapter is structured as follows. Since the state of economics research influences what is taught in economics departments in many ways, the next section briefly reviews the main debates about pluralism in research in the UK, especially focusing on the impact of the Research Assessment Exercise (RAE) on training and recruitment in British economics departments. Section 6.3 describes the background institutional setting of teaching quality assurance in the UK. This is necessary to have a good understanding of the reasons why subject benchmarking statements were introduced and how the economics community has dealt with it. Section 6.4 analyses the Economics Benchmarking Statement in more detail, focusing on its likely impact on the wide economics curriculum in British universities. The final section offers some conclusions and reflections about the general picture of pluralism in economics in the UK.

6.2 A BRIEF LOOK AT THE IMPACT OF QUALITY ASSURANCE ON PLURALISM IN BRITISH ECONOMICS RESEARCH

6.2.1 The interdependence between research and teaching

In order to understand why quality assurance procedures in teaching, and in particular the introduction of the Economics Benchmarking Statement, might lead to a reduction of pluralism in economics teaching, it is necessary to briefly review the impact that the introduction of quality assurance had on economics research in the UK.

There are various reasons why investigating what has happened in research is likely to lead to a better understanding of the impact of quality assessment in teaching. First, both teaching and research are carried out by essentially the same people. If the RAE is making economists work mainly in mainstream economics it is likely that their teaching will be influenced in the same direction because of what they have in their minds. The research agenda contributes to determine what the important questions and topics are. These, in turn, influence what theories are taught to students.

Second, even if economists were completely instrumental and carried out research in mainstream economics against their beliefs in order to improve their standing in the profession whilst being more open to pluralism in teaching, they would still have a duty to students to teach orthodox theory in depth. If they did not teach orthodox theories and methods adequately they would offer a disservice to their students who might want to go on and carry out research in economics. This means that little space, if any, would be left for alternative approaches in the degrees.

Third, the introduction of the RAE in Britain has led to the concentration of research funds in a few mainstream departments both because existing mainstream departments received more funds and because other departments that were less mainstream have explicitly changed their recruitment policies and hired mainstream economists in order to improve their RAE scores. This conclusion was reached by Fred Lee and Sandra Harley (1998), who argued that the introduction of the RAE in the UK was leading to the demise of non-mainstream economics.[1]

Given the experience of the negative impact of quality assurance on pluralism in research, it is necessary to investigate whether similar processes will take place as a result of quality assurance in teaching.

6.2.2   The introduction of the RAE in the UK

Until the 1980s the bulk of research funding in the UK was linked to the funding of teaching. This funding was provided by the University Grants Committee, later replaced by the Higher Education Funding Councils (HEFCs) of England, Wales, Northern Ireland and Scotland, and was intended for staff salaries, premises, and other infrastructure such as library costs. This arrangement assumed that scholarship was common to both teaching and research. Researchers could obtain additional research funding for particular projects either from research councils (the Economics and Social Research Council, or ESRC) for economics projects, and other funders, such as industry, government agencies, charities and international organizations such as the European Union[2].

Following a decline in research funding per student, there were concerns that the top research institutions would suffer and it was decided that it was desirable to be more selective in the distribution of funds in order to preserve excellence in research. It was therefore necessary to assess the quality of research carried out in the funded institutions. This thinking led to the birth of the RAE, which explicitly 'measures research quality in order to determine where funds should be applied' ('A Guide to the 2001 Research Assessment Exercise')[3]. Five RAEs have been carried out so far, in 1986 1989, 1992, 1996 and 2001. Already in 1992, over 90% of the HE funding councils funds were assigned through the RAE.

The assessment of the quality of each unit of submission[4] is carried out using a peer review system, where panels of experts in the subject 'use their professional judgement to form a view of the overall quality of the research in each submission within their unit of assessment, using all the evidence presented in the submission.' ('A Guide to the 2001 Research Assessment Exercise', 2001:5). The evidence used in the review is partly quantitative, including indicators of peer esteem, sources of research funding and research studentships, and partly qualitative.

There is little doubt that the introduction of the RAE has had a deep impact on research activity in the UK. The guide to the 2001 RAE argues that 'the policy of selective funding for research has contributed to improvements in the quality of research in the UK, [and] the effectiveness and productivity of the UK research base has increased substantially' (p2). Other benefits claimed in the guide include effectiveness 'in significantly increasing the conscious management of the research environment [and an increase in] research activity in the UK ... at a faster rate than funding, indicating an increase in efficiency' (p3).[5]

The RAE, however, has been severely criticized for the amount of resources spent in each exercise. The 2001 RAE required the appointment of 685 panel members and covered the work of around 56,000 researchers, with around 250,000 pieces of research work being cited. Many researchers feel that too much of their time is wasted in showing how good their research is rather than doing good research. This has led to a review of the RAE, and still today it is not completely clear how the next RAE, to be held in 2008, will operate.

Criticism of the RAE not only points to the bureaucratic costs involved, but also to the effects on the type of research being carried out.

6.2.3 The impact of the RAE on pluralism in economics research

In an influential article, Fred Lee and Sandra Harley (1998) argue that the introduction of the RAE is leading to an entrenchment of the domination of the neoclassical paradigm in economics research at the expense of other schools of economic thought.

They argue that the orthodox approach to economics has 'captured' the process of peer review in order to ensure that funding of research in orthodox economics is ensured, and this is leading to the demise of heterodox economics. The main points in their argument are the following:

- The main funds for research infrastructure are distributed according to RAE scores, so there are high financial rewards attached to good scores. Given the limited amount of funds, the funds of each department also depend on the performance of other departments (and other subjects). In turn, this means that 'peers may have an interest in the outcome of their deliberations'.
- It is possible to divide economic research in mainstream (neoclassical) and non-mainstream fairly accurately, and mainstream research is 'closed', which means that articles in core mainstream journals[6] tend to cite mainly other articles in the same journals.
- Mainstream economists have managed to control the process of peer review in the RAE because the selection process for the formation of the panel of experts who judged the research of the economic departments was not open and democratic.

Lee and Harley conclude that this institutional arrangement has led to the penalization of non-mainstream research in the RAE. Departments where non-mainstream research was taken seriously were penalized in the RAE and their research funding suffered as a result.

As a direct result of the RAE, therefore, many departments revised their recruitment policies in order to 'emphasise mainstream research and de-emphasise and discriminate against non-mainstream research' (Lee and Harley, 1998: section 7). Lee and Harley provide data on recruitment that shows how 'the impact of the RAE on hiring has been to reduce the employment possibilities of non-mainstream economists in British economics departments, and to "pressure" those departments most open to non-mainstream economists to hire mainstream economists as well' (section 7, table 4 in their paper).

Given these conclusions about the impact of quality assurance on the type of economic research carried out, it is natural to ask whether quality assurance in teaching, and in particular the introduction of the Economics benchmarking Statement, may have similar effects.

6.3 TEACHING QUALITY ASSURANCE IN BRITISH UNIVERSITIES

6.3.1 Quality assurance in the UK: a brief historical background

Following the increase in the number of people taking up higher education and therefore the transition of higher education (HE) from elite to mass provision, the British government has acknowledged that the standards of academic teaching are a matter of public interest. It is therefore necessary to monitor the quality of the provision of higher education, in order to ensure that the expectations of the various stakeholders, such as students, teachers, employers and parents, are met and that public expenditure on education is used effectively.

In 1992, the Further and Higher Education Act gave the task to assess the quality of higher education to Higher Education Funding Councils (HEFCs). In 1993, the Higher Education Funding Council of England (HEFCE) started a series of assessments of the quality of teaching in university departments, an exercise formerly known as Teaching Quality Assessment (TQA), then as Subject Review (SR), and more recently as Academic Review. Following the recommendations of a Joint Planning Group set up by the HEFCs and representatives of HE institutions, in 1997, the task of assessing the quality of teaching in HE departments was transferred to a new agency, the Quality Assurance Agency for Higher Education, or QAA. The QAA absorbed the quality assurance activities of HEFCs in England and Wales, and completed a series of SRs for all subjects in 2001.[7]

Through the Subject Reviews, the QAA aims to ensure that the education funded by HEFCE reaches at least a satisfactory level of quality, 'major shortcomings' in the quality of the provision are corrected, and funding is therefore used effectively. The publication of Subject Review reports is also supposed to create incentives for university departments to improve the provision of education, to help share best practice, and to give the public information about the quality of education in the various institutions.

It is important to stress that the impact of the Subject Review on funding is very different from that of the RAE on the funding of research. In the case of the RAE, the distribution of funds is very (and increasingly over the years) skewed: most of the funds go to the few institutions with the top score. There is therefore a substantial financial difference between being good and being excellent in research. The Subject Review, however, mainly affects teaching funds by making sure that funding goes to departments that receive at least satisfactory scores in their aspects of provision. The difference between good and excellent provision does not directly affect the funds received.

Indirectly, the scores received in the Subject Review might have an influence on the demand for education, and therefore the revenues, in single departments or institutions as league tables are compiled by the press and are used in advertisements by the top institutions. This happens despite the fact that the QAA explicitly warns that SR scores are not intended for use in league tables because of their meaning and limitations.[8]

6.3.2 The Subject Review process

When units of assessment (usually departments, but sometimes groups of departments, even across faculties) have to undertake the Subject Review, they have to prepare a self-assessment document (significantly known as 'SAD'), which illustrates their provision and briefly evaluates the student experiences and achievements according to six aspects:

- Curriculum Design, Content and Organization
- Teaching, Learning and Assessment
- Student Progression and Achievement
- Student Support and Guidance
- Learning Resources
- Quality Management and Enhancement.

The key part of the SAD is the presentation of the aims and objectives of the unit of assessment. These two terms have a specific meaning in the context of the subject review:

- 'The aims express the providers broad educational purposes in providing the programmes of study in the subject. These aims address the question "why is the education provided?"
- 'The objectives set out the learning outcomes and experiences that demonstrate successful completion of programmes of study. These objectives address the questions "what are the intended learning outcomes" and "how are these achieved (in terms of the learning experiences provided)?"'

Source: Quality Assurance Agency (2000) Annex B

Traditionally, institutions have had freedom in stating their aims and objectives, so long as they are coherent with their overall mission statements. This is important in the case of economics as it means that economic departments could, at least in theory, explicitly include the adoption of a non-technical and pluralist approach to economics teaching as one of their aims. This aim would shape the review, and the reviewers would not be able to criticize the department for not teaching advanced mathematical or econometric techniques and teaching instead, say, old institutional theories. Similarly, a department would be able to offer an economics degree that focuses on Marxist theories, at least in theory.

Once the SAD is sent to the QAA, the agency organizes a visit to the host institution by a review team that carries out an in-depth analysis of the provision of education in the unit of assessment. The review team is made up of especially trained subject specialists (economists in reviews of economics departments), led by a chair who is specialist in a different subject and only checks that the reviewers follow the QAA procedures correctly. The visit usually lasts nearly five days, during which the reviewers have access to a room literally full of documentation (the so-called 'base room'), observe lessons, materials, infrastructure and student work, and meet students. In this time, they 'evaluate the extent to which the student learning experiences and student achievement in each of the aspects of provision contribute to meeting the objectives set by the subject provider. Reviewers also evaluate whether the objectives set, and the level of attainment of those objectives allow the aims set by the subject provider to be met' (Subject Review Handbook). The scores (from 1 to 4 in each of the six aspects of provision, with a maximum of 24) are given at the end of the review visit and no appeal is allowed. In order to pass the review, a unit of assessment must get a score of at least 3 for each aspect of provision. If at least one aspect is marked as a 1 or 2, the provision is not deemed as satisfactory, even if all the other aspects have scored a 4.[9] In this case, the institution will receive feedback on possible ways to improve its provision and will have to show in a future inspection that the main issues identified in the Subject Review have been successfully addressed.

6.3.3 The role of subjects in the Subject Review before the introduction of benchmarking statements

So far, it appears that subject specific issues are not particularly relevant in the Subject Review. Indeed, it is true that most of the review is concerned with educational issues that are generic rather than subject specific. If we exclude the first of the six aspects, Curriculum Design, Content and Organization, the others address questions that apply to all subjects, such as 'are the learning outcomes indicated in the Objectives taught and appropriately assessed?', 'are the rates and trends in student progression and completion satisfactory?', 'are students given adequate information about their programmes?'

Even the curriculum aspect mostly addresses generic issues, and it has to be interpreted with reference to the aims and objectives mentioned in the SAD. The main questions the reviewers have to answer about the curriculum are:

- How appropriate are the curriculum design, organization and content in relation to the intended learning outcomes and experiences?
- Are the learning opportunities provided appropriate to the intended outcomes in terms of knowledge, skills, employability, further study and personal development?
- To what extent does the evidence of actual progression and achievement confirm that the learning opportunities provided are appropriate to the intended outcomes?
- Is there evidence that curriculum design and renewal are informed by recent developments in teaching and learning, recent subject/interdisciplinary developments, including research, industrial and professional changes, or developments in learning resources (library, IT)?

These questions do not ask reviewers to assess the intended learning outcomes and experiences set by institutions in their objectives. They rather ask reviewers to make their assessment given the learning outcomes stated by the institution. Furthermore, the QAA explicitly writes that 'the aims and objectives of programmes having the same or similar subject titles, but offered in different institutions, will vary. Programmes will reflect the particular research interests of individual institutions, and some may have more explicitly vocational aims than others'.

6.3.4 The role of subjects in the Subject Review after the introduction of benchmarking statements

With the introduction of benchmarking statements for each subject, however, the situation is changing. Subjects are becoming more important, and the content of programmes, namely their intended learning outcomes, are becoming themselves object of closer scrutiny. Already the change of name of the whole process from Teaching Quality Assessment to Subject Review indicated an increasing importance of subject specific issues. However, it is the introduction of subject benchmarks that makes it possible to give disciplines a more important role in the review.

Before the introduction of the subject benchmarking statements, as we have just seen, judgements about the intended learning outcomes (that is, the content, in terms of knowledge and skills, of programmes such as degrees or diplomas) could only be criticized indirectly, if at all. In order to pass judgements about the appropriateness of the learning outcomes set by departments in their programmes it was obviously necessary to define which learning outcomes would be appropriate in each subject. So, for example, in order to decide whether the knowledge and skill taught in each degree in economics are appropriate, it is necessary to agree on what an 'appropriate' degree in economics might look like. The subject benchmarking statements have been introduced to provide reviewers with this information.

With the introduction of benchmarks, the definition of quality adopted by the QAA can effectively identify two distinct dimensions:

- the appropriateness of the standards set by the institution;
- the effectiveness of teaching and learning support in providing opportunities for students to achieve those standards.

The first dimension is clearly subject-specific. The QAA explicitly states that 'reporting on programme outcome standards is concerned with the appropriateness of the intended learning outcomes set by the institution (in relation to relevant subject benchmark statements, qualification levels and the overall aims of the provision), the effectiveness of curricular content ...'

The importance of the role that subject benchmark statements are expected to play in future reviews is also explicitly illustrated in the QAA approach to judgement of standards. They write on their website:

Reviewers will assess, for each programme, whether there are clear learning outcomes which appropriately reflect applicable subject benchmark statements and the level of the award. Subject benchmark statements represent general expectations about standards in an academic discipline, particularly in relation to intellectual demand and challenge ... If the intended learning outcomes were found not to match those expectations, it is unlikely that reviewers could have confidence in the standards of the provision.

Although the QAA also allows for differences in aims and objectives, makes provisions for interdisciplinarity and innovation, and says that 'making consistent judgements about the appropriateness of the intended outcomes of academic programmes does not mean that reviewers will look for a dull uniformity rather than intellectual curiosity', it seems likely that pluralism within a subject might be negatively affected by the new QAA approach.

It is difficult to envisage how the introduction of benchmarks will not lead to decrease of diversity in the offerings of economics (and other subjects), and therefore to less pluralism in economics programmes. In practice the devil lies in the detail, and the actual content of the benchmarking statement can either legitimize or make it difficult for departments to teach economics adopting a pluralist approach.

6.4　PLURALISM AND THE ECONOMICS SUBJECT BENCHMARKING STATEMENT

6.4.1　Some considerations about economics in the UK and the benchmarking statement

There are various considerations that we have to keep in mind if we want to understand the impact of the introduction of the economics subject benchmarking statement on pluralism. First, status in research matters in teaching as well, and, as Lee and Harley's analysis of economics research suggests, mainstream economists have higher status in the discipline than non-mainstream ones. This means that the potential threat of a narrow mainstream interpretation of what economics – and therefore also Economics teaching – are about, is realistic.

A second consideration that might be important is that the benchmark was strongly wanted by the QAA, and there was no obvious agenda of orthodox economists to 'appropriate' the teaching of economics. This is because the financial and status incentives in teaching are not the same as in the case of research. In the RAE, the score achieved and the amount of funding received are tightly linked, whereas a bad score in the Subject Review does not lead to immediate loss of funding, and a good score does not lead to financial gains. This means that the incentive structure of the agents will be different.

Third, the recent increase in monitoring of teaching quality is not always seen as a positive development by academics. Whilst many economists would recognize that the Subject Review offers opportunities for self-reflection and useful external feedback about teaching practices, there are significant negative aspects associated with increasing monitoring of teaching quality. The major complaint moved to the QAA is that the increase in the workload due to teaching quality assurance is excessive compared to the benefits achieved. Such is the power of this argument that the QAA decided to move towards a 'light touch' approach with the end of the rounds of Subject Reviews in 2001 and the advent of the Academic Review.[10]

Complaints are also moved towards the bureaucratic costs of the RAE, but in the case of research there is the very significant difference that the RAE scores are directly linked to funding.

A fourth important consideration is that single honour economics degrees are in decline, and the great majority of students take economics courses within joint honours or combined programmes[11]. It is obvious that the learning outcomes of students taking a straight economics degree will be quite different from students taking a generic degree in business or social sciences with only some economics modules. The definition of economics in the benchmarking statement, therefore, has to consider carefully how economics should be defined (what theories, methods and techniques) in interdisciplinary programmes.

The split between single and joint honours in economics teaching is important because it generated a choice between two strategies to defend and promote pluralism in economics teaching:

- to fight for a pluralist approach to economics to be included in the discipline core, and therefore in single honours programmes as well;
- to avoid a direct clash with mainstream economists, whose status is superior because of the RAE-generated situation in the field of research, and concede the 'core' of the subject to the mainstream orthodoxy, which therefore defines the curriculum of single honour programmes, and ensure that pluralism is recognized in joint honours programmes.

As we will see later, it seems that the outcome reflects the second strategy.

6.4.2   Pluralism in the economics subject benchmarking statement

A sub-group of members of the Conference of University Heads of Department in Economics (CHUDE) was assigned the task of preparing the subject benchmarking statement for economics. Unofficial information about the meetings does not mention conflicts between members of the panel, an outcome that many would expect if a similar exercise was carried out for RAE purposes.
Among the issues that the panel had to tackle were:

- whether in economics there is a rigid core that must be taught,
- the role of formalism and, in particular, mathematical techniques in economics,
- the differences between teaching economics as a single subject (in single honours degrees) and in interdisciplinary settings.

Boxes 6.1 and 6.2 report some sections of the economics benchmarking statement. The whole document can be found on the QAA website (www.qaa.ac.uk).

The nature and context of economics

Box 6.1: Extract from Section 1 of the economics subject benchmarking statement

---

1.1 Economics is the study of the factors that influence income, wealth and well-being. From this it seeks to inform the design and implementation of economic policy. Its aim is to analyse and understand the allocation, distribution and utilisation of scarce resources. Economics is concerned both with how present allocations arise and how they may change in the future. Study of Economics requires us to understand how resources are used and how households and firms behave and interact. This understanding is required at both the individual (micro) and the aggregate (macro) level. The analysis is both static (dealing with output, employment, income, trade and finance) and dynamic (dealing with innovation, technical progress, economic growth and business cycles). The study of Economics requires an understanding of resources, agents, institutions and mechanisms. Moreover, since virtually no economy operates in isolation, it is important that these phenomena are studied in an international context.

1.2 Economics is a key discipline in the social sciences. Its subject matter engages with other subject areas such as psychology, politics, sociology, anthropology, geography, history and law. It also uses mathematics and statistics and is engaging increasingly with sciences such as biology, environmental science and medicine. Furthermore, since knowledge of economics is essential for an understanding of business behaviour, strategy and corporate performance, it is one of the central disciplines underpinning the study of business and management and related areas. Recognition of these interrelationships, and the increasing number of students who are choosing to study economics jointly with another subject, or as an integral part of a business and management degree, have led to new and imaginative degree programmes. Their design has been influenced by the appreciation that a training that includes Economics provides significant employment opportunities in a variety of careers in addition to working as a professional economist.

Virtually any economist can recognize in these paragraphs the strong presence of mainstream economics. The centrality of the allocation of scarce resources, the key role of mathematics and statistics, and the identification of resources, households and firms as main blocks of microeconomics are features associated with the competitive general equilibrium theory. Mentions of dynamics, innovation, economic growth and the importance of institutions, however, broaden the scope of the subject and gives room for the inclusion of alternative approaches.

It is worth mentioning that paragraph 1.2 acknowledges the growing importance of interdisciplinary degrees for the subject.

The aims of degree programmes in economics

Section 2 of the benchmarking document lists the aims that should be included in degrees where economics is a major component. The list mainly includes generic aims, such as 'to stimulate students intellectually', 'to equip students with appropriate tools of analysis to tackle issues and problems of economic policy' and 'to provide a firm foundation of knowledge about the workings of the economy'. It also clearly establishes the existence of a difference in economics teaching between single subject and interdisciplinary degrees as one of the aims is to 'provide training in the principles of economics and their application appropriate to the type of degree concerned: single honours, joint honours and combined studies'.

The section on aims, therefore, is far from prescriptive and leaves large room for interpretation.

Subject knowledge and understanding

Section 3 covers subject knowledge and understanding, that is the 'pieces of knowledge' that economics degrees are expected to include. It is therefore the part of the document where prescriptions about the topics and theories would appear.

Box 6.2: Extract from Section 3 of the economics subject benchmarking statement

---

3.1 To achieve these aims any single honours degree in Economics normally comprises the following elements.

- A coherent core of economic principles. The understanding of these might be verbal, graphical or mathematical. These principles should cover the microeconomic issues of decision and choice, the production and exchange of goods, the interdependency of markets, and economic welfare. They should also include macroeconomic issues, such as employment, national income, the balance of payments and the distribution of income, inflation, growth and business cycles, money and finance. The understanding should extend to economic policy at both the microeconomic and macroeconomic levels. In all these, students should show an understanding of analytical methods and model-based argument and should appreciate the existence of different methodological approaches.
- Relevant quantitative methods and computing techniques. These are likely to cover mathematical and statistical methods, including econometrics. Students should have some exposure to the use of such techniques on actual economic, financial or social data.
- A knowledge and appreciation of economic data, both quantitative and qualitative. Students should also have some knowledge of the appropriate methods that the economist might use to structure and analyse such data.
- The applications of economics. Students should have the ability to apply a core of economic principles and reasoning to a variety of applied topics. They should also be aware of the economic principles that can be used to design, guide and interpret commercial, economic and social policy. As part of this, they should have the ability to discuss and analyse

government policy and to assess the performance of the UK and other economies.

3.2 It is recognised that, in both single honours degrees and in many degrees that involve a substantial amount of Economics, content will be adapted to suit the nature and objectives of the degree programme. In degrees that are not single honours Economics, not all the core elements in 3.1 may be covered. It is also recognised that the forms of analysis chosen may differ and may be tailored to best serve the skills that students bring with them into their degree programme. It is neither the function nor the objective of this benchmarking document to prescribe what these forms of analysis might be; this is a matter for institutional choice and decision.

Section 3.1 covers single honour degrees, and it very much in line with mainstream economics. It talks explicitly of the existence of a 'coherent core of economic principles' which cover 'microeconomic issues of decision and choice, the production and exchange of goods, the interdependency of markets, and economic welfare': neoclassical microeconomic theory. Macroeconomics is slightly more open as it could include at least some Keynesian approaches, as the reference to issues about employment suggests, and there is a mention of the appreciation of 'the existence of different methodological approaches'. Section 3.1 also states the importance of techniques in single honours degrees and the primacy of mathematics, statistics and econometrics. This is a subject that is also reinforced in the section about skills, with a whole paragraph about the 'crucial skill of numeracy'.

Section 3.2 clearly highlights the difference between single honours and interdisciplinary degrees. The opening sentence of the paragraph confirms that in such programmes both the content of the economics taught and the form of analysis chosen are not prescribed, and are therefore matters in the hands of the various institutions. There is only one significant restriction for interdisciplinary degrees. Since the benchmark says that 'not all the core elements in 3.1 may be covered', there is presumption that at least some elements of mainstream theory should be taught.

Skills

Section 4 covers the skills that economics degrees should provide. Besides general key skills, common to virtually all degrees, and further emphasis on numeracy, the section identifies four 'transferable skills' specific to economics, namely abstraction, analysis (including deduction and induction), quantification and design (that is, working with data), and framing (defined as 'how to decide what should be taken as given or fixed for the purposes of setting up and solving a problem, i.e. what the important "parameters" are in constraining the solution to the problem').

All these four subject-specific skills refer to the construction and application of models, and therefore reinforce the technical nature of economics against a more discursive approach. Besides these skills, some 'transferable concepts' are identified, that are likely to be 'present in most of the decision problems that [students] are likely to face subsequently in their careers'. They are opportunity cost, incentives (and agents' rational response to them), equilibrium (including stability and disequilibrium), strategic thinking, expectations and surprises, and the relevance of marginal considerations.

Again, these main concepts reinforce the dominance of the mainstream approach as other important concepts that are used in other approaches are not included.

6.5   CONCLUSIONS: WHAT FUTURE FOR PLURALISM IN ECONOMICS TEACHING IN THE UK?

This chapter has analysed the possible impact of the subject benchmarking statement for economics on pluralism in economics teaching in the UK. Because of the close ties between teaching and research, the current trends in pluralism in research have been briefly discussed, mainly drawing on the analysis by Lee and Harley (1998). They conclude that the introduction of the RAE has led to the dominance of the mainstream school of thought and heterodox approaches are almost in danger of disappearing. One important trend they identify is the increasing recruitment of mainstream economists in the UK at the expense of heterodox economists.

Section 6.3 illustrated the background to the introduction of subject benchmarking statements and, more in general, the process of quality assurance in teaching in which they will operate. With the introduction of benchmarks, the QAA will be able to pass judgements on the appropriateness of learning outcomes of degrees in various programmes.

The previous section analysed the key sections of the subject benchmarking statement for economics, and found that whilst the mainstream approach appears to dominate single subject degrees, there is still considerable freedom in economics teaching for interdisciplinary programmes. For example, the benchmarking document acknowledges that it is possible to do good teaching of economics using a 'low-tech' approach, where by 'low-tech' is meant low-maths, still retaining analytical depth, using rigorous reasoning and abstraction, and achieving a significant degree of analytical complexity.

This finding is important because of the current trends in student numbers in economics, which show a decline in the number of students that take single honour degrees in economics and an increase of the proportion of students studying economics within interdisciplinary programmes. This means that for most of the British students that take economics courses it is possible to study economics with a pluralistic approach, although students taking single honours will see their training mainly confined to the mainstream approach.

On the other hand, it is true that 'real economists' are single honours students, and they therefore receive mainstream economics education. This means that it will be increasingly unlikely for the next generation of economists to receive an education that emphasizes pluralism. This is especially true because of the impact of the RAE on research funding has led departments to recruit mainly mainstream economists.

The hopes for pluralism are therefore twofold. One possibility is that the core mainstream theory will expand from within, with successful heterodox approaches being included in mainstream teaching and research. This already happens, but only slowly and selectively, with only theories that are not too incompatible with the core being included in mainstream teaching. Another possibility is that the decline of single honours students becomes so severe that either providers of single honours degrees have to review their curricula, or graduates that have taken a significant amount of economics in interdisciplinary degrees (and therefore have possibly been exposed to a pluralist approach) will be increasingly recognized as proper economists. Indeed, already today the Government Economic Service employs graduates who have as little as 50% economics in their degrees.

NOTES

[1] Recent unpublished research presented by Lee at the Association for Heterodox Economics in 2004 supports this conclusion.

[2] For more information on the 'dual support' system look at the RAE website: http://www.hero.ac.uk/rae/AboutUs/.

[3] Downloadable from RAE website: http://www.hero.ac.uk/rae/AboutUs/.

[4] The unit can be a department, but not necessarily. A number of economics departments have chosen to submit some staff in other disciplines.

[5] These conclusions are obviously dependent on the indicators of productivity and quality used. It is beyond the scope of this chapter to discuss the advantages and disadvantages of such indicators.

[6] Lee and Harley provide a list of core mainstream journals based on the more widely known 'Diamond list' (Lee and Harley, 1998: table 5).

[7] The agency is funded both by the HECFs, on whose behalf it assesses the teaching provision at subject level, and by the HE institutions themselves.

[8] A more detailed explanation of SR scores and their use in league tables is provided below.

[9] This explains why the overall score on its own is not particularly meaningful even though it is extensively used by newspapers in league tables. In fact, it is possible for a department to have an overall score of 22 (five 4s and one 2) and still fail the review because the provision is not satisfactory in one of the six aspects, or to pass the review with a score of 18 (all 3s). The QAA also explains that 'The graded profile relates to the aims and objectives set by the subject provider, and so should be read in conjunction with those aims and objectives ... When TQA scores are used in league tables to make comparisons between different institutions, it is important to remember that what is being measured is performance against each institution's own objectives.'

[10] Another reason for hostility towards the QAA is that any form of control and monitoring is seen by academics as an attack on their professional ethos and academic freedom.

[11] The crisis of the discipline, at least regarding single honours degrees, is well illustrated by the large number of economics departments that are merged in other units, especially business schools. Recent initiatives by the Royal Economic Society to improve the appeal of economics to potential students include a report on how to improve school economics textbooks and the creation of a website on 'why study economics'.

REFERENCES

Lee, F. and S. Harley (1998), 'Peer-review, the Research Assessment Exercise and the Demise of Non-mainstream Economics', *Capital and Class*, **66**, 23-51.

Quality Assurance Agency website, http://www.qaa.ac.uk/.

Quality Assurance Agency (2000), *Subject Review Handbook, September 2000 to December 2001*, QAA.

Quality Assurance Agency (2000), *Subject Benchmarking Statement: Economics*, QAA.

Research Assessment Exercise (2001), *A Guide to the 2001 Research Assessment Exercise*, RAE 2001 website, http://www.hero.ac.uk/rae/AboutUs/.

7. The Principles of Economics: An American's Experience

Daniel Underwood

> The art of teaching consists in large part of interesting people
> in things that ought to interest them, but do not. The task of
> educators is to discover what an education is and then to invent
> the methods of interesting their students in it.
> (Robert M. Hutchins, 1952: 49)

7.1   INTRODUCTION

Common to the intellectual journey of nearly all economists is Principles of Economics: as students, it is our first exposure to the discipline; as teachers, it is often our first duty station; as mentors recruiting disciples, it is here we seek to ignite that first spark to light the way for a new generation of economists. Yet, while Principles of Economics (Principles) provides a focal point for commonality, Principles is anything but a common course. Paradigms abound, even though a perusal of 'popular' texts suggests otherwise.[1] And history can be telling in this regard, and Samuelson's 1948 text revealing. It is here, in the first Principles text, we see a veritable absence of paradigms save for the 'Keynesian revolution', and the only exception is mention of Marx to illustrate the errors of his analysis, an 'ideological purge' consistent with the onset of the Cold War (Samuelson, 1948: 67-73). Thus, in the USA, Principles is generally Principles of Neoclassical Economics. For the majority – the 'mainstream' – debate between paradigms no longer exists, not because other paradigms vanished, but because a majority decided only a singular ideology is to be taught in the classroom (Siegfried and Meszaros). While agreement amongst the majority is one avenue to legitimate Principles as commonly construed in the USA, other decision criteria exist that might lead economic educators to consider a different approach to Principles.[2] Consider the question, 'Is Principles of interest to students?' Were our goal to pursue an answer in the positivist tradition, that is, to create a pseudo scientific framework to explore the question, the null hypothesis would be that there has been no change in student interest: economics continues to be relevant to undergraduates. The alternative hypothesis: economics is narrow, excessively mathematical, and increasingly irrelevant to contemporary undergraduates. Keeping in mind that in the positivist tradition theory need not be accurate – indeed, it should not be! – and only yield accurate predictions (Friedman, 1953), data (Siegfried, 1999) force us to reject the null and work from the alternative: yes, students find economics boring and irrelevant and thus pursue other lines of study. This leaves us with something of a quandary: adapt and soar in new directions to meet the changing demands of the academic environment and thus retain economics' historically vibrant presence in the student's educational experience; or, continue on the current evolutionary trajectory with the smugness of a mathematically adept but experientially irrelevant flightless bird.[3]

7.2   RETHINKING PRINCIPLES

For several decades economists in the USA have individually and collectively turned their scholarly interests toward economic education. Initially, this effort occurred exclusively under the auspices of the National Council of Economic Education (NCEE) and the American Economics Association's (AEA) Committee on Economic Education. The NCEE has engaged in a number of fruitful activities which have enriched economic education, including the *Journal of Economic Education (JEE)*, sessions conducted at the Allied Social Science Association's (ASSA) annual meetings, and its *Handbook on Undergraduate Economic Education*. Yet, the combined efforts of the NCEE have not reversed the 20 per cent decline in economics majors in the USA that led one NCEE leader to explain the outcome as a steady state equilibrium adjustment (Siegfried, 1999). Thought of in terms of our alternative hypothesis, the inward shift in the demand for economic education caused by a change in the tastes and preferences of students – they decided Principles had become boring and irrelevant – has stopped with a new equilibrium 20 per cent lower than in the past.

It is not difficult to discover why undergraduate interest has declined. First, in the late 1980s the AEA formed its Committee on Graduate Education in Economics (COGEE). Interviews with graduate students revealed dissatisfaction with the field because of excessive emphasis on mathematical theorems, narrowness of content, insufficient incorporation of real world problems, inattention to economic history, and failure to incorporate interdisciplinary knowledge (Knoedler and Underwood, 2003). And, of course, as most teach what they learned in graduate school, Principles has come to mirror the graduate experience. Second, participation in NCEE sessions at ASSA and the pages of the *JEE* reveal that many economic educators, in advancing the science of economic education, have focused predominately on pedagogy: new ways of teaching the same old stuff, the stuff COGEE reveals is increasingly not of interest to students. A third reason is to be found in cognitive psychology. It is well understood that the process of knowing requires the use of filters to block the flow of sensory data which makes possible focus on a particular phenomena of interest. These 'schema' determine that which we see and that which we ignore. Schema are products of experience guided by culture. Thus, for economic education to be of interest to students, it must resonate with their experiences, their interests. Failure to do so will make economics increasingly irrelevant to contemporary undergraduate students (Knoedler and Underwood, 2003).

For these reasons and others, in 1998 a small group of Original Institutional Economists (OIE) banded together to isolate the axiomatic tenets implicit in Principles, and then develop a parallel set of tenets that might enrich the undergraduate educational experience (Knoedler et al. 1998). The outcome was '10 Things Every Principles Student Should Learn?' and '10 Things Every Principles Student *Should* Learn!' presented in revised form in tables 7.1 and 7.2 below. This effort led two of the panelists to make their proposal for a multiparadigmatic approach to Principles, one that would systematically emphasize how alternative theories could be used to explore and understand economic phenomena (Knoedler and Underwood, 2003). Tables 7.1 and 7.2 help illustrate how NeoClassical and Original Institutional economic Principles can be systematically contrasted when using a multiparadigmatic approach Simultaneously, a series of economic education sessions were sponsored by the Association for Institutional Thought (AFIT) which presented innovative pedagogy, provided 'how to' templates to incorporate those approaches into the classroom, assembled collateral readings, and more (Knoedler and Underwood, 2004).[4] These efforts to integrate a multiparadigmatic approach to Principles do not end with the efforts of OIE, as economic educators complete similar exercises using other paradigms (Schneider and Schackelford, 2001; Cohn and Schneider, 2003).

Table 7.1: 'Ten Things Every Principles Student Should Learn?[5]'

1. Economics is the study of choice under conditions of scarcity.
2. Economic actors are motivated by rational self-interest to maximize their satisfaction from consumption (based on a given set of preferences).
3. Economic efficiency (technical and allocative) is the primary goal of an economy.
4. The market values (prices) established in a 'free market' economy are the critical guides to economic efficiency. Anything that 'distorts' free market values reduces efficiency, thus imposing costs on society.
5. Government 'interference' in the free market distorts market values, thus reducing efficiency. A policy of laissez-faire is optimal.
6. The history of economic thought began and ended with Adam Smith. The historical context shaping development of economic theory is not important.
7. Inequality and poverty are completely unrelated to race, gender and class. Thus, analyzing the recent 'welfare reform' – 60 months of total lifetime benefits, 'incentives to work,' etc. – does not require any knowledge of the history or structure of the programs involved or the characteristics of those who participate in these programs.
8. In an advanced market economy, money is used as a means of exchange, a store of value, and a unit of account. However, money is a neutral variable in analysis of the economy. Given this, the first objective of monetary and fiscal policy is combating inflation and stabilization of employment is a by-product.
9. Economics, practiced correctly, is a 'positive science' premised upon value-free, objective knowledge. Thus, practitioners of the discipline are one dimensional, *wertfrei*, value free economists who often share the same opinion.
10. The natural world, the source of all energy and materials and the repository of for all waste, is irrelevant in conceptualizing a materially expanding economic process.

Source: Knoedler and Underwood (2003:708)

Table 7.2: 'Ten Things Every Principles Student Should Learn![6]'

1. Economics is about social provisioning, not merely choices and scarcity.
2. Both scarcity and wants are socially defined and created.
3. Economic systems are human creations; no particular economic system is 'natural.'
4. Valuation is a social process.
5. The government defines the economy; laissez-faire capitalism is an oxymoron, a rhetorical concept of incongruous concepts.
6. The history of economic thought is critical to the study of 'basic principles' of economics.
7. Economic theory ('logical economics') and real world economics are often very different things.
8. Race, gender, and class shape economic processes, outcomes and policies in the real world economy.
9. There are many types of economists who do not agree on many things. This reflects the fact that economics is not "value free" and ideology shapes our analyses and conclusions as economists.
10. Ecological literacy – the economy↔ecology interface – between biophysical first principles and economic sustainability is essential to understanding the economic process.

Source: Knoedler and Underwood (2003: 714)

7.3   PRINCIPLES AND GENERAL EDUCATION

Before we can analyze why students find economics boring and irrelevant, we need to explore why students might take Principles, gateway to the major. Most students take Principles to satisfy a social science general education requirement. What then are the goals of general education? Answers parallel an institution's educational philosophy articulated through its mission statement: breadth of knowledge, an understanding of civilizations, appreciation of the arts; yet further examination reveals more, and that is exposure to and mastery of the knowledge–skill set necessary to effectively pursue a professional career and to practice the tenets of citizenship. In the USA this knowledge–skill set has traditionally consisted of 'reading, writing and arithmetic.' Today, arithmetic has metamorphosed into quantitative reasoning, and three additional knowledge–skill sets have emerged:

interpersonal communications, access and application of digital technology, and critical thinking.

While Principles has long advanced development of *quantitative reasoning*, understood as the ability to access, organize, and process data using quantitative and technological skills, it is my contention that Principles is in a unique position to similarly advance critical thinking skills. The education literature reveals that critical thinking consists of three elements (Underwood, 2004a). First, critical thinking is a process to evaluate goals and render a decision (Ennis, 1987; Siegfried et al., 1991; Borg and Borg, 2001; and Greenlaw and DeLoach, 2003). Second, for students to develop this critical thinking outcome – render a decision – their cognitive processes must be systematically developed moving from simple binary choice sets through comparative analysis (Ennis, 1987; Borg and Borg, 2001; Greenlaw and Deloach, 2003). Third, essential to development of this cognitive framework is integration of alternative methods of explaining the same phenomena (Siegfried et al., 1991; Borg and Borg, 2001; Greenlaw and DeLoach, 2003). These recursively interrelated elements can be integrated into a singular definition: *critical thinking is the use of empirically grounded quantitative reasoning to advance understanding of phenomena of interest to inform value driven judgment.*[6] Reliance upon a singular analytical apparatus necessarily decreases the number of alternatives that can be explored and thus reduces the choice set from which judgment is derived.

Crucial then, if the objective is to advance critical thinking, is for students to understand that multiple avenues exist to use empirically grounded quantitative reasoning to derive informed judgment. Many schools of economic thought exist, each capable of using internally consistent logic to sort, organize and empirically test the capacity of a theory to explain a phenomena of interest and derive conclusions. Yet, because these schools differ on the basis of underlying value systems, they use alternative theories to derive different conclusions about the nature of economic reality and the appropriate policy objectives and tools. Define this as the Values↔Vision↔Analysis↔Policy nexus (V↔V↔A↔P), a recursive interaction that is anything but *wertfrei* (Knoedler and Underwood, 2003; Underwood, 2004a).

Each economic paradigm has its own V↔V↔A↔P. Each uses different objectives and tools to create alternative realities. Which is right? The answer depends less on objective criteria – realism of assumptions or predictive power – and more upon the value system of the observer. Let us be honest: there is no such thing as objective *wertfrei* analysis. We all bring value laden modes of analysis to conduct inquiry and should remain cognizant of the inherent biases that shape our critical thinking. While students do too, they are also students with an intrinsic goal of learning. Furthermore, few students are likely to be predisposed to favor one paradigm over another during their general education experience – they need not deal with the dilemma of a career's worth of sunk costs becoming an expert in a singular paradigm. Use of a multiparadigmatic approach will greatly increase *their* critical thinking skills, not only through the systematic use of empirically grounded quantitative reasoning, but by comparing and contrasting how alternative paradigms lead to different explanations of the material world. They will learn to inform their judgment (Underwood, 2004a).

7.4   TOWARDS A MULTIPARADIGMATIC APPROACH

A multiparadigmatic approach to Principles utilizes two or more paradigms to explore economic concepts, analysis and policy prescriptions throughout the course. Fundamental is that these paradigms be used to study a phenomena of interest by explicitly examining how the V↔V↔A↔P operates to shape the nature of that study. For instance, a multiparadigmatic approach to macroeconomics could use Keynesian, Marxist, Monetarist, and Schumpeterian explanations for the business cycle (Underwood, 2004a). Each school of thought rests upon an alternative set of premises indicative of an underlying value system that leads to a unique explanation of the nature of the business cycle, how that cycle propels society, and what can – *should* – be done about it. As the policy prescriptions range from laissez faire to incitement of revolution, these paradigms are anything but *wertfrei*: rather, they are reflections of particular *Weltanschauungs* with an agenda of recreating culture in that image.[7]   The objective of a multiparadigmatic approach to Principles is to integrate the V↔V↔A↔P to foster development of critical thinking skills in a form relevant to students. It is not to indoctrinate students towards adopting one worldview over another.

If Principles is to be relevant to the student, the educational experience must resonate with their undergraduate experience while simultaneously advancing Principles unique contribution to general education: the development of critical thinking skills. One effective avenue to attain this objective is the use of 'Cognitive Rejoinders'. Cognitive Rejoinders are defined as 'explicit and deliberate returns to knowledge sets for further application, synthesis and evaluation' (Underwood, 2004a: 572-573). There are two types: 'Paradigmatic Rejoinders' and 'Theme Rejoinders'. A Theme Rejoinder is return to an important contemporary topic as the term progresses. Paradigmatic Rejoinders are explicit and systematic returns to a V↔V↔A↔P to further explore economic phenomena. Both Theme and

Paradigmatic Rejoinders should be employed within and between economics courses. Figure 7.1 depicts how energy can be used as a Theme Rejoinder, while Neoclassical Economics (NCE) and the Original Institutional Economics (OIE) can be used as Paradigmatic Rejoinders. It contrasts Principle 10 found in tables 7.1 and 7.2. One could analyze a number of important economic concepts in both macroeconomics and microeconomics using Figure 7.1 as a design template (Underwood, 2004a). In microeconomics NCE would explain economic rents as a reward to ownership, an institution necessary for the efficient allocation of the resource. OIE could emphasize how path-dependence on oil which creates those rents was a result of only one possible evolutionary trajectory: energy futures don't just happen; they are the result of deliberate choices (Underwood, 2003b). When exploring the impact of energy on employment in macroeconomics, NCE might emphasize NAIRU (the non-accelerating inflation rate of unemployment), whereas OIE would focus on social policies to guarantee employment to all willing and able to work.

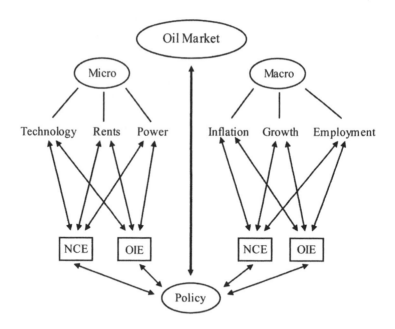

Figure 7.3 Energy and rejoinders within and between micro and macro

Let us return now to general education and, in particular, the 'breadth of knowledge' objective. While all institutions of higher learning package breadth differently, they all identify knowledge sets an educated person should possess. Within each set of courses, themselves drawn from discipline specific subsets, courses are clustered. Thus, for instance, we might find humanities with courses like art, literature, music and philosophy; natural sciences with biology, ecology, mathematics and physics; and social sciences with economics, history, political science and sociology. Students fulfill general education requirements by selecting courses that interest them, and one important way to interest students – make it meaningful – is to create linkages with other subjects. This can be accomplished using 'Intellectual Nodes' illustrated in Figure 7.2 (Underwood, 2004a).

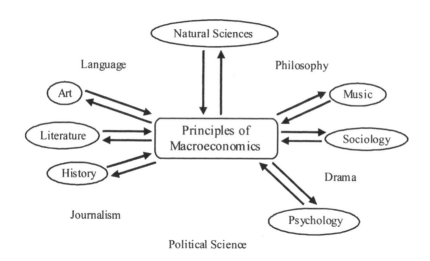

Figure 7.4 Nodes as an organizational template

'Potential Nodes' are general education courses that could be topically or analytically linked with Principles. 'Realized Nodes' are knowledge sets explicitly and systematically integrated into Principles (Underwood, 2004a). The directional arrows indicate the knowledge sets one course can build from, or feed to, knowledge sets in another course. When nodes become realized, they create experiential relevance for students by creating explicit connections with other elements of their general education.[7] We can enrich this experience by integrating historical nodes that illuminate how the economic process shapes historical events; we can explain how 'Vested Interests' use political institutions to advance their agenda thereby creating a political science node; we can even create Nodes with music and art: the key is to be imaginative while focusing on potential nodes in the student's general education experience. In so doing Principles becomes a part of their schema and economics will more likely become part of their interest.

7.5   SCHEMA, MULTIPARADIGMATICS, AND CRITICAL THINKING IN PRINCIPLES

Here, our goal is threefold. First, we want Principles to continue its time honoured role in general education: to use a rigorously applied and well defined epistemology to advance knowledge. Second, we need to integrate a multiparadigmatic approach to better advance critical thinking. Third, we need to modify our pedagogy to simultaneously achieve objectives one and two while penetrating the schema of today's undergraduate. In other words, the content and method of teaching Principles must be relevant to students and prepare them to make rationally tractable and empirically verifiable judgments about the world.

   The crucial first step in shaping the student's journey is a theory of knowledge: what is knowledge and how is it discovered? Economics has traditionally emphasized the application of the scientific method to advance knowledge. One might be surprised, however, to discover how few students understand what this involves and how seldom a rigorous treatment of what is and is not knowledge is encountered by students as they pursue general education. Of course, Principles as encountered in NCE treats its paradigm as *wertfrei*. Indeed, few popular texts even mention the so-called positive normative dichotomy! (Knoedler and Underwood, 2003). Those using a multiparadigmatic approach can address the fallacy of value free knowledge by emphasizing the problem of separating the knower from the known. Better, we can ask students, 'How do you know what you know is true?' The goal is for students to discover the tests they use to evaluate truth, to separate fact from fiction, where facts themselves can never be separated from the knower of the facts. Students find this line of abstract inquiry fascinating because it leads them to question authority, and questioning authority is an important part of the undergraduate experience! Go on then to explicitly introduce the V↔V↔A↔P and tell students this will be a regular platform from which to explore alternative explanations about the nature of the economic world: that as a professor you will not prescribe the correct choice, but help them find their own choice set. This is the second important part of the undergraduate experience: students must learn to make choices for themselves!

For some time pedagogy has emphasized that discovery based learning, where students actively and collaboratively participate in the problem solving process, results in a deeper level of understanding (Simkins, 1999; Johnson et al., 2000; Truscott et al., 2000). While recent developments in neural biology do not tell us why discovery based learning may create greater learning outcomes, it has revealed why students often prefer it to rote – 'chalk and talk' – forms of teaching and learning. Magnetic resonance imaging and electroencephalogram recordings are used to map and measure changes in the brain's neural centers when insight – cognitively assembling what were disparate pieces of information into a holistic solution – is used in problem solving. The result is a 'Eureka' or 'Aha!' experience.[8] Not only is a unique part of the brain used with insight problem solving, but a high burst of neural activity occurs. This creates a satisfying 'Aha effect'. Another way to make Principles resonate with students, then, is to design discovery based learning exercises that put them into a position where they make the mental leap to solve a problem. To accomplish this objective, the learning activity must help students gather the pieces, yet, simultaneously, the students must find the key to assemble them and solve the puzzle.

We can use this knowledge about the importance of discovery based learning to help accomplish our threefold goal. As the goal of higher learning is for *students* to inform their judgments, it is essential they determine which alternative explanation is preferred in a particular situation, and are not indoctrinated into a particular mode of explanation.[9] Essential in this regard is empowerment of students to conduct empirical study of the economic world through discovery based exercises. Fortunately technology makes possible access to databases at the click of a mouse: sometimes a left, but when copying files it's a right! Early in the term it is instrumental to create what I call 'Empirical Adventure Teams' (Underwood, 2004a). After a tour of the web, where students are exposed to comprehensive databases available and are shown how data can be used to not only test hypotheses but form hypotheses, they are randomly assigned into teams. Teams receive a multi-part assignment that requires them to learn the history and objectives of each database, compile predetermined cross-sectional and time-series data, and look for patterns and formulate hypotheses. Crucial in assignment design is careful consideration of the Theme and Paradigmatic Rejoinders to be subsequently employed so that students experience Aha! moments as the term progresses (Underwood, 2003a). Done properly, students will have the data to examine and derive informed judgment when studying the business cycle, or variants of the natural rate of unemployment hypothesis, or the distribution of income, or – the potential list is constrained only by our pedagogic imagination. I like to do this assignment early in the term, before students are exposed to any paradigms. Later, they receive additional Empirical Adventure Team assignments. While these assignments are demanding, at each juncture students find the results interesting and exciting. Occasionally they will share how they were able to use the results, or build upon those studies, when taking on assignments in others classes. Empirical Adventures promote attainment of all three goals in a discovery based environment. First, students have employed a rigorous epistemology to determine what knowledge is. Second, by using Rejoinders to explore and test alternative paradigms, students work through all three levels of critical thinking. The outcome is an informed judgment. Third, when they share the results of their inquiry, especially when those results are linked with other courses using Intellectual Nodes, we know Principles has entered their schema: thus we have achieved relevance. Empirical Adventures create a rigorous analytical and empirical backdrop for continued study throughout and even after the term. Consistent return to Theme and Paradigmatic Rejoinders should make use of empirically grounded quantitative reasoning to understand phenomena of interest and make informed judgments: critical thinking thus becomes a regular part of their lives.[10] And this all the more so if we employ nodes to extend the use of this critical thinking into other courses.

There is one more pedagogic innovation to share in this chapter. It too emphasizes attainment of our three-fold goals: use of a rigorous epistemology, development and application of critical thinking skills, and penetration of students' schemas. One important element of the student's world and one emphasized in nearly every class they take are changes in the world outside academia. Call this 'current events'. We want our students to be aware of current events and we often believe our academic discipline has something to say about those events, from causality to policy response. For decades the way this is accomplished is to photocopy a news story, or more recently access the print medium through the internet (Bredon, 1999).[11] Standard operating procedure is to have students study the story, maybe analyze it using NCE theory; it is highly unlikely the story will be empirically tested! Of course, if one employs a multiparadigmatic approach to Principles, it is essential these current events be analyzed using the $V\leftrightarrow V\leftrightarrow A\leftrightarrow P$. Yet, even still, this approach may not be exciting to today's students who have come to expect knowledge packaged as entertainment. Not only this, theirs is a digital world full of marvellous gizmos that all too often detract from the higher learning. How then to integrate current events, use the gizmos they have come to expect, and create an entertaining educational delivery system (Underwood, 2004b)?

I am a frequenter of National Public Radio (NPR). It is there I learn about the world, be it from programming originating in the USA or from other nations. Often, while commuting I'll hear a story and say, 'That would be perfect to illuminate upon an economic concept: the story could be analyzed from multiple perspectives; students could go to the CENSUS and test those propositions.' Then I drive onto campus and the story is over. Yes, NPR has a digital archive but the files are protected, our classrooms are not wireless, so how to 'bring it to class'? The digital revolution offers a solution. One can use an MP3 recorder; play the story from the internet into the recorder, then carry the pocket size device to class.[12] Because the story is in audio form, the students must listen. To assist with focus, it is useful to summarize how the story fits into current themes and give them a few short questions to seek answers for. To make this work it is essential one consider student schema in selecting these stories. The story needs to be important to them, not us! Our role is to figure out how to bring the economics we deem important to explain their world. Yet this is not hard to do. The best way to discover what interests students is to ask; even better, listen! Recently I experimented with this approach, building an MP3 digital archive of current events topically relevant to students (Underwood, 2004b). With gasoline prices soaring they had an inherent interest in stories about oil: OPEC, Iraq, big oil companies, futures markets; spring break is a ritual so any story about the airline industry and air fares is a winner; and finally, Wal-Mart, a retailing juggernaut transforming the world into its image. Each of these examples can be integrated within and between Principles using Theme and Paradigmatic Rejoinders, and even nodes to establish knowledge interchange across disciplines. A Google search makes it possible to build visual support materials to create the context for a 'great story': current events of relevance to students, alternative $V{\leftrightarrow}V{\leftrightarrow}A{\leftrightarrow}P$s to identify and explore the issues involved, and the need to make an informed judgment (Colander, 2000; Knoedler and Underwood, 2003; Underwood, 2004a). Together these current events created the context for a case study students eagerly took on (Underwood, 2004b). Imagine students excited about taking on a difficult project!

7.6   CONCLUSION

My contention in this chapter is that for Principles to resonate with today's student, it must be relevant to their experiences, it needs to emphasize economics' rigorous adherence to a well defined epistemology while systematically developing critical thinking using a multiparadigmatic approach, and it must use discovery based learning. I and many colleagues believe this and practice it on a daily basis. We have found it successful. Yet my conclusion is not about the pedagogy and content of Principles and how the economics curriculum could be improved.

We began with the challenge of Hutchins: decide what an education is and then invent ways of interesting our students in it. As educators, succeeding in this challenge is the core of our mission. Yet, all too often, we leave campus frustrated with the day's results. Maybe we can't reach all of our students while that is our goal. And so, each day upon returning to campus, like Don Quixote, I arrive to confront the forces of darkness and ignorance with the torch of knowledge: it is a relentless quest, 'The Impossible Dream', with little chance for victory.[13] What I have learned about teaching in this struggle is that I am not alone, and it is my students who are my best allies: if they know I will stand with them, through the best and worst of times, they will rise to meet any and all challenges to master economics because we are doing it together. You may think me foolish, call me the 'Man of La Mancha' and retort that 'My classes are too large'; 'My students aren't motivated'; 'My students, my students, my students...' I teach at an open admission community college. My students come from all walks of life, with no to excellent preparation for higher learning; they range in age from 16 to 60. Some have had life easy; others have been pounded by life's hammer; a few have Standardized Aptitude Scores that rival those admitted to the most select private institutions while many begin their studies in remedial English and math, sometimes at the arithmetic level! Our students are not the problem. Forget not the words of Hutchins with which this chapter began: it is our charge. We can all approach becoming great economics teachers when we come to understand we have great economics students, and a rigorous multiparadigmatic approach will get us there. But don't believe me, test the hypothesis. All you have to gain is the lifelong thanks and admiration of students for making their educational experience real and meaningful. It doesn't get any better than that!

NOTES

[1] For a survey of paradigmatic coverage in 'leading' textbooks, see Knoedler and Underwood (2003: Appendix 1).

[2] Outcomes are always shaped by the particular legitimization process used, and that process is often the result of implementation of rule sets designed to advance the interests of a predominate group.

[3] Yes, the dodo comes to mind.

[4] These materials can be found online at http://www.orgs.bucknell.edu/afee/AFIT/teaching_institutionalism.htm.

[5] At our institution, critical thinking often takes the form of what I call *feeeeeeeelings*, which involves the expression of emotional reactions using the written and spoken word. The objective is to create agreement over the relative relevancy of emotional reactions and, once it is agreed that all relatively relevant emotional reactions are legitimate, i.e., everyone has them; the emotional reactions become descriptions of the external world. While experientially entertaining, the resulting knowledge-skill set is economically useless, which among some, is the goal of the higher learning! Principles can help students rise above this pedagogic nonsense.

[6] Students find Marx and Schumpeter fascinating in this regard. Both argue capitalism will undermine its own existence, yet get there following remarkably dissimilar pathways.

[7] This template, at least in the ideal world, could create an avenue for meaningful discourse between colleagues across disciplines to advance the higher learning. My experience, limited thus far, is that many educators seem locked in ceremonially encapsulated disciplinary boxes, and are often reluctant to engage in cross-disciplinary integration of knowledge.

[8] Yes, this is the technical jargon used in the literature. The Eureka experience is traced back to Archimedes, who supposedly shouted it out, then ran home from a public bath naked, after observing water overflow from the tub upon his entry. From this observation he solved a problem posed by a monarch: how can you tell if a coin is gold without damaging that coin (Jung-Beeman et al., 2004).

[9] I recognize that my position is in contrast to some (Siegfried and Meszaros), though I suspect Orwell would side with me.

[10] It has been my experience that once students have learned to do this, they become increasingly dissatisfied with the less rigorous approach to knowledge characteristic of many other academic disciplines and more interested in economics. For instance, last month I received the following comment: 'Dr. Underwoods approach to Economics caused me to rethink what was going to be an English major and subsequently shift my direction toward two of my other interests: Economics and Forest Ecology. I realized I could work toward a valuable major that would incorporate the things I loved to do with worthwhile job opportunities. The class did not change my interests; instead, it showed me how to fulfill them' – Rebekah Gentry.

While this is obviously a biased observation, I have never asserted a separation between the knower and the known.
[11] 'Readings' books of current events are also available; the 'currentness' becomes increasingly problematic after publication.
[12] It is easy to create web-based links so students can complete such assignments outside of class.
[13] Yes, 'The Impossible Dream' is my Principles theme song. You can find the lyrics at http://www.varian.net/dreamweavn/neverending/impossible. html.

REFERENCES

Borg, J.R. and M.O. Borg, 'Teaching Critical Thinking in Interdisciplinary Economics Courses', *College Teaching*, **49**, 20-29.
Bredon, G., 'Net News—Old Wine in a New Bottle?', *Journal of Economic Education*, 28-32.
Colander, D., 'Telling Better Stories in Introductory Economics', *American Economic Review*, **90**, 76-80.
Cohn, S. and Geoff Schneider, 'Heterodox Hypertexts: Using the Internet to Knit Together Heterodox Economics', *International Confederation of Associations for Pluralism in Economics conference on the Future of Heterodox Economics*, Kansas City, Missouri, http://www.facstaff.bucknell.edu/gschnedr/Heterodoxpercent20Hypertexspercent20vpercent205.doc.
Ennis, R.H., 'A Taxonomy of Critical Thinking Dispositions and Abilities', *Teaching Thinking Skills: Theory and Practice*, edited by Joan Boykoff and Robert J. Sternberg, New York: W.H. Freeman and Company, 1987.
Friedman, M., *Essays in Positive Economics Chicago: The University of Chicago Press*, 1953.
Greenlaw, S.A. and Stephen B. DeLoach, 'Teaching Critical Thinking with Electronic Discussion', *Journal of Economic Education*, 36-52.
Hutchins, R., 'The Great Conversation: The Substance of a Liberal Education', *Great Books of the Western World*, 1, edited by Robert Maynard Hutchins, Chicago: Encyclopedia Britannica, Inc., 1952.
Johnson, C.G., Richard H. James, Jenny N. Lye, and Ian M. McDonald, 'An Evaluation of Collaborative Problem Solving for Learning Economics', *Journal of Economic Education*, 13-29.
Jung-Beeman, M., Edward M. Bowden, Jason Haberman, Jennifer L. Frymiare, Stella Arambel-Liu, Richard Greenblatt, Paul J. Reber, John Kounios, 'Neural Activity When People Solve Verbal Problems with Insight', *PLOS Biology*, 2, 0500-0510.
Knoedler, J.T. and Daniel A. Underwood, 'Teaching the Principles of Economics: A Proposal for a Multi-paradigmatic Approach', *Journal of Economic Issues*, **37**, 697-725.

Knoedler, J.T. and Daniel A. Underwood, 'Suggestions to Effectuate a Multi-paradigmatic Approach to the Teaching of Principles of Economics, A Reply', *Journal of Economic Issues*, **38**, 843-845.

Knoedler, J.T., Jennifer Long, Reynold Nesiba, Janice Peterson, Geoff Schneider, James Swaney, and Daniel Underwood, '10 Things Every Principles Student Should Learn But Probably Does Not', *Preceedings*, Western Social Science Association, Denver, Colorado, 1998.

Samuelson, P.A., *Economics, An Introductory Analysis*, New York: McGraw-Hill Book Company, Inc. 1948.

Schneider, G. and Jean Schackelford, "Economics Standards and Lists: Proposed Antidotes for Feminist Economics, *Feminist Economics* **7**, 77-89.

Siegfried, J.J., 'Trends in Undergraduate Economics Degrees', *Journal of Economic Education*, **30**, 325-330.

Siegfried, J.J. and Bonnie T. Meszaros, 'National Voluntary Content Standards for Pre-College Education', *American Economic Review*, **87**, 248-253.

Siegfried, J.J., Robin L. Bartlett, W. Lee Hansen, Allen C. Kelley, Donald N. McCloskey, and Thomas H. Tietenberg, 'The Status and Prospects of the Economics Major', *Journal of Economic Education*, **22**, 197-224.

Simkins, S.P., 'Promoting Active-Student Learning Using the World Wide Web In Economics Courses', *Journal of Economic Education*, 278-291.

Truscott, M.H., Hemant Rustogi, and Corinne B. Young, 'Enhancing the Macroeconomics Course: An Experiential Approach', *Journal of Economic Education*, 60-65.

Underwood, D.A., 'Principles of Macroeconomics: Toward a Multi-paradigmatic Approach', *Journal of Economic Issues*, **38**, 571-581.

Underwood, D.A., 'Tidal Innovations in the Principles of Economics', *Proceedings*, Western Social Science Association, Salt Lake City, Utah, 2004b).

Underwood, D.A., 'Energy Security in the 21st Century?', *Proceedings*, Western Social Science Association, Las Vegas, Nevada, 2003a.

Underwood, D.A., 'Multipliers, Deficits, and Applied Political Economy in Principles of Macroeconomics: An Exercise in Critical Thinking', *Proceedings*, Western Social Science Association, Las Vegas, Nevada, 2003b.

8. A Practitioner's Perspective on Interdisciplinarity in Education: The MBT Case

Wolter Lemstra

8.1 INTRODUCTION

Delft TopTech, the School of Executive Education of the Delft University of Technology, has successfully provided a sector specific MBA programme to the ICT industry for well over a decade. This programme started as a mono-disciplinary programme, focused on strengthening the engineering knowledge and skills of engineers, and is evolving into an interdisciplinary programme that intends to deepen and broaden the insights of ICT executives. In the evolution of this programme a parallel can be drawn with the education of economics and the role of its practitioners in business and government. The engineering and economics disciplines have in common a strong mono-disciplinary core as the source of their historical successes. However, with the increasing complexity of real world problems, it has been recognized that these problems cannot be solved by a mono-disciplinary approach. The experience obtained with the design and management of the Master of Business Telecom programme could therefore provide useful points of learning if an evolution of the education of economics into an interdisciplinary curriculum is being considered.

8.2 THE INITIATIVE

New initiatives often come up at times of change. The trigger for the design of a new telecommunications programme came at the time of liberalization of the telecom operator market in the mid-1980s[1]. One of the objectives of the liberalization was, and still is, to give telecom users the choice of telecommunication service providers. Although competition already existed in the handling of international traffic, the need to choose among providers had been limited *grosso modo* to the telecom managers of large multinational companies. Through liberalization the choice of provider would be extended to all (national) businesses and consumers. Recognizing the increasing importance of telecommunication in modern business operations and with telecommunications increasingly becoming a 'means of production' for many entrepreneurs, the assessment at the time was that a need would arise for postgraduate education in telecommunications, in particular for senior telecom managers and executives.

In the mid-1980s the function of telecom manager and IT manager were mostly separated. Hence, the target audience for the new course became the telecom managers in medium to large business. Most of these telecom managers had a background in engineering, with a strong operational focus. The objective of the new course would be to provide them with an update of the latest technological developments whereby the emphasis would be put on the transfer of knowledge and skills in the application of these technologies in the design and management of telecommunication networks, with a keen eye for optimizing the return on investment with respect to dimensions such as make or buy, rent or lease.

Delft TopTech, the School of Executive Education at the Delft University of Technology in the Netherlands[2], took on this challenge and developed the Chartered Telecom Engineering (CTE) programme, which was first delivered in 1987. Graduates of the programme received the Certificate of Chartered Engineer. The university would ascertain and ensure the quality of the educational programme at the chartered engineering level.

8.3   FROM MONO-DISCIPLINARITY TO INTERDISCIPLINARITY

In the good tradition of a technological university, technology constituted the core of the CTE programme. Updates were provided on topics such as packet networks, mobility and satellite communication. The skill development was centred on systems engineering and network design. And as liberalization was the trigger, the first element of multidisciplinarity appeared in the programme around the topic of regulation.

In line with the progress of liberalization the needs of the market started to change. Incumbent players became subject to competition and became interested in a broader perspective of the industry. New players emerged and generated the need for skilled telecom personnel. The pace of change accelerated providing increasing opportunities for consultants to participate in the growth of the industry. The entrepreneurial spirit took to the telecom industry and it resulted in a shift of emphasis from engineering acumen to business and financial acumen. This was reflected in the change in the profile of the course participant over time. As a gross generalization, the programme came to cater for two types of participants. One category included the telecom engineers. They had seen a successful development of their career based on their technical knowledge and skills. But they had arrived at a point where further progress would require them to take on broader responsibilities in general management and hence they had to broaden their perspective beyond technology into these other dimensions of the telecom business. A typical example was a very bright researcher, and proud owner of a number of patents in the field of information security, finding his career prospects limited to the confines of the laboratory of an incumbent operator.

The other category consisted of staff that had been recruited for their business orientation, most of them having an MBA or equivalent type of education, who after a successful career start came to realize that they were lacking the necessary background in telecom technology to successfully pursue their career further. This became particularly apparent when they were pursuing new business opportunities in the field with clients and prospects[3].

As a result the Chartered Telecom Engineering programme was in need of adjustment to cater to the changing demands in the market. The challenge for the programme managers was to retain the values of the CTE program while extending it to include the business dimension more fully.

In the new model the course consisted of three main building blocks: a technology, network engineering and operation oriented block, also called the T-Block; a block focused on the business disciplines, the B-Block; and a masters block with the emphasis on the graduation project, the M-Block. Depending on the background of the participants, the T- and B-Blocks would provide for either an update or the foundation of the disciplines being covered. The entry into the T-Block was facilitated by an introductory block on Telecommunication Principles. The intake interviews would indicate whether attending this preparatory block would be mandatory.

As a result of this fundamental change the certification based on the chartered engineering regime became inappropriate and the new course became accredited as Master of Business in Telecom.

As a result, the programme became multidisciplinary by design; the challenge remained to make it an interdisciplinary programme in practice. The MBT course was first delivered in 1995.

8.4 A PARALLEL WITH THE EDUCATION OF ECONOMICS

At this point it may be useful to draw a parallel with the education of economics. Comparing different disciplines and trying to determine common characteristics is not a trivial affair. And given the variety within the engineering discipline and the existence of many schools of thought within economics, any attempt will have to remain inconclusive if judged by scientific standards. However, the engineering and the economics discipline have in common a strong mono-disciplinary core as the source of their historical successes. Therefore drawing a parallel may provide useful insights for the development of future curricula.

Using stereotyping, one could argue that for engineers each real world problem is a new challenge to solve. And being fully aware of their well equipped 'technological toolbox' they are generally convinced that there is a solution to be found; it may be only a matter of time. The (neo-classical) economist brings along a range of often very sophisticated models and tools to discover that the real world is much more stubborn than most theories suggest. This growing discrepancy between theory and practice was the main reason for the transformation of the Chartered Telecom Engineering programme into the Master of Business Telecom programme, the latter taking the multi-disciplinary nature of business and policy as the starting point for the design of its curriculum.

For a proper assessment it should be noted that the MBT programme is a postgraduate programme, attended by participants having in general between 5-10 years of work experience. Transposing the postgraduate experience into a graduate programme, although this could be the masters phase of the new bachelor-masters regime, poses additional challenges. Nevertheless, I would argue that any early opportunity for an exposure of students to the practices and challenges of real live business and policy should be seriously considered for implementation.

This need for multidisciplinarity and interdisciplinarity in the field of engineering, especially at graduate level, has been broadly recognized within the Delft University of Technology. In 1992 it resulted in the establishment of a new school under the name of Faculty of Technology, Policy & Management. This school operates at the intersection of technology, business management and public policy. It takes the technological complexity and the complexity of managerial decision-making and public policy as the premise for its curriculum and its research. The programme of the school is dedicated to the design and management of infrastructures and infrastructure related services using a multidisciplinary approach[4].

8.5   THE DELFT TOPTECH APPROACH

As a School of Executive Education, the attention of Delft TopTech is focused on postgraduate types of education. It is established to leverage the wealth of knowledge and expertise of the academic staff at the Delft University of Technology and to combine this with faculty drawn from business and policy sectors to create and deliver a broad portfolio of structural and topical programmes. The Master of Business in Telecom and the Master of Business in Energy programmes are examples of structural programmes, delivered once a year over a period of many years. Delft TopTech assures a close fit of each programme with market developments and market requirements through two organizational bodies: an Advisory Board and a Curriculum Committee. The Advisory Board is composed of industry representatives and is aimed at the long-term development of the programme. It assesses the changing needs of the industry and validates the course fit through monitoring the progression of its alumni. The Curriculum Committee consists of the course manager(s) and representatives of the course faculty. It takes the input of the Advisory Board and other sources as the basis for its main task: constant tuning of the programme to the changing market demands and recruiting the appropriate faculty for delivering a high-impact course.

8.6   THE STRUCTURE OF THE MBT PROGRAMME

The early CTE programme was very modular in design and consisted of two-week modules dedicated to a specific topic. These modules were provided over a period of 18 months. The programme concluded with a graduation project aimed at integration of knowledge and skills being transferred during the course.

The MBT programme is delivered in modules of 5-8 days over a period of 12 months to minimize the impact on the 'day-job' and facilitating participation by students from abroad. The content of the blocks are individually managed, the Technology Block by a staff member of the Delft University of Technology, the Business Block by representatives of the industry[5].

The participants are supposed to follow the course in the sequence: Technology, Business, Masters; consequently the B-Block builds on the knowledge transferred in the T-Block on technology, network design and network operations.

To provide a logical structure to the multidisciplinary nature of the B-Block, the choice and flow of topics were essentially modelled after the major disciplines required in business:

- Perspectives of the industry and the industry value chain,
- Strategy development[6], including environmental scan and company assessments,
- Business financials and managerial economics with the emphasis on the telecom practice,
- Marketing of services, including the e-dimension,
- Liberalization and the regulatory dimension,
- Managing cultural differences, with emphasis on globalization.

Short contributions on topical subjects would be interwoven or included in the M-Block depending on the specific need at the time. Examples of such topics are:

- Business planning
- Billing
- Venture capital
- E-government
- Innovation management

The MBT course is based on a variety of learning formats of which short assignments and case work are an important component. In particular the case format allows for the very valuable exchange of experience among participants, which is an essential element of the programme. The case work is concentrated in the evening sessions, supporting the integration as well as the application of the information, knowledge and skills transferred during the day sessions.

8.7   THE FACULTY

Underlying the design of the programme is the paradox of rigor and relevance[7]. On the one hand it is essential to provide a proper foundation for each discipline. On the other hand the course content has to be relevant for the day to day practice of the participants. This means finding and creating the appropriate synthesis.

Within the B-Block this is being pursued by first of all drawing faculty from the academic, business and consulting sectors. In some parts of the programme academics and business people have jointly delivered a segment of the programme. The programme manager is responsible for achieving alignment between the contributions. The identification and selection of the faculty is a crucial element in creating a multidisciplinary programme. The ability of the faculty to view the topic at hand from different perspectives and to create a linkage with other components of the programme, both within the B-Block and the T-Block, are essential. The programme furthermore relies on case work to provide a high level of integration of theory and practice. For this purpose the cases are selected on their relevance to the telecom field or have been specially developed for the MBT course[8].

Providing multiple perspectives, as a principle of design, is further extended by the international cast of faculty members[9] and the broad range of cultural backgrounds[10] that the participants bring to the course. The global nature of the telecom industry and the need to manage across cultures has become a core part of the programme design. This emphasis has moved the course away from a singular (engineering) mindset and has made the participants receptive to different approaches to solving (business) issues.

8.8   CREATING INTERDISCIPLINARITY

At this point it may be useful to make a small side step toward the theoretical context of interdisciplinarity.

The quest for understanding nature in ever increasing detail results in ever increasing specialization in scientific research. Also the increasing complexity of business and society in general is leading to further specialization. However, real world problems require holistic solutions. This means an increasing need for building bridges or closing gaps that are growing between disciplines. A first step is bringing the disciplines together; an important next step is providing some form of integration of the underlying theories.

In this context multidisciplinarity can be defined as cooperation between different disciplines aimed at the same business activity or the same topic of research, but applying the theories, methods and tools of each discipline independently. While in the case of interdisciplinarity there is also a form of integration of the theories of the disciplines taking place, resulting in a theoretical foundation of the (new) interdiscipline. In the 1970s a group of German scholars, known as the Starnbergers, defined the distinction more precisely[11], see also Figure 8.1.

- The Starnbergers speak of an interdisciplinary science if external triggers, for example societal needs, lead to the development of an independent theoretical framework or foundation. They use the term 'finalized science' as the formation of the theory serves an explicit societal purpose and is independent of the theory development of the related mono-disciplines. See Figure 8.1a.
- The Starnbergers talk about 'applied science' when the theories of the individual disciplines are applied without the integration or creation of an independent theoretical framework. See Figure 8.1b.
- They also distinguish another form of 'applied science' whereby the theory of one discipline is combined with empirical findings from another discipline. This is termed: transdiscipline. See Figure 8.1c.
- When only empirical inputs of the mono-disciplines are combined the Starnbergers identify this as 'instrumentalism'. See Figure 8.1d.

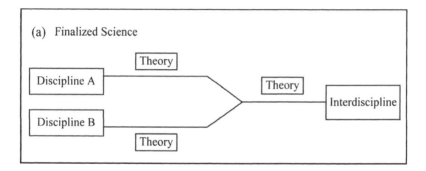

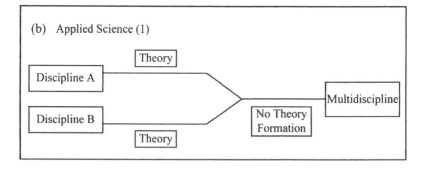

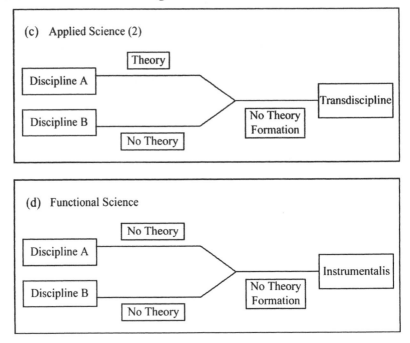

Figure 8.1: From multidisciplinarity to interdisciplinarity

Creating this integration of disciplines is the core objective of the relatively new schools focused on business management and policy[12]. This is where they are expected to provide the greatest value-added.

By bringing together faculty from different disciplines, Delft TopTech provides a multidisciplinary environment that is conducive to the application of interdisciplinarity. By drawing on academic faculty Delft TopTech intends to leverage the development of interdisciplinary theory into its course program. With respect to the MBT programme, interdisciplinarity is still in an early stage of development and application.

Turning a multidisciplinary course by design into an interdisciplinary course in practice hinges on the capability of the faculty to create the appropriate environment for participants to explore solutions through the different 'lenses' provided by each discipline. This implies that each discipline is allowed the time needed to provide its particular view on the world (the theory). Each discipline is allowed to establish its credibility, that is, they are provided with the opportunity to show the type of problems they can solve and how they would solve them. Reflecting on the paradox of 'rigour and relevance', the approach adopted allows for a first level of integration by the participants individually – allowing them to compare and contrast the materials presented with their own knowledge base and experience. They should be able to come to some type of judgement, to develop a first sense of applicability and feasibility of the theory in their specific (business) environment. The next step is illustration, validation and integration through short assignments and case work.

The challenge for the course management and the faculty is to continue this process and push it to the next level and provide the integration of the various disciplines being introduced as the course unfolds.

To support this process of integration at the next level, a Case and Game is being used in the B-Block of the MBT programme. This Case and Game is executed in the evening sessions and extends across almost the full length of the B-Block. It is different from typical HBS or INSEAD cases because it is open-ended. As it explores the future, there is not necessarily one correct answer or solution. It is also a game, as role play is part of its design[13].

The objective of the Case and Game is to invite (if you will: force) the participants to apply the learning of the daytime sessions and combine it with their personal knowledge and experience. And, to make this process explicit and hence accessible for other participants, as part of the teamwork activity.

In the Future Casting Case and Game the participants represent senior managers of a company operating within the telecom industry. An attempt is made to represent the various types of companies operating in the industry and to reflect, albeit in a very coarse way, the value chain or value network as it is applicable within the industry. Typically the companies represented are an incumbent and a new entrant, a traditional equipment provider and a new entrant, a mobility player and a large-scale user of telecom services. The assignment of companies to participants is made so that each will act on behalf of a player that is their counterpart in real life. This forces the participants to 'live and act' according to another discipline than the one they have come to be accustomed to through education or business practice. To ensure that the typical business tensions within a company are played out in the game, and to ensure involvement by all participants (that is, to avoid the free-rider problem) the participants can choose among the roles of senior executives: for example Chief Executive Officer, Chief Financial Officer, Chief Sales and Marketing, Chief Manufacturing and R&D. Here the integration of the T-Block finds its way into the B-Block explicitly through the R&D role. Moreover, the role play provides a further push toward 'acting out' the various disciplines.

The Case and Game then evolves in stages, as much as possible in step with the teaching material presented during the daytime sessions. The assignment of the Case and Game is to develop a perspective of the future and to design a strategy to arrive at the perceived target position, taking into account the interactions in the industry, the moves of the other players. In terms of strategy paradoxes, the strategy formation is chosen to be 'deliberate', the aspect of strategic thinking and strategic change are left open to the teams[14]. Moreover, the teams are free to take a broad or a narrow perspective; they can operate at the business unit level or choose to act at the corporate level.

8.9   THE LEARNING PROCESS

Being confronted with assignments much akin to real life appeared to be a major learning point for the course participants. The large degree of freedom and the open-endedness of for example the Case and Game forced the issue of choice: which approach should be taken to develop the solution, which discipline would provide the answer. But would this also provide the right answer? How would we know it to be right? There were many approaches that could be taken, many perspectives to be considered. Understanding the power and the limits of each discipline became important. In the process an appreciation for different approaches resulting from different cultural backgrounds developed. A need to be able to 'talk the other language' as a means to be understood and as a means to bridge the gap between disciplines started to grow.

8.10   THE REALITY CHECK

A close linkage of the course with the day to day reality of the industry is further assured through the participation of industry executives in the evaluation of the results of the Future Casting Case and Game.

For each company represented in the Case and Game a senior director participates in the evaluation committee. They will evaluate the recommendations in the context of the current industry and the plans for the future of the company. They will provide feedback in particular on relevance and feasibility of the recommendations made by the course participants. This external evaluation and the competitive nature of this final session of the B-Block have shown to be a major incentive for the participants to deliver high quality results.

8.11 THE OPERATIONAL CHALLENGES

The design of the MBT programme poses a number of special challenges for the Delft TopTech programme managers.

This is first of all the challenge to create a cohesive programme using a very diverse faculty, sourced from a wide range of (international) organizations. The challenge manifests itself in the coordination, the alignment of the programme and the creation of course documentation. While academics are used to developing course materials, business executives and consultants are often hard-pressed for time and course documentation frequently remains limited to a copy of the presentation materials.

For structural programmes that are intended to run for many years, such as the MBT programme, establishing a level of continuity among the faculty is another challenge that impacts both the course quality and the time and effort required to create a new edition of the course. Moreover, long development cycles are hard to accommodate with essentially a freelance faculty. However, the flip side of this has the benefit of a large degree of flexibility in tuning the programme to changing demands in the market. Using the Curriculum Committee and the Advisory Council in step with the course cycle, Delft TopTech assures its programmes stay tuned to the evolving industry requirements.

8.12 PERSPECTIVE ON THE FUTURE

In the aftermath of the Internet bubble the Delft TopTech MBT is subject to the severely reduced spending of the players in the telecom industry. Moreover, the certainty of yesterday has become the uncertainty of tomorrow. Perspectives of the future are becoming more diverse, and the need to explore the future even more pressing. For future MBT programmes the inclusion of a scenario-building element as a tool to more structurally exploring the future is being investigated, building on the work of De Geus, Van der Heijden, Schwartz and others[15]. The need to develop comprehensive and cohesive perspectives of the future is another way to stimulate and create interdisciplinarity.

Reflecting on the challenges ahead, the view articulated by Carlota Peréz in her recent book *Technological Revolutions and Financial Capital – the Dynamics of Bubbles and Golden Ages*[16] is considered relevant. In this book, which builds upon her earlier work and the work by Freeman and Louçã[17], she describes the importance of recurring surges and the related change of techno-economic paradigms. The periodicity of these changes is linked to the

Teaching Pluralism in Economics

fundamental tensions around technological change, economic change and institutional change: once more an example of the organized complexity of real world problems and a plea for an interdisciplinary approach. See Figure 8.2 for an illustration[18].

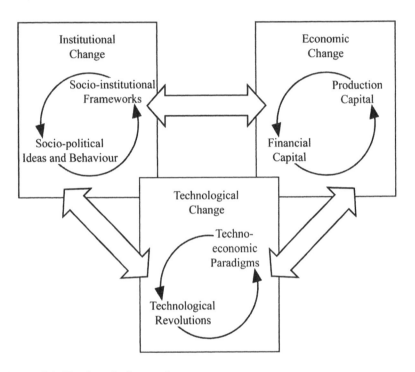

Figure 8.2: The three fundamental tensions

NOTES

This chapter is based on the author's experience obtained within the telecommunication industry, in particular within the management of a large equipment, software and services supplier and his experience with the Master of Business Telecommunication (MBT) programme at Delft TopTech. The objective of the chapter is to present the particular case experience. As in any other case materials, the aim is to provide information as a basis for learning, not to express an opinion on or judge the behaviour of the company and/or its management. The author joined Philips Telecommunicatie Industry in 1978 and has been subsequently engaged with

AT&T and Lucent Technologies. He has been involved in the MBT programme since 1989.

[1] Instrumental in this initiative was Prof Dr Jens Arnbak, the first Chairman of OPTA, the Dutch National Regulatory Agency for Post and Telecom and Chairman of the European Regulatory Group.

[2] For more information on Delft TopTech see: www.delft-toptech.nl.

[3] Observation by the author, when employed with AT&T at the European Headquarters, that many MBA graduates were recruited to offset the dominance of engineers within the firm.

[4] Infrastructures have been taken in the broad sense and include domains such as ICT, energy, water and transport. The disciplines covered include policy analysis and management, business management and organization, systems analysis, economics, regulation and law. See for more information: www.tbm.tudelft.nl.

[5] The author has been instrumental in the design of the B-Block from 1995 until 1999, and has been a faculty member since 1989. The program management of the B-Block is being assumed by Dr B. De Wit, founder-director of the Strategy Academy, see also www.strategy-academy.org. The linkage with the IT side of the industry has been assured through the involvement of Ing. R. de Boer, member of the Stratix Consulting Group, www.stratix.nl.

[6] The strategy component of the programme builds upon the paradox approach adopted by De Wit and Meyer described in their book: *Strategy Synthesis – Resolving Strategy Paradoxes to Create Competitive Advantage* (1999).

[7] This paradox is derived from the contribution by Dr B. De Wit of the Strategy Academy to the 23rd Annual International Conference of the Strategic Management Society in Baltimore, November 2003.

[8] A typical example has been the MFS-case, originally developed in cooperation with Erasmus University. This case addressed the strategy of the Metro Fiber Systems company and evolved over the years to include its acquisition by MCI and subsequently by WorldCom.

[9] The faculty has typically been drawn from the UK, Germany, Sweden, France and the Netherlands.

[10] Course participants have come from a wide range of countries and different continents, including South Africa, Indonesia, Saudi Arabia, Finland, Poland, the Czech Republic and The Netherlands.

[11] Derived from Chapter 4 of the 'Syllabus Methodologie' [syllabus Methodology], by Essers, Erasmus University, Rotterdam, The Netherlands. (1992). See also *Interdisciplinarity – History,Theory and Practice* by Klein (1990).

[12] In the Dutch terminology: 'bedrijfskunde en bestuurskunde'.

154   *Teaching Pluralism in Economics*

[13] More information on the use of games and simulation in the specific context of infrastructures can be found in: *Games in a world of infrastructures – Simulation-games for research, learning and intervention* Mayer and Veeneman (eds.). (2002).
[14] For the use of paradoxes in strategy see De Wit and Meyer: *Strategy Synthesis – Resolving strategy paradoxes to create competitive advantage.* (1999).
[15] De Geus (1997, 2002); Van der Heijden (1996); Schwartz (1991).
[16] Peréz (2002).
[17] Freeman and Louçã (2001). *"As Time Goes By – From the Industrial Revolutions to the Information revolution".*
[18] Peréz (2002: 156).

REFERENCES

De Geus, A. (1997, 2002), *The Living Company – Habits for Survival in a Turbulent Business Environment*, Boston, Mass.: Harvard Business School Press.
De Wit, B. and R. Meyer (1999), *Strategy Synthesis: Resolving Strategy Paradoxes to Create Competitive Advantage*, London: International Thomson Business Press.
Essers, J.P.J.M. (1992), *Syllabus Methodologie (Syllabus Methodology)*, Rotterdam, The Netherlands: Erasmus University,
Freeman, C. and F. Louçã (2001), *As Time Goes by – From the Industrial Revolutions to the Information Revolution*, Oxford, UK: Oxford University Press.
Klein, Thompson, J. (1990), *Interdisciplinarity – History, Theory and Practice*, Detroit: Wayne State University Press.
Mayer, I. And W. Veeneman, (2002), *Games in a World of Infrastructures – Simulation-games for Research, Learning and Intervention*, Delft, The Netherlands: Eburon.
Peréz, C. (2002), *Technological Revolutions and Financial Capital: The Dynamics of Bubbles and Golden Ages*, Cheltenham, UK: Edward Elgar.
Schwartz, P. (1991), *The Art of the Long View – Planning for the Future in an Uncertain World*, New York: Double Day.
Van der Heijden, K. (1996), *Scenario's – The Art of Strategic Conversation*, Chichester, UK: Wiley and Sons.

9. Interdisciplinarity and Problem-based Learning in Economics Education: The Case of Infonomics

Rifka Weehuizen

9.1 INTRODUCTION

Education is not only an informative process of acquiring knowledge, but also a formative process of acquiring a certain perspective, a certain approach to things, a set of mental models to understand the world with. This chapter is concerned with the formative effects of economics education on the receivers of this education, economics students. There are concerns about these formative effects. Critics argue that the economics that is taught to students often is at best irrelevant to real world problems, and at worst in fact causes real world problems. The approach taught in economics would lead to misinterpreting the nature of problems and consequently to arriving at ineffective solutions, which may be even more problematic than the problems they were intended to solve. The criticism of economics education concerns not only the content but also the form. Economics education is said to be an almost dogmatic, one-way affair, not stimulating critical reflection – which is the more serious given the doubts of the real world validity of what is being taught.

This is not an academic issue, but a very real and serious problem. Economic insights and the economic approach to problems are influential on real world decisions, both in business and in policy. The quality of these decisions depends on the quality of the economic insights and the economic approach that the decision-makers have been taught. If these are dubious or even misleading, this will have direct, concrete, detrimental effects in real life, for real people. As Fullbrook (2004) writes, 'we live in a time when bad economics probably kills more people and causes more suffering than armaments'.

The criticism is well known, and the interesting question is what the alternative is or should be. There is much debate about what should not happen in economics education, but much less about what should happen. How should economics education change for the better?

This chapter reports on an attempt to innovate economics education at the University of Maastricht. Some years ago, a new track was started at the economics faculty of this university, that was set up to be multidisciplinary and to some extent interdisciplinary and that was taught according to a method not often used in economics, the method of problem-based learning (PBL).

The chapter aims to use the experiences of this undertaking to illustrate the more general problem of changing economics education.

The chapter starts with a brief discussion of the educational experiment at the University of Maastricht (Section 9.2). It then sets out to sketch the broader context of change in economics education. The function of education will be briefly discussed (Section 9.3). The problems associated with the content of economics education will be described and analysed (Section 9.4), and the possible solution in terms of interdisciplinarity and the problems related to this solution will be discussed (Section 9.5). Next, the problems associated with the form of economics education will be touched upon, and it is discussed to what extent a different teaching method, problem-based learning, can overcome these problems. The discussion of these issues will be illustrated by the experiences with introducing an interdisciplinary curriculum in combination with the PBL method at the Faculty of Economics of the University of Maastricht.

The conclusion (Section 9.6) will put forward that both interdisciplinarity and problem-based learning in principle are real and superior options for economics education, but that in order for their potential to be realized, a number of conditions must be fulfilled. Without this, an interdisciplinary curriculum offered with the PBL method of education may in fact be worse. Given the current situation at universities in Europe, in which faculty are rewarded for their research rather than for their teaching and in which budgets for universities increasingly get constrained rather than expanded, it is not to be expected that these necessary conditions will be widely realized.

9.2   THE CASE OF INFONOMICS

Some years ago, the Faculty of Economics and Business Administration of the University of Maastricht started an interdisciplinary programme, an educational track called 'Infonomics'. The starting point for this undertaking was the observation that, due to the accelerated development and diffusion of information and communication technology (ICT) to almost all spheres of life, many things are changing at the same time, and that these changes are interrelated to such a degree, that one could speak of a 'systems-change'. The idea was that these changes could not be understood in a meaningful way if they were studied solely from a singular, disciplinary perspective. Infonomics was to be the multi- and interdisciplinary study of the information society. While for several reasons economics formed the core of Infonomics, it was explicitly intended that concepts, insights and methods from other disciplines would form a considerable part of Infonomics. The method of 'problem-based learning' (PBL), which was already in use in the Faculty of Economics, was thought to offer unique possibilities to realize the goals of multi- and interdisciplinarity. In addition, due to the subject matter of the track – information and communication technology (ICT), the information society – special attention was paid to the way students made use of the Internet in their studies.

After four years, it was decided to evaluate the Infonomics track. How did it work out? What was it like for undergraduate students to get an interdisciplinary education? Did they become broad-minded, curiosity-driven, critical, creative 'out-of-the-box' thinkers, superior in dealing with the more complex questions and issues in the outside world than the more narrowly educated 'normal' economics students? Or was a confused group of individuals raised that was even less clear on what the world is about and how to deal with its complexity? How did the students experience their interdisciplinary education? Was the problem-based learning system at the University of Maastricht conducive to interdisciplinarity or not? Did making use of the Internet enable and facilitate interdisciplinarity and PBL, or did the combination of these three factors turn students into clueless postmodern knowledge-shoppers?

All the Infonomics students (4 years, 54 persons) were given a questionnaire, and the results of these were discussed in a brainstorm with Infonomics students from each year. In addition, interviews with eight staff members teaching Infonomics students were held. Three of these teach mainstream economics modules offered to all students, both Infonomics and non-Infonomics (such as microeconomics and electronic markets), and five teach courses that were either interdisciplinary or from another discipline altogether, and which were only offered to Infonomics students (courses on WWW-technologies, on the network society, on law, and on institutions, culture and behaviour).

The interviews were open interviews; questions were minimized and mainly served the function of getting the stream of impressions and experiences going. The aim was to 'tap' the experiences of the staff as naturally as possible. The issues that came up were discussed with the Infonomics students in the brainstorm mentioned before. In this way, the subjective impressions and experiences of the staff were put into perspective and balanced with the equally subjective impressions and experiences of the students about the same courses and the same meaningful incidents within these courses. The results of the evaluation and their broader implications were discussed at a session on interdisciplinarity during the European Association for Evolutionary Political Economy (EAEPE) conference of 2003.

In the following sections, the findings of this will be used to illustrate the broader problems at stake. In order to understand what to expect of proper economics education, we start in the next section with the question of what actually the function of education is or should be.

9.3   THE FUNCTION OF EDUCATION

There has been a long, ongoing discussion inside and outside of academia about what education should be about, and what it should achieve. Generally it is stressed that education is, or at least should be, an important goal in and for itself, being a form of intellectual enrichment and self-development. In addition to this 'intrinsic' value of education, it is clear that education has important 'instrumental' value: it has an important economic and social function. Education has always been seen as a means to improve society, by emancipating minorities, by helping to create equal opportunities, and more in general by 'enlightening the masses', liberating them from the 'chains of ignorance'. Not only the social importance but also and increasingly the economic importance of education is being recognized and emphasized. Education is increasingly seen as an important supplier of human capital, producing workers with knowledge and skills that are of important use in the economy.

Though the intrinsic and the instrumental view on education do not exclude each other, they are different things, and there is a trade-off. Education that aims at maximizing intellectual enrichment will often not fully maximize direct social and economic relevance at the same time and vice versa. In this chapter we are primarily interested with the instrumental view of education, though it will become clear that, slightly paradoxically, an overly instrumental view of education may in fact be counterproductive to the instrumental value of education.

An important related question is to what extent education should be reactive – responding to demands from society – and to what extent it should be pro-active, in the sense of actively shaping society, through shaping its participants. In the 1980s and 1990s there has been a shift to emphasizing a reactive, demand-driven view of education. This shift is related to the increased recognition of the economic value of knowledge and skills as being the main engine for economic growth, and consequently of human capital, being the origins of and often the carriers and applicants of knowledge. Since education is one of the main determinants of human capital, the education system was 'discovered' as a key factor to economic growth. This has strengthened the instrumental, demand-driven view of education as a supplier of skills and knowledge needed in the 'knowledge economy'.

Although the instrumental view of education has gained considerable strength because of economic considerations regarding the economic value of education, it seems that economics education itself does not take its instrumental, society- and economy-serving role very seriously. More than in any other discipline, there is long-standing, increasing, serious criticism concerning the lack of relevance of economics education for dealing adequately with real world problems, but nevertheless the providers of this education, economic faculties, generally do not seem inclined to change the content and form of their programmes.

Without overestimating the effect of education on the thoughts and actions of students in their future life, it cannot be denied that education has a strong formative influence on students. There is growing evidence that economics education equips people with problematic concepts and approaches. An education system is responsible for its formative impact on the individuals in the system and thereby by implication also to some degree for the actions of these individuals; at least, to the extent to which these stem from the ideas that they were imprinted with during their education. The lack of interest in many economics faculties in the consequences of the education they provide cannot be excused. There should be more debate about economics education, and this debate should not have the character of only 'preaching to the choir', in which critical economists largely complain to other economists that already share their viewpoints and concerns anyway. The debate should be broad and it should have a concrete impact in terms of adjustment of curricula in economics education. This chapter hopes to contribute to this debate.

The next section will look at the nature of the criticism on economics education, and will discuss some explanations of the present unsatisfying situation in economics education.

9.4   CHANGING THE CONTENT OF ECONOMICS EDUCATION

9.4.1   The problem of the lack of relevance

One of the main problems of economics education is the relevance and validity of the approach, and of the insights derived through that approach, that are being taught to students. These are doubted by many, including well-known economists themselves. The debate on the perceived strengths and weaknesses of economics is long-standing and ongoing. In this chapter it will only be briefly discussed in order to provide insight into one of the main problems with economics education. An important driver of the debate is the criticism of the neoclassical approach in economics, which is thought to be narrow and based on assumptions that are only minimally related to the real world. As the famous joke goes, 'for an economist, reality is a special case'.

Fine (2002) summarizes a key problem in observing that economic research has got the character of a 'journal game', in which the aim is not to be relevant but to get published in certain economic journals. Many critical observers point to the excessive use of mathematics too often having little or no added value in terms of offering additional understanding and insight. Economic research is based on stylized rather than real facts, and seems to be designed to demonstrate cleverness rather than address real problems, complicating issues rather than clarifying them. Blaug (1997) comments on these developments:

> Modern economics is sick. Economics has increasingly become an intellectual game played for its own sake and not for its practical consequences for understanding the economic world. Economists have converted the subject into a sort of social mathematics in which analytical rigor is everything and practical relevance is nothing ... I am very pessimistic about whether we can actually pull out of this. I think we have created a locomotive. This is the sociology of the economics profession. We have created a monster that is very difficult to stop. (1997: 3)

Also the 'users' of contributions of people educated in economics indicate a lack of relevance and express their surprise about the apparent lack of concern about this among the people responsible for economics education at universities. Henry Aaron (1992) collected views and comments of 'people who use economics but are not "doing economics"'. He and a colleague were puzzled about the 'blissful unawareness among leading academic economists of a particular piece of rather bad economics that was threatening to result in extremely costly, welfare reducing legislation'. Rather than 'elicit more economist-bashing screeds from people who had one brand or another of axe to grind', they invited people who worked with economists to express what they think economists could do differently to increase their effectiveness.

Many comments of 'users' were related to the lack of skills of economists to communicate their views and the underlying arguments properly, because economists are stuck in 'sophisticated jargon and convoluted technical shorthand learned in graduate school' while in fact 'the most helpful advice seems often to rest not on complex theory but on the sorts of economic principles taught to beginning undergraduates; [for example] that distribution matters' (Aaron, 1992: 60). Economists seem unable to translate even basic well-founded insights to real life contexts, and users point to the important 'need to translate into plain English the usually complex and sometimes counterintuitive insights that economists bring to the policy debate' (Eizenstat, 1992: 69). Sometimes economists do manage to be good communicators, but in that case other problems arise. Due to the rather disconnected and abstract nature of economic knowledge, there is the risk of 'the selective use of evidence on behalf of deep-pocketed clients' and 'intellectual corruption' (Weinstein, 1992: 75). Hamilton (1992: 63) observes: 'Every politician understands the impatience that led Harry Truman to wish for a one-armed economist. But the nation is not well served with economic advice that conceals scientific disagreement or genuine uncertainty about the economic consequences of particular actions.'

In addition, economics students themselves are increasingly and fiercely critical of the education they receive. In 2000, economics students in Paris were so dissatisfied with the economics education they received that they started a movement, which they called the 'Post-Autistic Economics Network' (www.paecon.net). These French students wrote their concerns down in a petition, which was short but clear. The first part, 'We wish to escape from imaginary worlds', kind of summarizes what they were protesting against (Fullbrook, 2004).

It was argued that neoclassical economics sheds light on an ever-smaller proportion of economic reality, leaving more and more of it in the dark for students permitted only the neoclassical viewpoint. This makes the neoclassical monopoly more outrageous and costly every year, requiring of it ever more desperate measures of defence, like eliminating economic history and history of economics from the curriculum. For the purpose of this chapter it is useful to quote part of the students' petition, because it gives a good formulation of the general critique on economics education:

Most of us have chosen to study economics so as to acquire a deep understanding of the economic phenomena with which the citizens of today are confronted. But the teaching that is offered, that is to say for the most part neoclassical theory or approaches derived from it, does not generally answer this expectation. Indeed, even when the theory legitimately detaches itself from contingencies in the first instance, it rarely carries out the necessary return to the facts. The empirical side (historical facts, functioning of institutions, study of the behaviours and strategies of the agents) is almost nonexistent. Furthermore, this gap in the teaching, this disregard for concrete realities, poses an enormous problem for those who would like to render themselves useful to economic and social actors. (www.paecon.net)

The Parisian students were concerned about the narrowness of their economics education, and their desire for a 'broadband approach' to economics teaching that would enable them to connect constructively and comprehensively with the complex economic realities of their time. Their concerns hit a chord with French news media (Fullbrook, 2004). Major newspapers and magazines gave extensive coverage to the students' struggle against the 'autistic science'. Economics students from all over France signed the petition, and a growing number of French economists started to speak out in support and launched a parallel petition of their own. The French government decided to form a commission to investigate the issues put forward, and this resulted in the so-called 'Fitoussi report', which supported the criticism of the students at a number of points. News of these events in France spread quickly via the Web and email around the world. In June 2001, almost exactly a year after the French students had released their petition, 27 PhD candidates at Cambridge University in the UK launched their own, titled 'Opening Up Economics'. In August of the same year economics students from 17 countries who had gathered in the US in Kansas City, released an 'International Open Letter' to all economics departments calling on them to reform economics education and research by adopting the broadband approach. In March 2003 economics students at Harvard launched their own petition, demanding from its economics department an introductory course that would have 'better balance and coverage of a broader spectrum of views' and that would 'not only teach students the accepted modes of thinking, but also challenge students to think critically and deeply about conventional truths' (Fullbrook, 2004).

It is worth citing in some detail what these economics students of many countries think is needed and why, because it gives a good insight into the problem of economics education and thereby also some clues about what should be changed:

> This debate is important because in our view the status quo is harmful in at least four respects. Firstly, it is harmful to students who are taught the 'tools' of mainstream economics without learning their domain of applicability. The source and evolution of these ideas is ignored, as is the existence and status of competing theories. Secondly, it disadvantages a society that ought to be benefiting from what economists can tell us about the world. Economics is a social science with enormous potential for making a difference through its impact on policy debates. In its present form its effectiveness in this arena is limited by the uncritical application of mainstream methods. Thirdly, progress towards a deeper understanding of many important aspects of economic life is being held back. By restricting research done in economics to that based on one approach only, the development of competing research programmes is seriously hampered or prevented altogether. Fourth and finally, in the current situation an economist who does not do economics in the prescribed way finds it very difficult to get recognition for her research. (www.paecon.net)

There are a number of well-developed, compelling arguments against mainstream economics which cannot be ignored, but that nevertheless seem to have few concrete consequences in terms of changes of curricula of the economic programmes at universities.

There are a number of factors that may explain this. Universities have already for some decades been struggling with a kind of 'identity crisis'. Universities have a double function, they are expected both to do research and provide education. Although the idea is that these activities complement and enrich each other, in practice they turn out to be quite different activities and increasingly so. Teaching requires a different mindset and different skills. The economists that are good at research are by no means automatically also good at teaching. Since it is research and the resulting publications that determine the career of individual economists and the prestige of (European) universities, most economists populating economics faculties are not selected for their interest in and talent for teaching. This may to some extent explain the lack of interest in the problematic nature of economics education on the side of the people that are primarily responsible for it in the economics faculties.

Universities provide education to a growing, increasingly heterogeneous population of students. Both the heterogeneity and the scale pose problems. Whereas originally universities supposedly were places of reflection mainly aimed at training researchers, with a small scale setting of students and teachers, now most universities seem more like educational factories, mass-producing graduates. At the same time they claim to be 'centres of excellence' and are required to uphold high academic standards, even for the students that will not enter research careers, which is the majority of the students. Combined with the need for cost-cutting and consequently decreasing financial resources to achieve this excellence, and an incentive system in which careers mainly are related to research efforts rather than teaching quality, the result is inevitably an overall decline in the quality of education. Again, this does not contribute to the willingness or opportunities to face more fundamental problems in economics education.

It seems to be extremely hard to change economics education. There seems to be a kind of 'lock-in' situation not only intellectually but also organizationally and socially, in terms of communities of practice organized among disciplinary lines, populated by economists who all have an interest in keeping things as they are, or at best do not have an interest in changing things. In the Infonomics evaluation, one of the interviewed faculty members said that he wondered why people expected him to be interested in change. Faculty members are generally overloaded with work, fulfilling their research and teaching obligations, so there is no spare time in which to contemplate and initiate change. Even if they see a need for change, the opportunity costs of putting effort into change are too high since it will take away time from fulfilling the conditions for professional survival: publishing in economic journals. In addition, most faculty members obviously did not make it to their position because they were not convinced of, or at least not fiercely opposed to the way things are.

Nevertheless, there are attempts at changing the content of curricula of economics education. Often these attempts come from non-standard scholars at the faculty. The main ingredients needed for change are vision, initiative and organizational skills; in other words, entrepreneurship. In combination with consciously allocated 'money for change' and a generally positive attitude towards the change at hand, the minimal conditions for successful innovation of research and education practices are met. However, vision, initiative and organizational skills are not typical characteristics of the average academic scholar; on the contrary these are scarce and hard to find in the academic population. In addition, individuals that have these qualities are often not valued by economic faculties, and have to have the energy and stamina to fight through pervasive 'office politics' and basic inertia. The overall conditions for successful innovation in economics research and teaching are seldom met, and the result is that innovations in research and education often only partially succeed – thereby confirming the already existing scepticism and strengthening the negative attitude regarding change.

The case of Infonomics is an example of an attempt to innovate education in economics. It aimed at broadening the scope of economics education under the labels of multi- and interdisciplinarity, while making use of the special characteristics of the particular teaching method in use. The next section will discuss the need for multi- and interdisciplinarity, and the problems associated with realizing this in education.

9.4.2 Interdisciplinarity

The case for interdisciplinary research has long been made in the literature on this topic; it will be only briefly summarized here. Basically it boils down to the insight that although we need disciplines to 'discipline' (control, conceptually manage) the complexity of the multitude of observations about reality that we are confronted with, 'reality' itself obviously is not organized along disciplinary lines. A number of important problems of knowledge are neglected because they fail to fit in with disciplinary boundaries and fall into the interstices between them. In order to not let our attempts to discipline our perceptions of reality work against the actual understanding of reality, which supposedly is the real goal, it is important to not draw the lines between disciplines too strictly and to not stay within disciplinary boundaries too rigidly or too exclusively. Disciplines provide us with conceptual tools, the forks, knives and spoons to capture parts of reality that we are interested in. Often it makes sense to use different tools (multidisciplinarity) to get the best hold on the issue; and ideally these tools are used in combination (interdisciplinarity).

However, disciplines and sub-disciplines largely form their own small worlds of methodology, assumptions, language, meaning and identity; and incentive systems in science are still rewarding vertical specialization rather than horizontal integration. There is a trend of ongoing further specialization, resulting in numerous sub-disciplines and a fragmentation, with specialized scientific communities who increasingly do not know each other's bodies of knowledge and who are rewarded for publishing within their own social and conceptual context. This has lead to a fragmentation of knowledge and of perspectives. Disciplines are like tribes, they have a specific culture and specific habits, norms and rules, and they do not easily accept outsiders. This poses problems for cooperation between disciplines, both in research and in education (Spanner, 2001).

Whereas there is a lot of discussion on interdisciplinarity in research, the issue of interdisciplinary education is much less discussed. However the problem is essentially the same: economics students going out into the real world will be confronted with problems that do not stay within disciplinary boundaries, and if they have learned a disciplinary approach they will be less equipped to deal with these properly. 'Properly' means in a way that does not create more problems than are solved.

The problem is that we cannot do without disciplines in education; we need a perspective from which to study phenomena, and we need a community of practice in which to discuss and further analyze phenomena in depth, and that is what disciplines are about. So although 'reality' could be described as 'non-disciplinary', our cognitive dealing with it will always be in some way rather than in another. Can a student learn to think in an interdisciplinary way if he never learned to think in a disciplinary way first? Many of the faculty interviewed in the evaluation of Infonomics held the view that a disciplinary approach in education is unavoidable, but that does not mean that we need to mediate our reality only by mono-disciplinary means. On the contrary, it is important that students learn to recognize that they use a certain approach, which helps them to see certain aspects of the reality they are dealing with. Therefore multi- and interdisciplinary education is needed. This was at least the underlying thought of Infonomics.

Infonomics as an educational track was defined by its subject area, similar to for example communication studies or international relations. Like these, Infonomics was built up by taking elements of different disciplines that are relevant to the area, and combining these. Infonomics was defined in principle as a thematic study on the information society (Figure 9.1).

The ideal envisioned future for Infonomics (Figure 9.2) was that in the end it could grow out into a real, autonomous thematic discipline by itself, fed by other disciplines but with a body of knowledge and methodology of its own. This discipline would study changes in the basic patterns of human behaviour as the result of information and communication processing, and deal with how digital information and communication technology changes these in all domains: in the economy (for example electronic markets), in law (information law, intellectual property rights), in the political domain (e-government, e-democracy), and in the social domain (new forms of community). The conviction was that the changes in the different domains are related to such an extent that they needed to be studied together, not separately – comparably to for example the study of the Industrial Revolution.

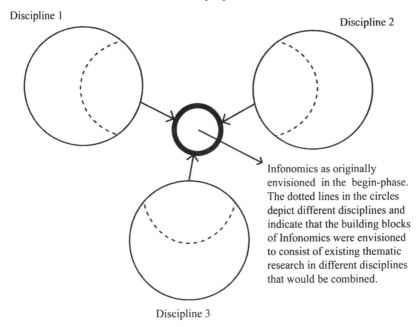

Infonomics as originally envisioned in the begin-phase. The dotted lines in the circles depict different disciplines and indicate that the building blocks of Infonomics were envisioned to consist of existing thematic research in different disciplines that would be combined.

Figure 9.1: Infonomics in the begin-phase

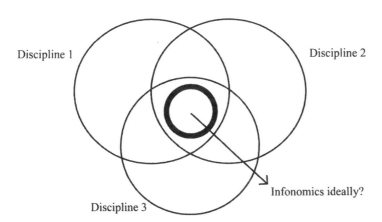

Figure 9.2: The envisioned ideal Infonomics

However, it was hard to find an organizational framework for this. Ideally it should not be attached to any one of the constituting disciplines. That however was very hard to arrange at the university. Because the idea originated from economists who held positions in the Faculty of Economics of the university, Infonomics then was brought under the wing of economics.

Some staff members involved in the programme regretted this, because it seemed to make Infonomics into just another thematic subfield of economics. The disadvantage of this was that the students were obliged to fulfil the end-terms of the study of economics, meaning that the emphasis would be very much on economics and that there was only limited space for other approaches. It was hoped that Infonomics could develop and acquire more and more an identity of its own. Other staff members thought it was good that Infonomics was part of economics at least in the beginning, because you need an established basis that you can offer to students. The students themselves thought it was good that Infonomics was broader and offered different perspectives, because it seemed more realistic and useful. Still, at the same time they appreciated being part of an established discipline, because it provides an identity and a story to the outside world (relatives, friends, future employers) about what they were actually studying, it offered an established recognizable label and thereby a form of safety.

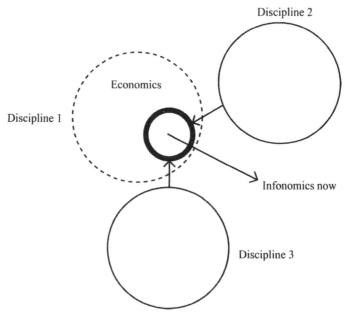

Figure 9.3: Infonomics now

9.4.3 Interdisciplinarity or economic imperialism?

In the interviews it became clear that the staff felt that Infonomics was more multi-disciplinary rather than interdisciplinary, and that it was inevitably dominated heavily by economics. The staff felt that it was harder for the students to get some overall idea of how things are related to each other, because they had to mainly create the links between the different courses themselves.

The staff was divided in two 'camps' that had different ideas of what the function of social science is; whether it is the attempt to resemble natural sciences as much as possible, or whether it is of fundamentally different nature and should be shaped as an instituted process of reflection on human behaviour. Both strategies require looking over the borders of disciplines. However the first is a form of economic imperialism, in which economists are crossing disciplinary borders to go into foreign areas to 'hunt' for interesting insights to take home and use in their theories. The second resembles a form of multi-disciplinarity, with an underlying ambition to interdisciplinarity.

The staff had diverging opinions on how to interpret the expansion of the field of economics. Some viewed it as a form of economic imperialism, economic science entering more and more domains and appropriating them. Others felt that the expansion of economics was in fact making economics more 'enlightened' and some saw it as taking in intellectual 'Trojan horses' from other disciplines, changing economic science from the inside by infiltrating it.

A central question seems to be: should you start disciplinary and then cross the borders? Or should you immediately go broad? Should an educational program look like a 'T' or like a 'T turned upside-down'? The majority of the staff interviewed think that it is important to first learn how to think properly in a certain way, with a certain, given toolset of concepts, methods and terminology. In the case of economics, one should start to teach students to think analytically within stylized models with simplifying assumptions, and only after that start to relax the constraints, broaden the area and make the assumptions more sophisticated and complex.

Some staff members felt that mathematics is the perfect tool to help students to learn how to think, to adequately and clearly represent problems and from there come to solutions; they had a rather purist idea of economics, wanting to have a 'clean' science. In principle non-economic elements can be added, but only if they are prepared in the right way, if they are translated into the format of stylistic thinking, in the form of (additional) assumptions. Infonomics to them should be an exciting new subfield of economics.

More in general, there was clearly the idea that you cannot get a real, deeper understanding of parts of reality when you are not prepared to try to make assumptions. The understanding you gain when doing that is of course bound to and limited by these assumptions, but it is better than not gaining any real understanding at all. The idea was that if you are not prepared to work with assumptions you will be paralyzed in your thinking and always stick at the level of 'many things are important and they are all related'.

Therefore, the majority of the staff members think it is best to achieve interdisciplinarity in education by starting from one or maybe two disciplines and after having control over it, to start looking over the borders, to relax constraints, to adapt assumptions and to look for integration of insights. This means that interdisciplinary education ideally starts after a couple of years of disciplinary training. When including different disciplinary approaches, it is important to first give a real understanding of the specific approach in the discipline, so the students know what they are dealing with and how to understand it, and how to relate it to other disciplines. In the Infonomics program it was too much left to the students themselves to make these connections.

The experiences of the staff with the students seem to reflect and support their already chosen standpoint to a considerable extent, possibly indicating selective perception.

The part of the staff that strongly believed in a broad approach noticed the motivation of students to do so and felt that it was very worthwhile to present a problem in its many dimensions without necessarily 'solving' it. Their aim was to raise awareness of the complexity and the many sides of real-life phenomena. The students confirmed that their awareness was raised but felt slightly left alone with no clear way of dealing with the issues that were raised.

The part of the staff that believed in the importance of a home-discipline and more specifically in the value of the approach of economics, also found confirmation of their ideas. They experienced the Infonomics students as being 'even worse than the other economics students'. They found that the Infonomics students had difficulties with strict, consistent, rigorous analytical thinking. They seemed quite unable to think within a model with assumptions; they kept questioning the assumptions rather than trying to reason within the constraints of the assumptions in order to at least get somewhere. They liked discussion and tended to talk a lot. With this, they took a lot of time of the course without helping themselves and the others to get more into the subject of the course. The impression was that to some extent their talking had to make up for their lack of effort to really work for the course and to really get into the topic and acquire the skills.

The students had mixed appreciation of the courses offered by the more disciplinary-focused economics staff. Many were not so taken by it, because it seemed abstract and far removed from reality. It did not seem to make sense to spend an awful lot of work on modelling and solving something that was little related to reality anyway, because of the unrealistic assumptions in the first place. Why bother? Some of the students that felt this way did not like the application of math but others did not mind the math so much but disliked the abstraction math brought, in the sense of getting too far removed from reality. The students admitted that they did not spend enough effort on getting 'to learn the craft' and that they therefore may not be able to fully appreciate the gains of having a specific, rigorous approach to problems.

An interesting example of the problems of interdisciplinarity and multi-disciplinarity that was given by both staff and students involved the law course in the Infonomics program. This course in the beginning was very problematic. Students struggled with the different approach that is taken in law, it has a different language and concepts and a different 'style', which was described as less analytical and more descriptive. The students had problems with positioning and understanding the law-texts they had to read and had little affinity with the approach that is taken in law. No clear connection was made to the rest of the Infonomics program. They did not like it that there never seemed to be a clear answer to their questions, the answer they always got was 'it depends'. It was just too different from the other things they were learning and they could not really connect it to these other things.

The law course was clearly a disciplinary not an interdisciplinary course. The solution that was found for this course was not to make it more interdisciplinary but rather to stress even more the disciplinarity of the course, by starting with a more general introduction about law as a discipline: what it is about, what kind of questions, how it is studied, and so on. After a 'mini-crash-course' in law, the students got the original core of the course, focusing on specific aspects of law related to the information economy. This has solved many problems. Surprisingly, even the group that was so problematic in this law course, the first year of Infonomics students, who indicated that they did not relate much to the course, a few months later, when asked which course they appreciated most, answered that it was the law course. It seems that they liked the disciplinary approach and that they felt they learned a lot through it, contrary to the more interdisciplinary courses such as the Network Society, which touched all kinds of interesting subjects but left them with the feeling they had learned only a little.

This suggests that when offering disciplinary modules, it is important to make clear at the start that this is a 'different ball game', to avoid frustration and misunderstanding.

This helps students to understand and appreciate what the course offers them. However this does not mean that the effort spent on broadening students' perspectives such as was done in the thematic course, was not successful. It may merely have been less recognized because it has become internalized by the students who consequently do not attribute their changed way of thinking to their educational program; it becomes a 'natural' part of their own development rather than a clear identifiable acquisition of knowledge.

9.4.4   The importance of discipline

When confronted with the complexities of social reality, it is impossible to simply take in all the information that comes to you. You need a filter, to select what is relevant and to determine how to interpret the information, what it means, how it is related to other information and how to act upon it. Our contact with 'reality' is always mediated and controlled by mental models or 'schemata' that make us see things in a certain way and not in another way (Markovitz and Barrouillet, 2002). This enables us to deal with all that comes to us rather than to be paralyzed by it.

Academic disciplines are in fact pre-structured mental models of dealing with (measured, processed) input from reality. The fact that the term 'discipline' is also used for indicating the process of creating order and control shows what the basic function of a discipline is: it is a way to order and control social reality, to canalize the flood of information about this reality, to get a hold of and 'tame' the complexity of the world around us. What happens if you offer no clear canals for containing the informational floods, if you take away the 'shark-cage' that enables you to observe complexities without being absorbed by them? This is a crucial question for interdisciplinary education.

Often, disciplinary approaches are seen as closed off and locked in. However, the risk is that not disciplinary but interdisciplinary dialogues run the risk of going stale. The interdisciplinary community can become 'cut off from fresh infusions of disciplinary knowledge'. It can slide into naive, superficial generalism with little in-depth insight, problem-solving capacity and analytical skills (Nissani, 1997). The interdisciplinary student may become a 'jack of all trades, master of none'.

However, a strictly mono-disciplinary approach is not an option. Advanced industrial societies are increasingly faced with both the intended and unintended consequences of economic and technological development (Giddens, 1990). Education should prepare people to respond to an ever-increasing range of dilemmas that cannot be solved by recourse to existing schema, routines and procedures. People will have to understand why they will need and how they should use ideas that originate from one context to resolve the dilemmas experienced in another.

The idea that solid research results can be reached only by strict specialization dominated the epistemic climate of the last century, according to Kahn (1973). In academic life and scholarship it was postulated that serious knowledge about any area was obtained only by highly specialized research. And with the rise of the modern institutionalization of science there was almost 'no scholarly market for integrated, overall work unless the author was a recognized "authority"– or an elder statesman' and there was not even a non-scholarly market for such work, 'except for authors with a facility for dramatizing and popularizing' (…). This is the hostile environment that interdisciplinary approaches face, and counterweight is needed, both in content and in method.

Attempts to deal with complex and wide-ranging issues are trapped between the danger of either being myopic and biased due to specialization, or of risking superficiality by being too generalist. With the modern trend towards increasing intellectual specialization, the academic type of research, especially in social sciences, has less and less contact with the decision-making process and thus it slowly lost sight of long-term and complex issues that represent the ongoing challenge to modern policy-makers both in the public and the private sector.

For practical or policy matters there is always a need for a broad analytical picture, regardless of what the 'experts' think. In the absence of a systematic and well informed approach, people and decision-makers will construct their own intuitive, misinformed and non-systematic pictures and will act on their basis.

Education is to some extent responsible for the consequences arising from the mono-disciplinary, fragmented nature of human action, addressing one aspect of a problem but neglecting another. Education should help to prevent this from happening, at the least by not being a cause of fragmentation itself because of mono-disciplinary curricula.

Disciplinary approaches are constraining, but as long as one is aware of this, it may in fact be enabling, by presenting a clear, structured approach to tackle messy, complex reality. Not having such a structure may be more detrimental than having one. The Infonomics experience shows that multi- and interdisciplinary education should be more structured than disciplinary education, to compensate for taking away the disciplinary 'intellectual hand-holds'.

9.4.5 The need for intellectual, institutional and social identity

An important problem for interdisciplinary scholars is the lack of clear identity and a lack of a sense of belonging. In the world of learning as it is presently constituted, committed 'interdisciplinarians' typically find themselves in a disciplinary environment to which they never fully belong. Disciplines not only serve as convenient ways of dividing knowledge into its components, but they also serve as a basis for organizing the institution into autonomous fiefdoms. Specialized scholars tend to view with suspicion people lacking a firm anchor in any discipline. To prove themselves, to gain credibility and get their work accepted, they have to be better than a disciplinary scholar.

According to the staff, the Infonomics students did not seem very different from other economics students. There may be a certain selection effect, the students being less risk-averse in terms of uncertainty, since the Infonomics study was new and unknown. An obvious attraction is the broader set-up of the study. It seems that a number of students may have chosen Infonomics because they expected that there would be less mathematics in the programme. There were fewer electives: Infonomics had more of a fixed curriculum than the other options. They had to do courses that they may not particularly have liked because they were part of the programme. The Infonomics programme does seem to have some added value in its set-up, but in terms of courses, it could in fact have been a track within another study variant.

However, the fact that the students were not part of yet another track within economics, but were part of what was conceived to be in many ways a separate 'thematic discipline', had some additional effect. The students attended most of the courses in the same group, and this created strong bonding within the group of students. They were identified as 'the Infonomics students' and this gave a strong sense of identity, strengthened by the bonding due to sharing similar experiences only with other Infonomics students. In most years, the Infonomics group was really tight and close. This increased the influence of group dynamics, for the better and for the worse. A positive effect seems to have been that Infonomics students started to study together in groups, actively helping each other and stimulating each other to discuss learning material and to study as a social activity. At the same time, they turned into a small sub-society, which made them harder to control.

Contrary to the staff, the students had a strong sense of being different from the other students, even though this had not much real basis. For example in terms of content they did not differ more from other students than students within different tracks in the other study variants of the faculty differed from each other.

The group identity came from both internal and external forces. Internal was the fact that they shared most of the courses, and shared experiences are bonding. Also they had the feeling they shared some characteristics, that they were less risk-averse. The idea of being together in a kind of 'adventure' contributed to the group feeling, according to the students. The students had the idea that they were different from the other economics students in terms of their motivation for the study; they indicated that, supposedly contrary to 'normal' economics students, their motivation was not primarily making a lot of money. They seemed proud to be part of Infonomics and they seemed to exaggerate the differences between them and the other students at the faculty. They felt they were more open, less fixed in their future plans. Many of the students did not seem to have clear, set plans for the future, in terms of career. The group may be relatively undecided. They were attracted by the fact that Infonomics was something different. International Business (IB) you can do everywhere but Infonomics is quite unique. Some non-Infonomics students apparently expressed a certain jealousy because Infonomics was more special and exotic and there seemed to be more personal attention and interaction with the staff members for Infonomics students. In addition, in at least two of the four annual batches of students, the Infonomics group seemed a very close group that enjoyed being a group.

The students did not have a clear professional identity; they were students in a subject area that had no clear contours, that was and still is not yet 'mature', and unknown outside of the circle of the University of Maastricht. The students themselves also expressed mixed feelings about this; in principle they were proud to be doing something special, but in practice, when asked what they study, they usually answered 'economics', because it would take too long to explain. The students do think that having done something different, something unique, will look good on their CVs; it will attract attention and curiosity and will give them the chance to explain.

Intellectual identity is an important product of an academic discipline. The students seemed to have responded to being singled out and not having a clear identity by actively creating an identity of their own, which consisted mainly of being in the same position and having the same experiences. In doing this, the students tended to magnify the differences with other students and actively construct similarities between the Infonomics students.

9.4.6 Conditions for successful curriculum change

None of the staff members denounced the intellectual and the social and economic importance of interdisciplinarity. What they seem to indicate is not that interdisciplinary education is not the way to go, but rather, that it only works under a number of conditions. According to the staff, these conditions are:

- A high level of capabilities, motivation and involvement of both students and staff
- A well-designed, thorough educational programme, more structured than normal educational programmes, to make up for the complexity within the programme
- More support for the students and staff, for example actively coaching the staff
- Active creation of reflectiveness on what students learn and on what staff members teach

It will be hard to fulfil these conditions at most universities. For example, it would require selection of students to sort out the most motivated, which is at least in the Netherlands a debated issue. More problematic is that it would demand much more time and effort of the staff, who often are already burdened by the increasing pressure to publish research, and who are rewarded for their research publications, not for their educational achievements.

Therefore it may not be realistic to attempt to give interdisciplinary education, at least not at the bachelor's level. At the master's level, this may be more realistic and desirable. Consequently, it was decided that Infonomics should be a master's programme, which can be entered after finishing a bachelor's degree in economics.

9.5 CHANGING THE FORM OF ECONOMICS EDUCATION

9.5.1 The need to change the way we deal with knowledge

The criticism of economics education does not only concern the content but also the form, the way in which economics is being taught. One reason for this lies in the need to change the way we deal with knowledge more in general.

The students that started the Post-Autistic Network expressed their discontent with the present way education is organized, pleading for a broad spectrum of analytical viewpoints instead:

> Too often the lectures leave no place for reflection. Out of all the approaches to economic questions that exist, generally only one is presented to us. This approach is supposed to explain everything by means of a purely axiomatic process, as if this were THE economic truth. We do not accept this dogmatism. We want a pluralism of approaches, adapted to the complexity of the objects and to the uncertainty surrounding most of the big questions in economics (unemployment, inequalities, the place of financial markets, the advantages and disadvantages of free-trade, globalization, economic development, etc.). (www.paecon.net)

This is indicative of a general perception that the world and its problems have become more complex. The basic idea is that technological development, globalization and an overall increase in the degree of specialization and organization in society have changed the scale and interdependency of problems.

The degree and nature of uncertainties have changed and insights developed in one time and in one particular context are of less value in understanding phenomena in other contexts or in the future. That means we can rely less on solving problems by 'tapping' existing knowledge acquired in some earlier phase, and that we increasingly need to look at questions and problems where and when they arise, finding whatever knowledge that is available and relevant at that point of time for that issue.

This poses enormous challenges to social science, not least because it is the application of social science itself that has led to increased complexity of interaction and decision-making (Giddens, 1990). The application of more science to deal with this complexity may make the complexity even worse – unless the way knowledge is applied is changed.

The cure for unintended consequences of the use of social science may lie in 'relaxing' our ideas about knowledge as reflecting objective truths. Instead, a more instrumental view of knowledge may be both more useful and truthful. Knowledge, especially in social science, reflects a selective set of observations, acquired through a certain approach, analysed with certain assumptions and interpreted from a certain perspective. Realizing this is important. It is essential to make students aware of the character of the knowledge they learn, and to stress the care with which they should apply this knowledge, and the limits to its application. As one of the staff members interviewed in the Infonomics evaluation said, economic knowledge or rather knowledge derived through the methods of economics, should always be labelled with some sort of warning, such as 'don't try this at home'.

If we manage to teach students to use the conceptual tools and the knowledge that they derive in a careful, sophisticated, context-sensitive way, we may increase the chance that the applied knowledge may solve more problems than it creates.

All of this has implications for the way knowledge is transferred; it requires a different approach, in which the emphasis shifts towards a more dynamic understanding of knowledge. The main responsibility of education is no longer the mere transmission of some existing stock of knowledge, but rather training students in dealing with new knowledge in a meaningful way. Since we neither know what kind of knowledge will be available in the future, nor what kind of problems students will face in their future, transmission of knowledge has been reduced from being the main function of education to being merely a part of it. Students have to learn how to learn.

As in the case of interdisciplinary, this is not a new idea, but the application to economics education to some extent is. One method that is supposed to increase the effectiveness of learning and especially the learning of learning skills is 'Problem-based Learning' (PBL), the method used in the case of Infonomics. PBL can both help students acquire much-needed meta-cognitive skills and to better apply theory to concrete problems and vice versa. In this section the PBL method is discussed, including its potential to accommodate a multi- or interdisciplinary content.

9.5.2 Problem-based learning

Most universities teach economics according to the 'transmissionist' or 'broadcast model' (Larkin, 2000). This model holds a number of (partly implicit) assumptions:

- Previous knowledge is not relevant (students are blank slates).
- Knowledge is binary (you either know it or you don't).
- The student is idealized (students are motivated, independent, and all have the same learning style). If the student differs from this image then it is their fault and their problem.
- Scientific thought and rational thinking are taken to be natural – even obvious.

Clearly these assumptions are problematic largely because they are simply not true. Problem-based learning (PBL) is based on cognitive learning psychology (Creedy et al., 1992), which has very different assumptions about learning. The main difference is that it assumes that learners are active processors of information rather than passive recipients of knowledge. This means that context, history and personal characteristics of the student matter in the learning process.

PBL, as it is known today, originated in the 1950s and 1960s in medical science. It grew from dissatisfaction with the common medical education practices in Canada (Barrows, 1996). PBL gained a foothold at a time when universities were disappointed in the effectiveness of learning, because so many students forget or fail to apply or integrate knowledge, and resist further learning. The underlying problem was that the curricula were based on a view of knowledge in which teachers were expected to tell students the 'truth' about what is known about medicine and science. This truth was primarily delivered by lecturing. Current views on human learning however are based on a view in which 'knowledge' is not absolute, but is constructed by the learner based on previous knowledge and existing mental models of the world. Learning is seen as a process that results from interactions with the environment. It is the learner who constructs new knowledge and who is at the centre of the educational process.

PBL is consistent with this 'constructivist' view of human learning. Students elaborate on prior knowledge in a meaningful context for future application of the information. This makes retrieval of knowledge easier once in practice (Creedy et al., 1992). In addition to this it is believed that PBL assists in integrating theory and practice and develops skills that can be transferred into a variety of settings and practices, such as team working and lifelong learning skills.

Six characteristics of PBL are distinguished in the core model (Barrows, 1996):

- Education needs to be student-centred.
- Learning occurs best in small student groups under the guidance of a tutor.
- The tutor functions not as an authority but as a facilitator or guide.
- The learning process is organized around problems.
- The questions encountered are used as a tool to achieve the required knowledge and the problem-solving skills necessary to eventually solve the problem.
- New information needs to be acquired through self-directed or self-regulated learning.

In PBL, teachers do not primarily disseminate information to students, but teach students to find their own answers to questions that they identify themselves. Teachers function as tutors who facilitate students' learning processes and provide students with feedback in order to safeguard the quality of the learning. In PBL students learn, how to learn which is thought to be crucial for functioning in a world characterized by constant flows of new information and knowledge and in which they must constantly identify new problems, acquire new skills and find new solutions (Dolmans et al., 1994).

PBL helps the development of Self-regulated Learning (SRL), according to the literature a crucial skill for successful economic performance of human capital, at the level of individual employees, organizations and national advanced industrial economies. SRL has emerged as an important new construct in education (Boekaerts, 1999). Self-regulation means being able to develop knowledge, skills and attitudes, which can be transferred from one learning context to another, and from learning situations in which this information has been acquired to real life situations.

The key issue in self-regulated learning is the students' ability to select, combine, and coordinate cognitive strategies in an effective way. It is important to know whether students perceive a choice among alternative processing modes. The perception of choice is a critical aspect of self-regulated learning (Winne and Perry, 2000).

Guile and Young (1999) put forward the concept of reflexive learning to encapsulate the sociological and educational dimensions of learning. Learning always takes place in specific contexts, but these contexts themselves are a product both of people's activities and of different historical circumstances, and the process of learning involves the transformation of contexts. Education should explicitly deal with the tension between the trans-contextual and context-specific nature of knowledge and skill.

9.5.3 The use of the Internet

An important development that radically changes the way we deal with knowledge is the rapid spread of information and communication technology (ICT). The impact of ICT on knowledge generation and diffusion is enormous, ranging from the increased possibilities to process large data-sets and the increased possibilities to communicate with others all over the world at low cost, to the tremendously increased access to information in general through the Internet. The direct access to large amounts of information about just about anything, through websites, electronic journals, and internet libraries shifts the emphasis from knowledge to knowing where knowledge can be found. An interesting question is to what extent this influences and changes the potential of multidisciplinary and interdisciplinary education, and to what extent it supports learning methods such as problem-based learning.

In the evaluation of Infonomics, the use of the Internet by the students and its effects was one of the issues addressed. Not surprisingly it was found that students use the Internet a great deal, but in a flexible and uncritical way which should raise some worries. The students are able to generate a lot of information about a topic in a very short time; but they do not seem to have a very coherent view of how different topics relate to each other and where to position what. In addition they seem to forget the information they gathered and the knowledge they acquired from it rather easily. The reason is that they know that if necessary they can find it again on the Internet. The result is that the Internet seems to function to some extent as an 'external memory', and knowledge is only temporarily stored in the 'working memory' of students.

The practice of 'cut-and-paste' is widespread. This is not in itself necessarily considered to be a bad thing, as long as the students are forced to understand what they cut-and-paste, and that is often not the case. They seem to be quite instrumental in finding material for their studies, not caring much for the truth in itself. To get some indication of the quality, the students seemed to use secondary signals, including a kind of 'brand' feeling. For example, something with the label of 'Harvard' on it must be good and legitimate. The use of special software to scan for cut-and-past plagiarism in papers has forced the students to reformulate and rephrase the information they found; and to do this successfully, they first need to understand it.

The effect of the Internet (unprecedented access, but danger of 'drowning', 'shopping', and copying) and specialist software (increasing processing power, but creating black boxes) on education is not well understood yet. There was moderate optimism among the staff about the use of the Internet enabling and facilitating interdisciplinarity and PBL. Internet, email and special software, all together enable easy and quick access to information, knowledge and processing power. Therefore it is, at least in theory, easier and less costly in terms of time to learn different approaches than in the past. In principle, interdisciplinary approaches, PBL and the use of the Internet can facilitate and strengthen each other.

However, in practice it seems that the combination of multi- and interdisciplinarity, PBL and the use of the Internet leads to a 'postmodern' attitude among students, who are collecting a 'patchwork' of partial insights taken out of context and interpreted freely, resulting in all kinds of semi-truths that start to live a life of their own.

9.5.4   Does problem-based learning work?

According to the Infonomics staff, PBL is hard for the students. The students have to read a lot of literature and they have to figure out how things fit together largely for themselves. In principle this is good for the development of learning and information processing skills, but in practice it often means that students remain at a fairly superficial level of knowledge. They read the literature, they don't study it. The drive to understand is not always present, and partly this is also a kind of defence against the mountain of literature they feel themselves confronted with. They feel it will be very hard to really understand and therefore do not allow themselves to try it, out of self-protection. What they then do may largely consist of instrumental information processing instead of gaining real understanding. On the other hand, it was observed that PBL clearly increases the involvement of students and increases their skills in terms of communicating, discussion, presentation, and application of knowledge.

Research on the effects of PBL shows that both for knowledge- and skills-related outcomes the expertise level of the student is associated with the variation in effect sizes, that is, it depends. In the *Lancet*, (Morrison, 2004) the overall finding in medical education is that PBL students show little or no improvement in written examination scores over students following conventional curricula. However, PBL students enjoy their learning more and give higher evaluations to their curricula. Additionally, if PBL curricula are compared with conventional varieties: staff prefer PBL; and students score better on clinical examinations. Also, PBL might enhance intrinsic interest in medicine and in self-directed learning skills, which may persist throughout their careers. Measuring examination performance is straightforward, but produces unconvincing evidence. More important outcomes of medical education include retention in medicine, career satisfaction, and commitment to lifelong learning.[1]

Evaluative research on the effectiveness of programmes or course with a PBL instructional approach does not present conclusive results. Segers et al. (2003) underline that the effectiveness of PBL as an instructional method probably depends to a great extent on the incorporation of a range of supporting variables. They find that PBL increases the pleasure of learning of students and seems to increase long-term retention of knowledge, but did not significantly contribute to student outcomes on exams (after controlling for prior knowledge and possible selection bias). The standard measurements of performance such as exams may not capture changed (meta-) cognitive approaches that may be more successful than standard approaches when applied to real life problems. Research suggests that educational innovations often lead to cognitive gains in the long term rather than the short term (Norman and Schmidt, 2000).

There is great variability in individual training gains: the so-called 'resistant students' may fail to develop the necessary self-regulatory skills to coordinate their mental processes and they did not take responsibility for their own learning, despite their increased meta-cognitive knowledge about the tasks (Dochy et al., 2003).

The main challenge for successful PBL is the balance between giving freedom to the learning process of students versus intervening in, structuring and directing the learning of students. Failure to achieve a good balance can lead to student and teacher frustration (Haith-Cooper, 2000). The evaluation of Infonomics showed that students can become confused and even angry when the facilitator does not provide enough information (also Alavi, 1995). On the other hand, too much intervention also can be counterproductive. It can be stifling for the students, who are on the one hand being encouraged to take control over the learning process themselves but on the other hand are constantly corrected and guided (Dolmans et al., 1993).

Weinert et al. (1989) pointed out that external regulation is a form of support that replaces or compensates for low meta-cognitive awareness and that students who are not skilful in orienting, planning, monitoring, or evaluating their own performance may rely instead on the teacher's meta-cognitive skills. Students are not used to managing their own learning process. They expect the teacher to tell them what to do, how and when to do it, and when to stop doing it. The point is that dependence on teachers works only as long as a teacher is available to take over, or to activate the students' poor self-regulatory skills. A decrease in achievement will be noticed as soon as these students have to study in an environment where they have to steer and direct their own learning process.

PBL also requires a lot from the teachers. Most teachers in economics have had primarily lecture-based experience and have hardly had any role models for tutoring. They have expertise in the discipline in which they have been trained and have had limited training in how to teach students. They are prepared as lecturer or subject matter expert with much knowledge about discipline-specific issues. With this background it is understandable that they feel uncomfortable with the tutor role in PBL.

To be a successful tutor in the PBL system, one needs to reconsider personal beliefs about the teacher's role in education. Facilitation styles may be influenced by the belief of the tutor about effective learning. Tutors felt that trusting that PBL works is essential to facilitate effectively. The success of PBL depended on the motivation and the skills of both tutors and students, and in addition to some extent on the content of what was being taught. PBL works better for some courses than for others (such as for example mathematics). It is important to not apply PBL to just any subject area, as now often happens, but to be selective when to use a more top-down approach, and when PBL is effective.

In principle PBL seems a better system than the more traditional top-down broadcast approach, but – similarly to the case of interdisciplinarity – only under some important conditions that are often not present.

Concluding, it could be said that the 'bandwidth' of results of PBL is broader: it is either much better or much worse than more traditional top-down approaches. It crucially depends on a number of factors (such as highly motivated and able students and tutors, a well-designed structure). If these factors are not present, PBL may be counter-productive.

9.6   CONCLUSIONS

There is serious, compelling criticism of what is taught in economics education and on the way it is taught. Economics education is accused of being narrow, based on unrealistic assumptions, dogmatic to the verge of indoctrinating, and increasingly irrelevant. This chapter has outlined the nature of this criticism and has discussed possible ways to change economics education for the better. Underlying this is the need for a different way of dealing with knowledge in general. Elements that should be part of the needed change are multi- and interdisciplinarity (content) and to some extent letting go of the 'broadcast model' of teaching. However these changes are not easy to make successfully and bring their own problems.

The case of Infonomics is illustrative for the type of problems that arise when trying to get away from both mono-disciplinarity (toward multi- and interdisciplinarity) and from passive knowledge transmission (toward active knowledge finding) at the same time. Infonomics was partially a success, since the outcome consisted of enthusiastic, motivated students, many of whom had gained a good understanding of a tremendously important insight about the character of knowledge: the need to interpret knowledge by looking at the context in which it was created, when, by whom and why, in which situation, with which methods and assumptions. This may be to some extent a selection effect, but at least the students themselves attributed it clearly and explicitly to the Infonomics curriculum. However the combination of multi- and interdisciplinarity and PBL (and in addition the use of the Internet) did not always have such positive effects, at least, not on all students. For some students, it resulted in a rather 'postmodern' attitude, the students collecting a 'patchwork' of partial insights taken out of context and interpreted freely, resulting in all kinds of semi-truths that start to live a life of their own. The difference mainly seems to lie in the quality and the personality of the students. It is not a good thing if the effect of an educational programme is too dependent on these elements.

Overall it can be concluded that introducing multi- and interdisciplinary elements (content) and a different method of teaching that recognizes the dynamic character of knowledge in principle represent a major improvement that could remedy many of the current weaknesses in economics education. However, in practice this is only the case if certain conditions are met. If these are not met, the result of trying to introduce these changes may have no positive effect or even a negative effect. So, either do it well, or don't do it. The latter however is no option. It is time that economists at universities take responsibility for what they send out into the world, both in terms of research and in terms of students and their thinking and acting as it is shaped by economics education.

NOTES

This chapter is based on a discussion paper for a special session on interdisciplinary education at the EAEPE conference in 2003. R.M. Weehuizen (2003), 'Interdisciplinarity and Education in the Information Society', EAEPE conference on the Information Society, 7-9 November 2003, Maastricht, The Netherlands. I thank Robin Cowan for comments. Special thanks go to the Infonomics students at the University of Maastricht, whose enthusiasm, idealism, honesty and involvement are a true source of inspiration for anyone involved in education. I am grateful to two students in particular, Nana Lohmans and Malte von Engelbrechten-Ilow, who were involved in the programme evaluation.

[1] It was concluded that PBL provides a challenging, motivating, and enjoyable approach to medical education, and may promote lifelong habits of self-directed learning. These effects may lead to better retention of graduates in medicine which possibly is the most important outcome measure in the long term. Longitudinal research to assess enduring outcomes of PBL, with long lasting follow-up across a range of medical schools, may provide convincing evidence that will justify the costs of these curricula in the long term (Morrison, 2004).

BIBLIOGRAPHY

Aaron, H.J. (1992), 'Symposium on Economists as Policy Advocates', *The Journal of Economic Perspectives*, **6**(3), Summer, 59-60.
Alavi, S. (ed.) (1995), *Problem-based Learning in a Health Sciences Curriculum*, London: Routledge.
Aligica, P.D. (2003), 'The Challenge of the Future and the Institutionalization of Interdisciplinarity: Notes on Herman Kahn's legacy', *Futures*, in press, corrected proof, available online 12 July 2003.
Barrows, H.S. (1996), 'Problem-based Learning in Medicine and Beyond: A Brief Overview', In L. Wilkerson and W.H. Gijselaers (eds), *New Directions For Teaching and Learning*, **68**, San Francisco: Jossey-Bass Publishers, pp. 3–11.
Beck, U., A. Giddens and S. Lash (1994), *Reflexive Modernisation*, Cambridge: Policy Press.
Bergin, C. and D. A. (1999) 'Bergin Classroom Discipline that Promotes Self-Control', *Journal of Applied Developmental Psychology*, **20**(2), June, 189-206.
Blaug, M. (1997), 'Ugly Currents in Modern Economics', *Policy Options*, September 1997, 3-8
Boekaerts, M. (1999), 'Self-regulated Learning: Where we are Today', *International Journal of Educational Research*, **31**(6), 445-457.
Bruner, J.S. (1959), 'Learning and Thinking', *Harvard Educational Review*, **29**, 184–192.
Bruner, J.S. (1961), 'The Act of Discovery', *Harvard Educational Review*, **31**, 21–32.
Creedy, D., J. Horsfall and B. Hand (1992), 'Problem-based Learning in Nurse Education: An Australian view', *Journal of Advanced Nursing*, **17**(6), 727–733.
Dewey, J. (1910), *How We Think*, Boston: Health & Co.
Dewey, J. (1944), *Democracy and Education*, New York: Macmillan Publishing Co.
Dochy, F., M. Segers, P. Van den Bossche and D. Gijbels (2003), 'Effects of Problem-based Learning: A Meta-analysis', *Learning and Instruction*, **13**(5), October, 533-568.
Dolmans, D., W. Gijselaers, H. Schmidt and S. Van de Meer (1993), 'Problem Effectiveness in a Course using Problem-based Learning', *Academic Medicine*, **68**(3), 207–213.
Dolmans, D. and H. Schmidt (1994), 'What Drives the Student in Problem-based Learning?', *Medical Education*, **28**, 372–380.
Eizenstat, S. E. (1992), 'Economists and White House Decisions', *The Journal of Economic Perspectives*, **6**(3), Summer, 65-71.
Fine, B. (2002), 'Social Capital versus Social Theory: Political Economy and Social Science at the Turn of the Millennium'. London: Routledge.
Fullbrook, Edward (ed.) (2004), *A Guide to What's Wrong with Economics*, London: Anthem Press.
Giddens, A. (1990), *The Consequences of Modernity*, Stanford, CA: Stanford University Press.
Guile, D. (2001), 'Education and the Economy: Rethinking the question of Learning for the "Knowledge" Era', *Futures*, **33**(6), August, 469-482.
Guile, D. and M. Young (1999), 'Beyond the Institution of Apprenticeship: Towards a Sociology of Learning as the Production of Knowledge', in P. Ainley and H.

Rainbird (eds), *Apprenticeship: Towards a New Paradigm of Learning*, London: Kogan Page.

Haith-Cooper, M. (2000), 'Problem-based Learning within Health Professional Education. What is the Role of the Lecturer? A Review of the Literature', *Nurse Education Today*, **20**(4), May, 267-272.

Hamilton, L.H. (1992), 'Economists as Public Policy Advisers', *The Journal of Economic Perspectives*, **6**(3), Summer, 61-64

Hughes L. and J. Lucas (1997), 'An Evaluation of Problem Based Learning in the Multiprofessional Education Curriculum for the Health Professions', *Journal Of Interprofessional Care*, **11**(1).

Kahn, H. (1973), 'The Alternative World Futures Approach', in F. Tugwell (ed.), *Search for Alternatives: Public Policy and the Study of the Future*, Camebridge, MA: Witrop Publishers.

Lepper, M.R., D. Greene and R.E. Nisbett (1973), 'Undermining children's Intrinsic Interest with Extrinsic Reward: A Test of the "Overjustification" Hypothesis', *Journal of Personality and Social Psychology*, **28**, 129–137.

Maccoby, E.E. (1992), 'The Role of Parents in the Socialization of Children: An Historical Overview', *Developmental Psychology*, **28**, 1006–1017.

Markovitz, H. and P. Barrouillet (2002), 'The Development of Conditional Reasoning: A Mental Model Account', *Developmental Review*, **22**(1), March, 5-36.

Marton, F. and R. Säljö (1984), 'Approaches to Learning', in F. Marton, D. Hounsell and N. Entwistle (eds), *The Experience of Learning*, Edinburgh: Scottish Academic Press, pp. 36–55.

Morrison, J. (2004), 'Where Now for Problem Based Learning?', *The Lancet*, **363**(9403), 10 January, 174.

Neufeld, V.R. and H.S. Barrows (1974), 'The "McMaster Philosophy": An Approach to Medical Education', *Journal of Medical Education*, **49**, 1040–1050.

Nissani, M. (1997), 'Ten Cheers for Interdisciplinarity: The Case for Interdisciplinary Knowledge and Research', *The Social Science Journal*, **34**(2), 201-216.

Norman, G.R. and H.G. Schmidt (1992), 'The Psychological Basis of Problem-based Learning: A Review of the Evidence', *Academic Medicine*, **67**, 557-565.

Pask, G. (1988), 'Learning Strategies, Teaching Strategies, and Conceptual or Learning Style', in R.R. Schmeck (ed.), *Learning Strategies and Learning Styles*, New York: Plenum, pp. 83–100.

Piaget, J. (1954), *The Construction of Reality in the Child*, New York: Basic Books.

Segers, M., P. van den Bossche and E. Teunissen (2003), 'Evaluating the Effects of Redesigning a Problem-based Learning Environment', *Studies in Educational Evaluation*, **29**, 315-334.

Spanner, D. (2001), 'Border Crossings: Understanding the Cultural and Informational Dilemmas of Interdisciplinary Scholars', *The Journal of Academic Librarianship*, **27**(5), September, 352-360.

Thompson Klein, J. (1990), *Interdisciplinarity: History, Theory and Practice*, Detroit: Wayne State University Press.

Thompson Klein, J. (1996), *Crossing Boundaries: Knowledge, Discipli-narities, and Interdisciplinarities*, Charlottesville, VA: University Press of Virginia.

Weinert, F., A. Helmke and W. Schneider (1989), 'Individual Differences in Learning Performance and in School Achievement: Plausible Parallels and

Unexplained Discrepancies', in H. Mandl (ed.), *Learning and Instruction*, 461-479, Oxford: Pergamon Press.

Weinstein, M. (1992), 'Economists and the Media', *The Journal of Economic Perspectives*, **6**(3), Summer, 73-77.

Winne, P.H. and N.E. Perry (2000), 'Measuring Self-regulated Learning', in P. Pintrich, M. Boekaerts, and M. Seidner (eds), *Handbook of Self-regulation*, 531-566, Orlando, FL: Academic Press.

10. Heterodox Economics and its Integration in Pluralist Teaching: a German Case

Wolfram Elsner

10.1 INTRODUCTION

The present chapter discusses a particular case of how diverse 'heterodox' economic approaches in a pluralist new MA programme are being implemented in a pluralist economics faculty in Germany. It is argued that such an implementation is feasible only if the approaches can prove their relevance and applicability to real world problems and their professional advantages to prospective students. The faculty that operates the programme has considerable experience with 'heterodox' approaches and with pluralist national master programmes. One of those experiences is a network of exchange agreements with other pluralist economics departments in Europe and the US. It illustrates the importance of international embeddedness. Some conclusions, generalisations and recommendations for the development of new European pluralist BA and MA programmes will be drawn in the final section.

10.2 SOME THEORETICAL CONSIDERATIONS

10.2.1 The 'single principle' orthodoxy

Economic mainstream orthodoxy is a 'single, or general, principle' science, which constructs an artificial world in order to utilize certain kinds of mathematics and be politically appropriate to the current status quo of the world of capitalist economies. It assumes and indeed requires one single, specific, uniform kind of behaviour, the maximizing *homo economicus*, one specific type of allocation mechanism (the 'market') and economic system (the 'market economy'), one single channel of information generation and diffusion (equilibrium prices), and finally it normally generates a single and specific kind of policy prescription.

The General Equilibrium Theory (GET) not only encounters theoretical problems in demonstrating the existence of unique and stable equilibria, but most of all it does not connect well with economic reality. It has been demonstrated during and after the 'Mirowski debate' (Mirowski, 1989) that the general 'market' approach of an economy does not generate nor admit enough structure to be able to fulfil its own research programme, which serves to prove the uniqueness and stability of a general equilibrium. On the contrary a general, unique, and stable 'market' equilibrium can normally not exist.

The interchange among individuals is restricted to a centralized and authoritarian vision of an auctioneer, in which agents' activities are allowed to take place only within the logical second of declared equilibrium.

10.2.2 The 'real-world' starting points of 'heterodox' economic approaches: their relevance

'Heterodox' economics, on the contrary, is real world economics; it is socio-economics in the widest sense. Specifically, institutional and evolutionary (socio-) economics (IEE/SE) begins with the real world pluriformity of individual behaviour, cultural conditioning of behaviour, as well as individual creativity. It reflects the real world of direct interdependencies among agents, where the outcome of A not only depends on his own decision, but also directly on the decision of B, and vice versa. Real world direct interactions are allowed to occur under conditions of different forms of non-perfect information, such as bounded rationality and strong uncertainty where no probability distribution of future events and risk calculation are feasible. Interactive socio-economics thus deals with genuine social decision problems where agents are uncertain in a 'strategic' sense, being unable to know at the outset the actions of others. Information then becomes a crucial issue in 'heterodox' economics. The imperfect nature of information influences present behaviour through expectations of the future.

'Heterodox' economics reflects complexity through many interrelated agents with a great number of potential relations among them. Furthermore, ubiquitous externalities, collective goods problems and different kinds of social dilemmas involved imply that any two agents have a multiplicity of kinds of interrelations between them. Those relations that promote problem-solving may only be feasible, however, through a process of collective learning. An environment that entails collective learning is far beyond the concepts of 'maximizing', 'efficiency', 'optimization' or 'stability'. However, it does not imply a lack of structure, regularity, or predictability.

Against the background of such properties, modern 'heterodox' approaches are able to provide more fruitful explanatory frameworks and research programmes for recent real world developments. They are more capable of explaining what is happening, for instance, in globally (functionally and spatially) fragmented value-added chains, the net-technologically based 'new' economy, ubiquitous net-externalities of individual (technological) decision-making, information as a collective good (having large economies of scale, near-to-zero marginal costs of information and its technical non-excludability), and finally, the 'complementary' and 'systemic' character of production and innovation (for more details see Elsner, 2005). Thus, for example, modern innovation and information economics has largely developed into an evolutionary and institutional framework.

'Heterodox' economics is also able to explain why the most developed parts of the globalized corporate economy – in contrast to its own rhetoric – is striving to establish conditions and relations of local proximity with their most important suppliers, and to constrain the 'market' through recurrent interaction, stability, structure, local cultural (re-)embedding and trust. Institutional dis-embedding under neo-liberal auspices and subsequent increased uncertainty drive even the largest corporation to take ever more control of their environment through the development of large hub and spoke networks (see for example Elsner, 2000).

'Heterodox' economics allows for complexity and collective learning to reduce complexity in order to enable agents to effectively coordinate, act, and innovate under fragmented conditions. 'Heterodox' economics permits analysis of learned institutions and complex interrelatedness of technology and institutions, including technological lock-ins on inferior technological paths (for example, the 'QWERTY' phenomenon). It permits roles for intra- and intercorporate routines, cultures, tacit knowledge, knowledge diffusion, and technology transfer.

Last but not least, it acknowledges that real time matters – for example in the processes of complex learning and adapting systems – and developments can be path-dependent and irreversible. For a rough illustration of some current key conceptions and theoretical developments, see Figure 10.1.

Figure 10.1: Theoretical strands and developments in economics: practical aspects of some heterodox approaches: a rough illustration

Macro	Meso	Micro
Classical and New Classical Political Economy Keynesianism/ Post-Keynesianism (Neoclassical) Ordo-liberal Ordnungs - Economics	Original Evolutionary and Institutional Economics (OIE); Neo-Schumpeterianism: • Direct Interdependences, • Strong Uncertainty. • Collective Complexity Learning, • Cumulative Technology, Institutional Arrangements, Marcofoundations • Institutional Emergence/Comparative • Institutional Design/New Economic Policy etc. **Practical Applications:** • **Net-Technologies and Innovation Economics, Externalities** • **Information, Uncertainty** • **Collective Learning, Tacit Knowledge, Social Capital, Trust** • **Contracting, Networking, Governance and Culture** • **Intra-Company-Routines and Culture** • **Innovation-Networks, Innovation Transfer** • **Clusters, Industries, Regions, Industrial + Regional Economics etc.**	Mainstream (Business Administration) Neoclassical Micro-Economics and General Equilibrium Theory New Institutional Economics (NIE); Evolutionary Institutional Micro: • Transaction Costs, Markets and Hierarchies • Uncertainty and Information Asymmetry • Contract-Governance • Network-Arrangements and Network-Governance • Principal-Agent, Governance • Evolutionary and Competence-base of Theory of the Firm Evolutionary Game Theory: • Externalities • Collective Goods, Social Dilemmas • Collective Learning, Complex Coordination etc.

Evolutionary Theory of Economics and Systems

Developing New Micro-foundations

10.2.3 Their greater specificity

'Heterodox' approaches enable economists to be more specific with respect to their understanding of the individual. Each individual has a personality 'fingerprint', an individually selected and adapted partial set of the universe of the social institutions. These institutions simultaneously operate at the 'micro-micro' (intra-individual) and the inter-individual and genuinely collective levels.

'Heterodox' economics also enables more specific analysis of the processes of emergence of institutions, of comparative institutions and collective learning, especially as they take place at the 'meso' levels and platforms (for example regions, agglomerations, industries, clusters, networks, professional or any other kind of 'mid-size' social groups (Elsner, 2000)).

10.2.4 Their policy orientation

Last but not least, 'heterodox' economics approaches have always had a strong policy orientation. Specifically, with modern IEE/SE approaches there is no suggestion that ideal evolutionary collective interaction and learning processes should be taken as proof of the self-regulative power and self-sustainability of individualistic 'market' economies.

On the contrary, the (according to the Veblen-Ayres institutionalist tradition) omnipresent ceremonial (that is, power and status preserving) dimension of institutions, the complexity of the technology-institutions systems, and ubiquitous technological lock-ins are instances which underlie the great amount of practical experience, theoretical analysis, model simulations and lab experiments which suggest interactive processes in an individualistic culture are often inferior or locked-in; the emergence of their collective outcomes is highly time-consuming and processes and results are fragile, if not blocked.

Consequently, there is a need for hybrid institutional arrangements of coordination with public, genuinely collective 'rationality' being specifically defined vis-à-vis the interactive processes of the private agents. The whole 'private' and collective goods structure of the socio-economy has to be socially and publicly evaluated and '(de-)meritorized', using criteria pertaining to the stability and certainty of the (useful) collective outcomes of private processes. For example, goods will have to be publicly evaluated on the background of their public effects and spillovers, according to R. Musgrave, as something to be either collectively supported or eschewed, in a process of collective participatory decision-making (for further details, see Elsner, 2001).

A new policy approach, a 'New New Deal' (de la Mothe and Paquet, 1999: 85) must be developed to initiate (de-block or un-lock), accelerate, and stabilize the processes that build institutions and that promote collective learning and innovation. The basic complexes hereof are the futurity of the interactions among the private agents (that is, their realization of the importance of their common future), which are indeed subject to policy control, and the development of incentive structures for these private agents. Such factors to be publicly shaped may be pecuniary, and also non-pecuniary, incentives for individual coordination efforts, as well as increasing the relevance and conscience of the common future (Axelrod, 1984; Elsner, 2001).

The different 'heterodox' economic approaches have developed a long-standing tradition of embedding policy intervention within the broader political-economic framework of participatory, transparent and publicly negotiated democratic regimes ('negotiated economies').

10.2.5 Their usefulness for students

In this way, the different 'heterodox' approaches are highly useful for the professional future of economics students, since they are appropriate to provide knowledge about strategic, coordinated and cooperative behaviour in complex systems of production and innovation (preferably in a non-invidious sense). They are useful to analyse the comparative advantages of different kinds of network structures and rules of 'good network governance'. Economics students in modern applied 'heterodox', especially IEE/SE, programmes and classes may learn and acquire superior 'strategic' competencies, or in other words, superior managerial basic knowledge.

10.3 'HETERODOX' ECONOMICS IS EFFECTIVE

The Economics and Business Administration Department at the University of Bremen has always been labelled the 'heterodox', and specifically, the left-wing economics department in Germany, from its very beginning in the early 1970s. Indeed, it is by far the most pluralist department in Germany and has included some well-known radical political economists, post-Keynesians, socio-economists, radical ecological economists, and institutional economists. Recently, the economics faculty has been downsized to about half the size it once was.

For instance, the department has been the organizing centre for annual national and European memoranda for alternative economic policies and against economic retrenchment since the mid 1970s, and these are largely developed in a post-Keynesian framework. Hundreds of economists, trade union representatives, social democrats and Green politicians and practitioners of all kinds sign these memoranda every year. The speaker of the national memorandum, a member of the Bremen economics faculty, is a well-known and frequently sought after commentator and discussant in the national media (see again for more detail, Engelen, 2005).

With this background, the Bremen department has had to struggle with its poor reputation within the established academic economics profession. In the economics departments rankings of the last ten or fifteen years, the department had a poor standing and low ranking, specifically as far as the economics profession's opinions came in.

In sharp contrast, empirical expertise on the professional success of the department's graduates has given the department high ranking in terms of effectiveness. In the Bremen department: Research output = effectiveness, OK. But heterodox economics: research output = effectiveness?

The latest (November 2002) national rankings of the economics departments, which have been said to be the methodologically most sophisticated ever, with all subjective valuations of economics professors being excluded, have ranked the Bremen department second out of 42 departments in the field of research output (see Centrum fuer Hochschulentwicklung, 2002). Notably, this is the view of one of the biggest German private commercial agents and transnational corporate players, the Bertelsmann corporation, which is not only the official monopolist national ranking agency but is also virtually responsible for the whole process of commercial university restructuring and university privatization in Germany.

A pluralist, critical, and largely 'heterodox' economics department cannot be ignored when it is effective – even in the sense of the narrow professional requirements and the rationality of the 'ideal' capitalist corporation (for the continuing high ranking of the heterodox and pluralist Bremen economics department, namely in terms of research, publications and PhD promotions, from the annual Bertelsmann national ranking procedures in 2003 through 2005, see, for example, www.che-ranking.de/allgemeines_fr.php and the detailed publications given there).

10.4 HETERODOX (IEE/SE) IS TEACHABLE - A CASE EXPERIENCE

10.4.1 A pluralist curriculum

The Faculty of Economics and Business Studies of the Bremen University introduced a new structure to its nine semester master programme in 1997. The structure included pluralistic approaches to micro and macroeconomics in its economics curriculum and placed institutional and evolutionary economics on an equal basis with advanced micro and macro in its graduate studies. In the applied areas, industrial and regional structural development and global processes of coordination and cooperation were added alongside ecological economics, international economic development and social policy.

Thus, the economics faculty has become experienced in teaching different institutional and evolutionary approaches, socio-economic micro, post-Keynesian macro and political economy. 'Heterodox' approaches have also been applied to subject fields such as globalization, fragmentation of value-added chains, clusters, networks, innovation economics, information and tacit knowledge, learned trust and institutionalization, corporate routines, knowledge diffusion and technology transfer, network structures and governance, and comparative coordination arrangements.

10.4.2 Attractiveness to business administration faculty

Some courses offered by institutional and socio-economists in the faculty have also proved to be particularly attractive to the business administration faculty. The economics curriculum complements that which they offer in their own courses.

For instance, the Bremen basic master programme requires large one-year applied teaching projects. Each project involves eight hours per week jointly coordinated by economics and business administration faculties. Economics projects must integrate at least 25 per cent of business administration courses and vice versa. Here, class offerings of IEE/SE economists turned out to be of particular interest to the business administrators who were looking to complement their own applied subject fields such as virtual companies, corporate innovation, corporate governance and culture, networks, innovation, and technology transfer.

Consequently, when the business administration faculty launched its own master programme 'MA Business Studies' they made an effort to include 'heterodox' economics courses on modern 'meso'-economics.

10.4.3 A pluralist new MA economics programme

Finally, as the faculty has now moved over to the bachelor-master structure and to launch three-year bachelor and two-year master programmes with economics majors (namely 'MA Global Economic Analyses – GlobE, recently re-termed MSc Socio-Economics), it was easy to get an agreement with the majority of business administration faculty to incorporate 'heterodox' courses into the curricula (Figure 10.2). Accordingly, the curricula of these new MA programmes contain modules such as advanced approaches to microeconomics, advanced approaches to macroeconomics, institutional and evolutionary economics and history of economic thought which together make up a pluralist economics programme. The applied modules contain courses on innovation and networks, trans-cultural issues, economic development and ecological economics, all of these being applied fields where 'heterodox' theories have considerable analytical leverage for substantiating the 'comparative advantages' of their research programmes.

Table 10.2: Curriculum 'MA Global Economic Analyses' basic structure

Module Areas and Modules
Module Area I: Theoretical Core
Advanced Approaches to Microeconomics   Advanced Approaches to Macroeconomics   Institutional and Evolutionary Economics   History of Political Economy
Module Area II: Methodological Core
Mathematical Methods and Modelling   Basic and Advanced Statistics and Econometrics   Applied Statistical and Econometric Modelling
Module Area III: Applied Analyses Core (Case Studies)
International Economics and Integration   International Finance   Globalization, Innovation and Networks   Trans-Cultural Management and Marketing   Economics of Development and Transformation   Global Ecological Economics/Global Environmental Governance

10.5 HOW TO IMPLEMENT PLURALIST PROGRAMMES

The process of development and departmental approval of the MA GlobE programme in Bremen has brought to the fore some experiences on the substance and processes of implementation of new pluralist programmes that may be generalized.

- First, a clear description of the relevance, high theoretical quality, empirical and practical applicability, cooperation potential of 'heterodox' economists vis-à-vis the business administration academic community, and its professional use for its future graduates is required right from the start.
- Second, the programme must be developed and presented as a highly 'modern' one. The degree of international cooperation is especially important.

Here, 'heterodox' economics has a comparative advantage, at least in Germany. The programme must include international partners, students and faculty exchange agreements. The Bremen MA GlobE was submitted to the faculty together with a list of current and potential future partners. Cooperation with for example US departments was extremely helpful in establishing this pluralist programme that otherwise could easily be dismissed as being outmoded, leftist, over-critical, or simply 'non-mainstream'.

Particularly, cooperation partners include some major 'heterodox' US departments such as those at the New School University (NSU), New York, and at the University of Missouri in Kansas City (UMKC). We have also offered the adoption of, and adaptation of where necessary, the long-standing agreement that we have had with the NSU since 1987 to other potential partners (such as the University of Utah (UofU) at Salt Lake City).

REFERENCES

Axelrod, R. (1984), *The Evolution of Cooperation*, New York: Basic Books.
Centrum fuer Hochschulentwicklung, (2002), *Das Forschungsranking deutscher Universitaeten. Analysen und Daten im Detail. VWL*, CHE-working paper No. 40. Guetersloh, November, http://www.che.de/html/ forschungsranking.htm.
Colander, D. (2001), *The Lost Art of Economics: Essays in Economics and the Economics Profession*, Cheltenham, UK and Northampton, MA, USA: Edward Elgar.

de la Mothe, J. and G. Paquet (1999), 'Structural Competitiveness and Interdependencies: Regional Patterns', in G. Royal and J. H. Dunning (eds), *Structural Change and Cooperation in the Global Economy*, Cheltenham, UK and Northampton, MA, USA: Edward Elgar, pp. 82-112.

Elsner, W. (2000), 'An Industrial Policy Agenda 2000 and Beyond - Experience, Theory and Policy', in W. Elsner and J. Groenewegen (eds), *Industrial Policies After 2000*, Boston, Dordrecht, London: Kluwer Acad. Publ. 411-86.

Elsner, W. (2001), 'Interactive Economic Policy: Toward a Cooperative Policy Approach for a Negotiated Economy', *Journal of Economic Issues*, **35**(1), 61-83.

Elsner, W. (2005), 'Real-World Economics Today: The New Complexity, Coordination, and Policy', *Review of Social Economy*, **63**(1), 19-53.

Engelen, K.C. (2005), 'Battle of Economists. The Inside Story of Germany's Internal Policy Knifefight', *The International Economy*, Winter, 22-62.

Klamer, A. and J. Meehan (1999), 'The Crowding Out of Academic Economics. The Case of NAFTA', in R.F. Garnett (ed.), *What Do Economists Know?*, London, New York: Routledge, 65-85.

Mirowski, P. (1989), *More Heat than Light. Economics as Social Physics, Physics as Nature's Economics*, Cambridge: Cambridge University Press.

Wellhoener, V. (2002), 'Institutionelle und Sozial-Oekonomie' Series, in W. Elsner et al. (ed.), *Oekonomik - Physik - Mathematik. Die Allgemeine Gleichgewichtstheorie im interdisziplinaeren Kontext*, **12**, Frankfurt/M.: Peter Lang.

11. On the Relevancy of Institutional Economics for International Economics

Ruud Knaack and Henk Jager

11.1 INTRODUCTION

After the fall of the Berlin Wall on 1 November 1989, in Central and Eastern Europe one country after the other broke away from the dominance of the Soviet Union and started a transformation process from a centrally planned economy into a market economy. In this process, most countries followed the often-used recipe that the IMF and the World Bank had formulated for developing countries (Taylor, 1993). This recipe was aimed at a rapid macroeconomic stabilization and the introduction of a liberalization process in which old planning institutions would disappear and new market institutions would arise. Implicitly, this recipe assumed that the market institutions would spontaneously arise the moment the old planning bureaucrats disappeared.

The economic results of the reform process were disappointing. Most countries were hit by a severe depression. Indeed, real GDP in 1999 surpassed 1989 levels in just two of the 25 transition countries, and in the most severe cases, in the countries that belonged to the Soviet empire, the observed cumulative output fall was more than 50 per cent of 1989 GDP (Campos and Coricelli, 2002). Moreover, one can perceive that especially in those countries that were formal Soviet republics an important part of the economic transactions took place on the basis of barter trade and other non-monetary forms of trade such as promises. In this chapter we will explore the causes of the recession. In addition we will search for an explanation for the fact that the disappearance of the old planning relations was not a sufficient condition for the rise of a full-fledged market economy.

An important thesis of this chapter is that the reform process in Central and Eastern Europe is based on an insufficient theory about the functioning

200

of a real market economy. For the underpinning of this thesis we will abandon the formal, neoclassical definition of a market economy in Section 11.2 and formulate the building blocks of a market theory with a more substantive content, namely a market as an institutionalized process (Polanyi, 1992). In Section 11.3 we will describe the real transition process in three different countries, namely East Germany, the Czech Republic and Russia. These descriptions reveal that the rapid demolition of the old planning institutions did not result in the building of a full-fledged market economy. It is true that East Germany imported the formal institutional structure of West Germany, but the informal institutions and routines of the past survived for a long time. In the Czech Republic the building of formal institutions took more time and also in this country the informal institutions of the past did not disappear quickly. In Russia, at this moment the country is still muddling through to a hybrid form of a market economy where the exchange relations often take the form of barter trade and other non-monetary forms.

From our analyses we can conclude that the creation of market relations might be a necessary condition for economic recovery, but not a sufficient one. Also the content of the pursued macroeconomic policy and the scope of manoeuvring of the medium and small-scale enterprises play an important role. We can ask ourselves the question whether or nor these empirical revelations will give some indication for a more integrated theory about a successful transition process. This problem will be discussed in Section 11.4.

11.2 INSTITUTIONAL ECONOMICS

In contrast with orthodox economics, which maintains that the central economic problems are the allocation of resources, the distribution of income, and the determination of the levels of income, output and prices, institutional economics asserts the primacy of the organization and control of the economic system (Samuels, 1998: 865). As in the other social sciences, institutional economists focus on the dependency and power relations between (groups of) human beings. These relations in an economic system originate from the division of labour. In a system characterized by division of labour, human beings need other human beings for their survival. Thus, where orthodox economists tend to identify the economy solely with the market full of independent subjects, institutional economists argue that the market coordinates dependency relations and that the market itself is an institution, comprised of a host of subsidiary institutions, which is interactive with other institutional complexes in society. The fundamental institutional position is that not the market but the organizational structure of the larger economy – including the market – effectively allocates resources. In short, institutional economists argue that orthodox economists have a too simplistic theory of the functioning of an economy in general and a market economy in particular.

The misconception regarding the functioning of a market economy stems from the orthodox formalization of Adam Smith's argument of the 'invisible hand' which induces self-interested agents to serve the common good. Orthodox economists investigate the conditions (taste, endowment, technology, and market structure) necessary for the existence of competitive equilibria that are Pareto-optimal. These conditions are summarized in the First Fundamental Theorem of welfare economics stating that if there are enough markets, if all consumers and producers behave competitively, and if an equilibrium exists, then the allocation of resources in that equilibrium will be Pareto-optimal (Ledyard, 1991: 407; Stiglitz, 1994: ch. 3). Moreover, by assuming that contract disputes are settled in court in an informed, sophisticated and low-cost way, the economic models have implicitly a 'legal centralist' point of view (Williamson, 1985: 20).

In these Pareto-optimal general equilibrium models power relations are defined away. The assumption of Pareto-optimality guarantees that the economic subjects participate voluntarily in the economy (assuming there is no jealousy effect), and the assumption of perfect competition guarantees that large corporations cannot set prices in a one-sided way.

The possible existence of an optimal, Pareto-efficient solution in a market economy is often cited as evidence against the functioning of a real planned economy. However, from a methodological point of view, it is only legitimate to compare the properties of ideal systems, or real systems. We cannot condemn the properties of a real existing economy by comparing it with the ideal properties of the alternative to it. In practice, however, this 'nirvana approach' is often adopted (Demsetz, 1969). When the properties of an optimally functioning market economy are compared with the properties of an optimally functioning planned economy, both based on utility maximizing individuals, it can be shown that under appropriate assumptions both regimes will lead to the identical allocation of resources (Pareto, 1966: 364). Following a different line of argument, Samuelson came to the same conclusion: 'under perfect competition workers can rent capital goods or capitalists can rent workers' (1972: 237). Hence, a competitive balance between market and planning can only shift to one side if we take a non-allocative efficiency point of view.

These general equilibrium models have several flaws. These models are only interested in the possible existence and properties of an equilibrium. The difficulties of what would happen if prices were not at the equilibrium level are often glossed over. When they are not glossed over the theory runs into trouble. When the economy is in disequilibrium it is often assumed that the equilibrium can only be restored with the help of a 'Walrasian auctioneer'. This solution can be criticized both from a theoretical and an empirical perspective. First, from a theoretical perspective, the market theory, using the auctioneer metaphor, is not self-sufficient. It needs an argument exterior to the market in order to stabilize the market. Secondly, when we think about the real content of the auctioneer on the level of a national economy, it can be argued that the orthodox equilibrium models are not models of a market economy, but models of a hybrid economy where central pricing agencies allocate resources of firms based on private property (De Vroey, 1998). Actually, orthodox economics provides a rudimentary theory of the state, imposed 'from above' on the economy.

The fact that social order can only be organized around an external point of reference is not satisfactory. Especially Hayek has tried to close the system with the help of his 'spontaneous social order'. This order arises from within, but remains nonetheless 'external' to the individuals who make up that order (Dupuy, 1996). Hayek's fundamental assumption is the unlimited variety of human gifts and skills and the consequent ignorance of a single individual of most what is known to all members of society taken together. On the basis of his limited knowledge the individual takes actions. When his perceived actions are in accordance with the actions as expected, he has no incentive to change his plans. When nobody's expectations are falsified, nobody has an incentive to change his plan and the plans of all individuals are consistent with each other. In other words, they are coordinated and the system as a whole is in equilibrium.

When the perceived actions are not in accordance with the expectations, the individual has to change its course of actions. By taking actions, structures emerge because successful interactions will be repeated more often than less successful ones. According to Hayek these efficient structures will stabilize themselves and form constraints to other individuals who have to adapt their plans. In this learning process, rules emerge which memorize behaviour that has proven beneficial over time. Hence, these spontaneous social orders are the result of human action but not of human design. By relying on these emerged structures, rules and institutions, individuals increase their capacities for actions without appropriating the logic of the combined knowledge these orders mobilize. It is in this sense that the system 'knows' more than the individuals of which it consists (Birner, 1996).

Unfortunately, Hayek's spontaneous social order has a teleological undertone. For Hayek the evolutionary process leads to the best rules, those of liberalism. He ignores the fact that his spontaneous order consists of persons that might have an interest to conspire against his best rules, or have an incentive not to obey these rules (Bianchi, 1994). However, Hayek's main improvements to the orthodox equilibrium models is his view that life is permeated by fundamental uncertainties and that the spontaneous collaboration of free men often creates things which are greater than their individual minds can ever fully comprehend. These institutions, which are characteristics of the system as a whole, are capable of performing tasks that are far too complex for individual human minds. Hence, rationality does not exist in the singular, as the rationalist approach seems to assume, but is a property of the system as a whole.

When we summarize our criticisms of neoclassical economics, we see that an economy is a hierarchical system. The properties of the system as a whole may be imposed by the state or induced as an unintended outcome of a spontaneous process. Moreover, at all levels of the economy life is permeated by uncertainties and many problems are too complex to be solved by standard optimizing techniques. Therefore, in order to get a more reliable picture of an economy, we have to study these uncertainties and complexities not only on the level of the individuals but at all levels of the economy.

In principle, there are two ways to deal with uncertainty and complexity (Knaack, 1996). First, we can try to reduce uncertainty and complexity by creating stabilizing institutions and organizations. Second, we can create more structural flexibility. Both ways are used at all levels of the economy.

At the micro level, Heiner (1983) has discussed the problem resulting from the gap between the competence of an individual and the complexity of the decision problem to be solved. He develops a Reliability Condition which states that individuals must ignore actions which are appropriate only for rare or unusual situations. This Reliability Condition resembles Simon's satisfying behaviour. It is also much more in line with biological research stating that our thinking is constrained by the structure of our neuron system (Maturana and Varela, 1984). With regard to firms, Alchian and Demsetz (1972) have advocated the monitoring of the workforce in order to minimize opportunistic behaviour. The problem of 'disciplining the labour force' can also be solved by other strategies. Modern organization theory stresses the importance of trust and loyalty for the efficiency of the firm (Simon, 1991). Many authors suggest that the relative efficiency of Japanese firms stems in part from long-established relations of give-and-take and trust (Imai, 1986). At the micro level the structural flexibility can be improved by building stocks and by learning new techniques.

At the meso level, many problems can also be solved by creating uncertainty-reducing institutions. Some of these institutions deal with asset specificity. Consumers will be protected from bad behaviour of firms by good inspectors, consumer agencies and quality marks. Firms are brought into contact with each other by chambers of commerce, auctions and fairs. Prices are published in newspapers, on radio and on television. Many firms work together on joint research projects. Also trust and personal relations are uncertainty-reducing devices. The structural flexibility can be improved when firms aim successfully for diversification and product innovation.

At the macro level too, there is a need for uncertainty-reducing institutions. In general, the need for coordination at the macro level stems from the 'fallacy of composition' (Hodgson, 1988: 233). In macroeconomics, relationships might be the reverse of the corresponding relationships at the micro level. For example, wage reduction may increase a country's competitiveness on the world market. But if every country follows this policy the overall demand for products will fall; this will lead to reduced business expectations, and a general decline in economic activity will ensue. Policy coordination, both national and international, might avoid these unintentional developments. On the other hand, also on the level of macroeconomics, structural flexibility can produce favourable outcomes. For example, the government can create more flexibility by stimulating schemes for *éducation permanente*, by improving the infrastructure and by deregulation.

Strangely enough the existence of uncertainty and complexity creates not only an impetus for the creation of uncertainty-reducing institutions, but also for growth and technological development. As a result uncertainty and complexity might increase again. Without these 'imperfections', entrepreneurs have no incentive to take risks. An incentive to invest, for example, depends in part on the belief that others do not possess information regarding the opportunity open to the investor. A profit opportunity which is known to everybody is available to nobody in particular. Hence markets have a double function. They are instruments for the coordination of activities and for the transmission of impulses to change (Kaldor, 1972: 1240).

From our analyses we may conclude that an efficient functioning market economy requires the stability and support of an overall institutional framework. Order and stability at the macro level are mainly brought about by stable political rules and by the norms set forth by tradition and culture. Order and stability at the meso level are realized by the stability of the organizational forms. Stability on the micro level is created if economic agents behave in an orderly way. This orderly behaviour is brought about by the permanent durability of the structure of human perception and behavioural rules (Nelson and Winter, 1982). The institutional forms on each level are not independent of each other. They have to 'fit'. The overall 'fit' is the result of an evolutionary process.

On the other hand, the new stability might not lead to rigidity. Entrepreneurs and the government must be able to adapt to changes in their environment. It is important to realize that these two kinds of response may contradict each other. Too much control may lead to gigantic principal-agent problems; too much flexibility may create a lack of coordination between the various parts. In short, in each economy there is a dialectic relation between the need for both flexibility and rigidity. This dialectic relation can be found on all levels of the economy.

The foregoing analysis leads to the conclusion that a dynamic and innovative economic system will require a structured combination of variety and rigidity, of statics and change, of centralized guidance and decentralized autonomy. Neither the liberal ideology of the free market nor the state power of Marxism-Leninism lends themselves to this type of conclusion (Hodgson, 1988: 169).

This conclusion has also some relevancy for institutional economics. Institutional economics must both have a theory about economic coordination and a theory about economic change. The institutionalist theory of economic change is worked out especially by the French Regulation School (Boyer and Saillard, 1995). They start from the widely-held view in social sciences that for an economy to function well, all parts of the economic system must be integrated. The parts must correspond to each other, they must support each other. The Regulationists assert that in order to obtain a harmonious development of society, the institutional structure and the technology structure must be fine-tuned to each other and both to the environment. They explain the 'golden age' of capitalism, the period 1950-73, as resulting from the 'functional fit' between the parts of the economic system and between the system and its environment.

As consequences of changes in particular subsystems or the environment, functional misfits may arise in the system as a whole. The changes stem from different sources (Lin, 1989). The institutional choice set may change (for example, privatization in Eastern Europe), the technology may change (the introduction of ITC), and the environment may change (for example, increasing share of elderly people). These changes may be the outcome of 'accidents', of economic laws, or of deliberate action. However, whatever the source may be, the question is whether or not they will induce adjustments in other subsystems.

As a result the institutional arrangements in society will change. However, these institutional changes may develop slower than expected. As a result, they may lag behind (Holesovski, 1977: 33). This delay might be very long because of inertia. Individual behaviour, the institutional arrangements among individuals, and technology may be 'locked' into formal and informal networks of social interaction from the past. The prolonged functional misfit among the subsystems is one of the major explanations for so many frustrated reform movements and defeated revolutions.

The fact that each subsystem has a different adaptation time may lead to the hypothesis that an economic reform that seeks to minimize transaction costs can only be an evolutionary process, one of learning-by-doing, of trial and error. What is needed is 'piecemeal social engineering', incremental improvements which can be continually improved upon.

In the next section we will demonstrate the dialectical relation between the institutional theory of economic stability and the institutional theory of economic change on the basis of the experiences of three transition economies, namely East Germany, the Czech Republic and Russia.

11.3 THE TRANSITION PROCESS OF THREE FORMERLY CENTRALLY PLANNED EUROPEAN ECONOMIES

11.3.1 Introduction

On 1 November, 1989, the Berlin Wall fell. From that moment on in Central and Eastern Europe one country after the other broke away from the Soviet dominance and started a process of conversion from a centrally governed economy to a market economy. On 30 June, 1990, the two parts of Germany were reunited and the German economic, monetary, and social union was created. In Czechoslovakia the Velvet Revolution brought the rule of the Communist Party to an end in November 1989. The new government of Prime Minister Klaus introduced a series of measures as from 1 January, 1991, aimed at the integration of the Czechoslovakian economy into the world economy. Also the Soviet Union was contaminated with this spirit of the time. After the breakdown of this country's economic system the new rulers strived for a rapid transition towards a new system characterized by market relations, private ownership, and a liberal democracy. On 2 January, 1992, the Gaidar administration brought a series of measures in that direction into force, which inflicted an enormous shock on the Russian economy.

The processes of change in Central and Eastern Europe were not based on a blueprint showing how a formerly communist country ought to be restructured as a capitalist country. According to prevailing opinion that was not necessary. Due to German unification, East Germany took the West German legislation and rules over at a stroke and East German enterprises were privatized at a quick pace. Other countries had the possibility to copy the existing and often-approved recipe as applied earlier by, for example,

Spain at the access to the European Union and developing countries at their integration in the world economy. It was the recipe developed by the IMF and World Bank (Taylor, 1993) and is dubbed the 'Washington Consensus'. The liberalization process was mainly oriented towards removing the old institutions. One fully trusted that many of the problems would resolve themselves naturally. Markets would develop as soon as the planning bureaucrats disappeared.

The economic results of the process of reform were considered to be very disappointing. Most countries experienced a severe depression. In one country it lasted longer than in another. In literature a lot of discussion was stimulated on the causes of this depression and of the growth differentials between the countries. Particularly, this tried to relate the growth differences to the intensity of economic reform.

The World Bank in its World Development Report 1996, for example, linked the pace of the stabilization and liberalisation processes and the economic results in the years 1989-95. It used a liberalization index constructed as the weighted average of the extent of liberalization of the internal and external markets and the extent of privatisation of state enterprises. On the basis of this index the World Bank distinguished four categories of transition countries and determined the scores per category on economic criteria, such as economic growth and inflation, and social criteria, such as average age and child mortality. On all the criteria the countries with a high value on the liberalization index scored best on average. In this research the World Bank left East Germany aside. Without any doubt this country would have had the highest score on the liberalization index in the period studied.

For individual countries and specific criterion variables however, the relation to the liberalization index appears to be much more differentiated. We will substantiate this view in the next sub-sections by means of a closer analysis of East Germany, the Czech Republic, and the Russian Federation, which endured very different transition processes.

11.3.2 East Germany

As already mentioned, the two parts of Germany were reunited on 30 June, 1990, after a separation of no less than 45 years. The Ostmark was replaced by the Deutschmark. Wages and a large part of savings in East Germany were converted from Ostmarks into D-marks at an exchange rate of one-to-one. The legal system, as well as the social security and tax systems, was adapted to the existing systems in West Germany. The latter had already proven their value. Moreover, all barriers to unrestricted capital and labour mobility were abolished. In this way, East Germany was spared a long process of economic stabilisation and erection of market institutions (Knaack, 2000: 179).

At first glance the economic results of this 'big-bang' were disappointing: between 1989 and 1991 real GDP in East Germany declined by as much as 35 per cent (Von Hagen and Strauch, 2000: 2). The quick restoration of economic growth is noteworthy. While real GDP still fell by 23 per cent in 1991, one year later the East German real GDP already displayed an impressive increase by almost 8 per cent, followed by a growth in the next two years of 9.8 and 10.4 per cent. Despite that, at the end of 1998 the level of real GDP was only 96 per cent of the level ten years earlier. One cause was the return of disappointing economic growth, in 1997 and 1998, at a level of 2 per cent, even lower than West German growth rates of 2.3 and 3.9 per cent in these two years.

The adjustment pattern consisting of an initial steep fall and subsequent quick recovery of economic growth, after which a period of near stagnation sets in, seems to have been characteristic for East Germany and, in any case, differs from the reform processes in other Central and East European countries. The Czech Republic, for example, encountered a stagnation of real GDP in the two years 1992 and 1993 – after a fall of 'only' 11.5 per cent in 1991 (EBRD, 1999: 213). In the Russian Federation real GDP fell every year of the period 1991-96, with an annual average of 8 per cent, although the decline in 1991 'only' amounted 5 per cent. End-1998 real GDP in the Russian Federation was 58 per cent of the end-1990 level. For the Czech Republic the corresponding outcome is 96 per cent, exactly equal to East Germany's percentage.

Paradoxically the unification of Germany resulted in a dichotomy between East and West Germany. In order to prevent a huge migration to the west, the decision was made to strive for a rapid upward convergence of the eastern wage level towards that in the west, although the low labour productivity in the eastern part did not give room for that. Soon after the unification a substantial unemployment came into being in East Germany and, partly as a consequence of that, a large and prolonged western financial support for the eastern part of the country appeared to be absolutely necessary.

The sky-high unit labour costs are mainly responsible for the near collapse of industrial production in the east. In 1990 labour productivity in East Germany was only 30 per cent of that in West Germany. Wages, however, were set at 50 per cent of West German wages. In the period until 1995 this percentage rose to 72 per cent, while labour productivity increased to 53 per cent of the West German level. This rise was substantial, but nevertheless not sufficient to compensate for the wage increase in production costs. While relative real wage rises in the period 1991-97 kept more or less in step with the growth of labour productivity in West Germany, in the east real wages doubled in value whereas labour productivity only increased by some 50 per cent (Von Hagen and Strauch, 2000: 4). With these high and increasing labour costs, the East German enterprises were not capable of competing successfully on the world market. For that reason, production in the east part declined and so did employment, principally in the industrial sector. In 1990, already, industrial production fell by more than 50 per cent. The light industrial and technological-intensive sectors suffered most. The share of the construction sector in East German production rose steeply, from 18 per cent to more than 34 per cent. The share of the services sector substantially increased too.

In the years 1990-94 almost four million jobs were lost through rationalization processes. An important part of these dismissals used an early retirement option. The remaining part of redundant workers became unemployed. In 1993 the unemployment rate was 16 per cent and in 1997 it was more than 20 per cent. Besides that, 20 per cent of the labour force had involuntarily accepted a reduction in working hours.

To prevent a movement of unemployed from east to west in Germany, the unemployment benefits were set high in the east. This combination of high unemployment and high unemployment benefits triggered huge social transfers from west to east (Von Hagen and Strauch, 2000: 11). Total gross financial transfers amounted to DM139 bn in 1991 and increased to DM189 bn in 1998. Between 40 per cent and 50 per cent of these annual amounts consisted of social security benefits. These financial transfers created a large difference between production and disposable income in the east. As an illustration: in 1995 the former was only 60 per cent of the latter.

In line with the data for 1997 and 1998 presented earlier, the more recent figures about production and unemployment in East Germany (until 2003) point to a more or less stagnating economy with the unemployment rate continuously at a high level of almost 20 per cent (Datastream). This situation and the preceding outline of German economic development since the reunification give support to the early suggestion of a 'German Mezzogiorno problem' (Hallett and Ma, 1993). Could this Mezzogiorno problem have been prevented?

First, the conversion at parity of the Ost- into the D-mark can be criticised. It made wages in East Germany at one strike much higher than in other Central and Eastern European countries. In contrast to those countries, East Germany could not take advantage of a cheap currency. Neither did the area have the policy autonomy to devalue its currency in order to counter the negative effect of an initially high inflation on the country's competitiveness.

In the years 1991-95 the consumer price index rose by one third! (Datastream). A more realistic conversion value would have strengthened East Germany's competitiveness, but would probably also have intensified the migration of people from east to west in the country.

Second, the government could have subsidized the production factor labour more intensively. In the years 1991-98 subsidies to East German firms in general were only 5 per cent to 10 per cent of the total financial transfer flows to the east. One can, however, question the effectiveness of this support instrument for, for example, shipyards in Mecklenburg-Vorpommern, mining in Thüringen or the Trabant factory in Saksen. Instead the government preferred to carry out a high wage/high tech policy. It tried to maintain an independent base for research and development in East Germany. It also spent a lot of money in the development of infrastructure. In the process of privatization however, most Eastern enterprises were sold to West Germans. They were not interested in the research and development departments of these enterprises. Their only interest was better access to the eastern market and reduction of their existing overcapacity. The number of employees in East Germany who dealt with research and development declined from 86,000 to 16,000 (Fleischer and Hornschild, 1999: tables 8.3 and 8.4).

The preceding analysis leads to the conclusion that the potential positive effect of the import of West German institutions for East Germany has been more than fully compensated by the negative effects of the conversion at parity of the Ostmark into the D-mark and the quick upward convergence of the wage rates in east and west in the country. The high growth rates in East Germany in the period 1992-96 are a response to the huge financial transfers from west to east. This money was used for a large part for infrastructure projects, the construction industry and the local government sector. One may fear that if most of these projects will be completed, the economic basis of East Germany will appear to be quite small.

11.3.3 Czech Republic[1]

For a long time, the transition of the Czech Republic towards a market economy was considered to be the example of a successful economic transition process. On 1 January 1991 the government led by Klaus took a number of important measures directed to a quick integration of the Czech economy into the world economy. These measures included the introduction of a fixed and unified exchange rate, liberalization of most prices, abolishment of most foreign trade controls, and a start of small-scale privatization. These measures covered liberalization, stabilization, as well as privatization of the Czech economy. To a certain extent this scenario reflected the package of measures that the Polish government had introduced one year before (Dyba and Svejnar, 1994: 99).

The substitution of the Ministry of Economic Affairs for the so-called Committee for State Planning was the basis of the Czech economic liberalization process. A direct result was that firms did not need to carry out their tasks assigned by the economic plan any longer. About 85 per cent of all prices were freed and the majority of the state subsidies abolished. The state monopoly on foreign trade was ended step by step. Monetary policy became restrictively aimed at two intermediary goals, namely a prolonged positive real interest rate and a restriction of the growth of bank credits. In order to ease the conversion of Czech exports from the former Comecon countries to the west, the currency was devalued by as much as 50 per cent against the US dollar in 1991.

It was clear that dismantling the institutions of the old planning system and laying the foundation for the institutions of a market economy should preferably be a simultaneous process. The way to realize this seemed to be privatization of state ownership as soon as possible. This privatization occurred in three ways, namely restitution of private properties appropriated after 1948, as well as the so-called 'small' and 'large' privatizations. The restitution programme delivered an important incentive to the development of the services sector. The small privatization had a similar effect. In a short period of time tens of thousands of shops, restaurants, and small firms were sold. Privatization of large firms was more problematic. Initially, the government tried to realize the 'large' privatization by direct sale. An example is Skoda, which was sold to Volkswagen in March 1991 after a tough process of negotiations. Other large state enterprises however, were privatized by means of the voucher system that began in May 1992. In this system the estimated value of the enterprises to be privatized was converted into so-called vouchers, which were sold to the Czech people at a low price. In the first years of its existence the voucher system hardly met any enthusiasm among the Czech population. Only after investment funds entered the market, sometimes offering a tenfold of the value for a voucher, vouchers started to be bought massively and resold to investment funds (Knaack, 2001: 88).

In the first half of the 1990s, all these transformation measures seemed quite successful. Although the Czech GDP declined by 11.5 and 3.3 per cent, respectively, in the years 1991 and 1992, in 1993 it showed a slight recovery of some 0.6 per cent (EBRD, 1999: 213). After a while, the fight against inflation also proved to be successful. After an annual inflation of almost 60 per cent in 1991, the annual price rise declined rapidly to a level of 11 per cent in 1992. The production slowdown was not associated with a quick rise in unemployment. The Czech unemployment was some 4 per cent end-1991 and even only 2.6 per cent at the end of 1992! In contrast, unemployment in the two other Viségrad countries, Hungary and Poland, was over 12 per cent at that moment. The Czech government's financial position also remained sound in the first years of the transition period, with an average financial deficit of 2.5 per cent of GDP in the first two years. In these same years, the Czech external sector showed a small trade deficit, on the balance of payments compensated by surpluses in international trade in services and an inflow of foreign direct investments (EBRD, 1999: 213).

The favourable unemployment figures in the Czech republic cannot have been caused by a favourable development in the demand for labour in the industrial sector (Munich and Storm, 1996). To the contrary: between 1989 and 1995 about 25 per cent of workers left that sector. Partly they left the labour process once and for all, particularly the pensionable. Other industrial workers easily found new jobs in the services sector or in the neighbouring countries of Germany and Austria. Many set up one-man firms in the services sector, in particular in trade and catering. Many jobs were also created in the tourist industry. Especially in the Prague area, this industry showed amazing growth.

It was very surprising that in the first years after the change of the economic system Czech international trade did not meet real problems. The business environment had changed dramatically through the collapse of the Comecon. Until 1989, 80 per cent of Czech exports were directed to the Comecon countries. After that year there was a radical fall in this sale of goods, as these countries were unwilling or unable to continue this import flow. It was therefore unavoidable that Czech exports were redirected to the western countries. This adaptation was eased by the substantial currency devaluation and the favourable location of the Czech Republic with respect to rich countries such as Germany and Austria. Mainly the exporters of raw materials and semi-manufactures succeeded in taking advantage of these two assets. Despite that, the Czech trade balance began to deteriorate mid-1990s. Its deficit grew to $3.7 bn in 1995 and $5.9 bn in 1996. In 1995 this deficit could still easily be financed by the surpluses in international services trade and foreign direct investment inflows. However, in 1996 this was no longer the case (EBRD, 1999: 213). In 1996 and 1997 the Czech Republic struggled with huge current account deficits of over 7 per cent of GDP.

This balance of payments outcome indicates economic problems for the Czech Republic from 1996. In the first half of that year the economic tide turned through a combination of a deteriorated competitiveness and a domestic demand that was too large. The international competition position had mainly been worsened through an inflation that had not fallen since

1992. On the contrary the inflation rate of 11 per cent in 1992 was followed in the years 1993-95 by inflation levels of 21, 10 and 9 per cent, respectively. Due to the deterioration of competitiveness, Czech exports stagnated and the growth of industrial output fell back to the low level of 2 per cent. In particular the large enterprises, privatized under the voucher system, got into trouble in the free market. An important reason was the uncertainty with respect to the privatization programme. From one day to the next the ownership could change. For that reason the owners had a short horizon and concentrated themselves on maximizing short-term profits. Growth of GDP declined further to a low 0.8 per cent in 1997, while there was a production reduction by 1 per cent in 1998 and a weak growth recovery by 0.5 per cent in 1999 (IMF). This recession undermined the trust of the foreign investors in the Czech economy. After an attack on the koruna – since February 1993 the Czech currency – a devaluation of 19 per cent against the US dollar followed. Another consequence of the depression was a large number of enterprises with annual losses. This caused a new wave of enterprise restructuring. Unemployment began to increase quickly to 8.7 per cent in 1999.

Only at the end of the millennium, ownership rights were crystallized sufficiently for enterprises to direct themselves again on the longer term (Myant, 1999). This changed attitude led to an improvement in the economic situation. The Czech economy began to grow again, with 3.3 per cent in 2000 and 2001, and the balance of payments deficit turned into a surplus, mainly through a restoration of confidence of foreign investors. A worrying by-product of this capital inflow was a large current account deficit of 5 and 4 per cent of GDP in the years 2000 and 2001 (IMF). Foreign investments in the Czech Republic are now larger than in the other Central and Eastern European countries. For the entire period 1989-2001 its cumulative inflow of foreign direct investments is second, only to Poland, in the amount of over US$26 bn. (*The Economist*, 2002: 5). This restoration of the investment climate is to a large extent the result of the drive with which the new social democratic Zeman administration, which succeeded the Klaus administration, is implementing the a*quis communautaire*, the law of the European Union. This energetic policy stance was rewarded with the EU decision to accept the Czech Republic as a member, effective as from 1 May 2004.

11.3.4 Russian Federation

After the collapse of the Soviet Union and the fall of communism, the way was paved for radical changes in the Russian economic order. On 2 January 1992, the new rulers, under the leadership of president Yeltsin, introduced a series of measures that upset the Russian economy. These concerned a liberalization of foreign trade and trade in foreign exchange, as well as all forms of private trade. Most prices became free market prices. A quick introduction of convertibility of the rouble with respect to the US dollar against a fixed exchange rate was pursued, as well as a swift privatizing of a large part of the state enterprises.

These measures did not generate the desired results. The Russian economy exhibited a massive contraction. As already mentioned in Section 11.3.2, Russian real GDP plunged in the years 1991-98 by 42 per cent. The decline in national income was even larger: 55 per cent in the period 1992-98. At the outset the fall in industrial production even exceeded that high percentage; later on its decline was closer. All in all, the drop of industrial production in the years 1992-97 amounted to 60 per cent. Chiefly the light industry and machine construction sectors were heavily hit. In 1996 their production dwindled to respectively 11.5 and 30.5 per cent of the 1990-level. In contrast, the energy and metal sectors were able to uphold a substantial part of their production. In the same period their production decreased 'only' 20-30 per cent. The corresponding figure for agriculture was 25 per cent. The poor economic outlook in that period explains the dramatic reduction in investments, with 80 per cent in the corresponding period.

Developments in domestic production were also reflected in the changing size and structure of foreign trade. Foreign trade fell by about 40 per cent in absolute terms in the period 1990-96. The reduction of imports was larger than that of exports. As a result the Russian trade balance soon displayed large surpluses. The structure of both exports and imports also altered in the first years of the reform period. In effect, trade with the western countries rose to 50 per cent of total Russian foreign trade, at the cost of the trade shares of the former communist countries. The goods composition of Russian exports changed to the benefit of the energy and raw materials sectors; their share grew to 80 per cent. The export share of industrial goods suffered. On the import side the share of durable consumer goods and food increased to some 60 per cent. It was a vast problem for the Russian economy that the export earnings were hardly used for the import of essential capital goods. Instead, they were used for large-scale capital flight. In the first years after 1991 the foreign assets of Russian inhabitants grew by US$10 bn per year (Chandra, 1995).

These negative economic developments in the 1990s had, of course, serious damaging effects on the living standard and the general well-being of the population. Although the labour force increased by about 1.5 million, the employed labour force decreased by 15 million, or about 20 per cent. Besides a loss of jobs, a part of the employed had to accept an involuntary labour time reduction that occurred in various forms. Unemployment gradually increased from 5.3 per cent in 1994 to 12.6 per cent in 1999 (Datastream). Apparently, firms did not really adjust themselves to the crisis situation by firing superfluous personnel, but by means of labour time reduction and even by late payments of wages or non-payments. Due to these measures average wages declined drastically. Real income of wage earners deteriorated further through a dismantling of subsidies on many products. For products that were supposedly free, such as education and health care, people had to pay informally.

Income distribution became very unequal. This explains, among other things, the steep rises in car sales and imports of durable consumer goods in the 1990s. But it explains too the 23 per cent of households in 1996 that received an income below the poverty line. As a pure survival strategy, the Russian population put much time and energy into cultivating food in the many allotments in the country. This line of food production is even estimated to be 43 per cent of Russia's total food production.

Through the economic contraction the nature of domestic trade changed. The role of money diminished, which was perceivable in the increase in barter trade and the rapid accumulation of payment delays (Ledeneva and Seabright, 2000). This also held true for government and businesses. There was a shift of transactions from the formal to the informal economy and in addition, an increase of self-supporting activities. All in all, in the first years of transition there were clear signals of a kind of 'primitivization' of the Russian economy (Hedlund and Sundström, 1996).

The phenomenon of 'privatization' has several possible explanations. First, a much-used argument is the inability of firms to attract loans, due to both the high interest rates and the uncertainty about the Russian economy. Second, the various forms of barter trade give businesses the opportunity to evade tax payments. Besides the usual reason for tax evasion, the non-transparent range of different taxes and the various tax exemptions are additional incentives. Tax evasion is further stimulated by the frequent change of taxes. Third, bankrupt enterprises usually continue producing. Mostly, a Russian enterprise is a link in a large production network, often of a regional nature (Boeva and Dolgopiatovo, 1994). Disappearance of a link may threaten both the entire network and the balance between management, workers and local government. In view of the economic uncertainties and the tight technological and economic ties between enterprises, the networks furnish individual firms a bigger chance of survival relative to an independent position of the enterprise in the economy (McDermott, 1997).

An important reason why the transition in Russia resulted in a prolonged reduction of production compared to the production in, for example, the Czech Republic is the very delicate position of Russia's small and medium-sized businesses. In the period 1995-97 employment in Russian businesses with a maximum of 50 employees reduced by 50 per cent! This cannot be explained by a disappointing productivity growth. To the contrary, these small firms often had a good performance (Commander et al. 1996: chapter 8). The true explanation is the behaviour of the Russian Mafia and the unreliability of the Russian government. Small enterprises are compelled to make regular payments to their 'protectors'. The presence of the Mafia however, also has advantages. As a consequence of the weakened tax morale and the lack of a well-functioning legal system, a frequently used method for settling payments is to call in the help of 'Judge Kalashnikov' (Knaack, 1999).

The Russian currency crisis in August 1998 was more or less a watershed for economic development in the Russian Federation. An outcome of that crisis was that the rouble depreciated strongly, from 5.8 roubles per US dollar in 1997 to 24.6 roubles per dollar in 1998.[2] The strong depreciation continued in 1999 to an exchange-rate value of 24.6 roubles per dollar. The concomitant real effective depreciation of the rouble over the two years concerned amounted to 31.3 per cent, despite high and increasing inflation of 15 per cent in 1998 and 55 per cent in 1999. In the next two years inflation remained at a level of some 50 per cent. Although the rouble continued to lose some value against the dollar, the real effective exchange rate of the rouble appreciated again by 33 per cent. The most gratifying economic development in Russia was the associated start of economic growth. The economic growth rate in the years 1999-2002 was between 4 and 5 per cent with an outlier of 9 per cent in 2000. In response, unemployment could fall, from a peak of 12.6 per cent in 1999 to 9 per cent in 2001. The real depreciation contributed to huge surpluses of the Russian current account of over 10 per cent of GDP from 1999. It seems that the Russian economy, after a long transition period with shrinking growth, through the shock of the currency crisis appeared to be able to find the upward path of transition with substantially positive economic growth. One remaining worrying feature of this new path is the alarmingly high inflation.

11.4 INSTITUTIONAL VACUUM

After the fall of the Berlin Wall in 1989, in principle all East European countries followed a liberalization process directed at the breaking down of the existing planning systems. It was expected that markets would arise spontaneously the moment the old planning bureaucrats disappeared. In other words, the policy-makers hoped that the political and economic institutions necessary for the functioning of a market economy would be created during a process of 'organic growth'. Obviously it was assumed that the fundamental propensities of mankind to barter and truck as postulated by Adam Smith were not foregone during the decades of communist rule (Knaack, 1999: 357).

However, this did not take into account the fact that properly functioning markets require an institutional infrastructure and that it takes a lot of time before the new institutional system and the persons who have to work in those markets are adapted to the new circumstances. Not only must new institutions be created, but they must prove their value during a time-consuming process of trial and error. Each economic transition process is fundamentally an incremental process, constant experiments with new forms, which finally keeps that form which is considered acceptable. In this way the existing institutional structure will be improved.

The at-a-stroke abolishment of the old planning system without construction of the new institutions of a market economy will irrevocably lead to an institutional vacuum. That vacuum has many forms (Knaack, 1999: 363). The old rules lose their meaning, but the enterprises have not yet learned how to behave in the new situation. Further, the information structure of the old system disappears, while at the same time the new market signals are not yet developed enough. The enterprises find it difficult to find new customers and when they finally succeed it is difficult to find out how trustworthy they are. As a result, the enterprises operate in an environment characterized by an extreme level of uncertainty.

As we have seen, enterprises might react in different ways to the uncertainty, either by creating and/or adopting uncertainty reducing institutions or by creating structural flexibility. In the first case the institutional vacuum is filled. In the case of East Germany, the institutions of West Germany were taken over in one stroke. In the case of the Czech Republic, the country profited heavily from the neighbourhood of Germany and Austria, and learned quickly from the international trade relations. Moreover, from 1995 onwards the Czech Republic adopted the *acquis communautaire*, the jurisdictional structure of the European Union. Russia did not have these advantages. As a large country, its international trade is a much smaller percentage of the national income. With regard to the possibility of the import of institutions it only had to fulfil the requirements of the IMF when it borrowed money. As a consequence, much more so than the small countries, Russia could fill the institutional vacuum on its own terms. Given the fact that the creation of new institutions is a time-consuming process, one can understand that it fell back into its old routines and that, given the weakness of the state, organizations such as the Mafia filled the vacuum.

Although the differences in institutions are important, they alone cannot explain the differences in growth figures. The success of the transition process was also dependent on the possibilities in the countries to improve the structural flexibility. Government policy with respect to the foreign trade and the medium and small enterprises was particularly important. The collapse of the Comecon trade and the resulting loss of jobs in the big state enterprises had to be counterbalanced by an increase of exports to the west and the creation of new jobs by the medium and small enterprises. Only the Czech Republic was successful in both respects. The strong devaluation of the crown resulted in a strong swing of foreign trade to the west and the process of the 'small' privatization contributed to the strong growth of employment in the private sector. The Czech Republic also profited from its geographical position and the possibilities of the tourist industry, especially in Prague. Compared to the Czech Republic, East Germany could not profit from devaluation. Given the politically motivated choice of a one-to-one conversion of the Ostmark for the Deutschmark, the terms of trade of East Germany worsened, creating mass unemployment. On the other hand, many young entrepreneurs could profit from the new circumstances.

Compared to both the Czech Republic and East Germany, Russia opted for the less successful road. It is fair to say that it had few other options. The choice for a fixed coupling of the rouble to the dollar under conditions of high internal inflation led to a strong appreciation of the rouble. This did not lead to a deterioration of the trade balance given the strong export of the gas and oil reserves. These developments resulted in the crowding-out of Russian industrial production. Industry became more and more expensive and lost its possibility to export. The industrial loss of sales became severe because the strong rouble stimulated Russian consumers to opt for cheaper foreign consumer goods. The loss of jobs in the industrial sector was not counterbalanced by a growth of jobs in the medium and small enterprises. Both the government and the Mafia are responsible for the lagging behind of the *de novo* enterprises in Russia. Both viewed the new enterprises as cash cows instead of centres of new economic initiatives that required stimulation.

This conclusion about the importance of the role of medium and small enterprises in the transition process agrees with one of the most important conclusions of a recent report of the World Bank regarding the first 10 years of the transition process (World Bank, 2002). According to this report the key for economic growth in the transition countries is the shift of means of production from the old, largely capital-intensive enterprises to the new, largely labour-intensive, enterprises. The last group consists overwhelmingly of small enterprises (with a maximum of 50 workers). The value added per worker in this group is much higher than in the group of old enterprises. It is interesting to notice that the differences became bigger when the old enterprises were heavily subsidized and protected.

According to the World Bank the transition process gains momentum when the share of medium and small-scale enterprises in the national employment is more than 40 per cent. The group of countries in Central Europe (including the Baltic states) reached this percentage in 1996. This group continued with the reform process. On the other hand, the countries that belonged to the former Soviet Union stayed behind. In these countries the growth of small-scale enterprises seems to have stagnated with devastating consequences for the whole economy. The share of small enterprises did not rise above 20 per cent.

The World Bank explains this stagnation in growth of the small-scale sector in the countries of the former Soviet Union with the help of a public choice type theory. In this theory the results of the transition process are determined by the power game between three groups of players in the former central planned economies: (a) the workers in the state enterprises; (b) the workers and managers who are able to work in the new sectors; (c) the oligarchs and insiders who enter the transition process with a tremendous amount of control over the state properties and close relationships with the old political establishment. An important hypothesis of the World Bank is that the power game between these three groups can result in three possible situations.

The first situation is that there will be no reform at all. At the start of the reform process all workers and managers lose, also those in category (b). Only category (c) wins, although the gain is relatively small. In fact there is no force that is strong enough to change the situation of 'no reform'. The only possibility for change is the prospects for category (c) of additional profits when they strive for a moderate reform. In that situation category (c) can aim for maximal profit. At that moment category (b) also starts to make a profit. In this second situation the joined profit of both categories is more than enough to compensate the loss of category (a). In that situation a moderate reform will end in a stable equilibrium.

The reform process would get a new impulse if the *de novo* enterprises would get much more room of manoeuvring. The prospect of much more profit can be a stimulus for category (b) to strive for this. But categories (a) and (c) will be opposed. This means that only a government that is strong enough to reform the institutional infrastructure can break through the deadlock. Part of the new situation must be a new coordination mechanism which helps the potential winners – the scattered small, new enterprises – to find each other in a joint effort towards a more radical reform process in which the power position of category (c) will be broken. In this third situation the profit of category (b) is already so huge that the losses of categories (a) and (b) can be compensated more than enough. At this moment the reform process gains momentum. The profits of category (b) increase without further losses to the other two categories. So to speak, the door is wide open for more reforms.

This picture corresponds to the analyses in Section 11.3. The reform process in Russia is stagnant because the oligarchs and insiders, together with the old political elite, are still in command. The Czech Republic had trouble reaching and passing the third situation in 1996/97. After some hesitation they succeeded and at the moment the country moves freely in the direction of far reaching reforms.

11.5 CONCLUSIONS

After the fall of the Berlin Wall in 1989, one country after the other in Central and Eastern Europe freed itself from Soviet dominance and started a transition process from a centrally planned economy to a market economy. In this transition process they followed the recipe developed earlier by the IMF and the World Bank for developing countries. In each country, the results were disappointing. In 1999, only two of all the transition countries surpassed the 1989 levels. Especially the countries that had belonged to the Soviet empire were struck by a severe recession. The recession was much more profound than expected.

The length and depth of the recession in most of the transition countries can be explained by the fact that the reform process was based on an incomplete theory about the functioning of a market economy. The policy makers were too late in recognizing the precondition for the functioning of a market economy, namely an institutional infrastructure, and the dynamics of the reform process, namely that it takes time for the new institutional infrastructure and the persons who are to work in it to adapt to each other and the new situation. The collapse of the old planning institutions placed the enterprises in an extremely uncertain situation, in which it was difficult to find new customers and decipher how trustworthy they were. From this perspective the length and depth of the recession depended on the time it took to build new institutions, for example the new private property rights, and the time it took for the market players to adapt to them.

This point of view seems to be confirmed by the experiences in East Germany, the Czech Republic and Russia. The depth of the recession can indeed be related to the speed of the introduction of new market institutions. However, our analyses suggest that the institutional infrastructure is not the only factor that can explain the differences in growth figures. Also of importance for the success of the transition process is the increase of structural flexibility in these countries. For example, given the collapse of the Comecon trade, in all Central and East European countries enterprises were forced to bend their trade to the west. A precondition seemed to be a depreciation of the national currency. Only the Czech Republic was able to do this. This explains why the collapse of industry in East Germany and Russia was much more profound than in the Czech Republic.

Our study also suggests that the speed with which the *de novo* enterprises can expand is also important for the success of the transition process. Especially in Russia the *de novo* enterprises were unable to expand. The government was not able to protect the new enterprises against the negative practices of the Mafia and the already existing large enterprises. Also the behaviour of the government itself was counterproductive.

From our story one can conclude that the success of a transition process does not only depend on the building of a viable market sector. It also depends on the existence of a strong government that is able and willing to create the necessary market institutions, fight the trusted interests, and formulate an economic policy that aims among others at a rapid switch in the trade relations with the west.

NOTES

[1] In the present analysis we neglect the subdivision of Czechoslovakia in the two autonomous countries the Czech Republic and Slovakia on January 1, 1993. The economic situation in Slovakia was then much more negative relative to the Czech Republic. Unemployment in Slovakia, for example, was over 10 per cent in 1993, whereas it was only 4 per cent in the Czech Republic.

[2] The data in this paragraph are derived from IMF and Datastream.

REFERENCES

Alchian, A.A. and H. Demsetz (1972), 'Production, Information Costs, and Economic Organization', *The American Economic Review*, **62**, 777-795.
Bianchi, M. (1994), 'Hayek's Spontaneous Order: The "Correct" versus the "Corrigible" Society', in J. Birner and R. van Zijp, *Hayek, Co-ordination and Evolution*, London and New York: Routlegde, 232-250.

Birner, J. (1996), 'Decentralization as Ability to Adapt', in B. Dellago and L. Mittone (eds), *Economic Institutions, Markets and Competition*, Cheltenham UK and Brookfield, USA: Edward Elgar, 63-89.

Boeva, I. and T. Dolgopiatova (1994), 'State Enterprises during Transition: Forming Strategies for Survival', in A. Aslund (ed.), *Economic Transformation in Russia*, London: Printer, 111-126.

Boyer, R. and Y. Saillard (eds) (1995), *Regulation Theory: The State of the Art*, London and New York: Routledge.

Campos, N. and F. Coricelli (2002), 'Growth in Transition: What We Know, What We Don't, and What We Should', *Journal of Economic Literature*, **XL**, 793-836.

Chandra, N. (1995), 'Economic Crisis in Russia and Contemporary Liberalism', *Lecture, Indian Economic Association*, Chandigarh, December, 28-30.

Commander, S., Q. Fan and M. Schaffer (1996), *Enterprise Reconstructuring and Economic Policy in Russia*, Washington D.C: World Bank.

Datastream,http://www.thomson.com/content/financial/brand_overviews/Datastream_ Advance.

Demsetz, H. (1969), 'Information and Efficiency: Another Viewpoint', *Journal of Law and Economics*, Vol. 12, 1-22.

Dupuy, J.P. (1996), 'The Autonomy of Social Reality: On the Contribution of Systems Theory to the Theory of Society', in E. Khalil and K. Boulding (eds.), *Evolution, Order and Complexity*, London and New York: Routledge, 61-88.

Dyba, K. and J. Svejnar (1994), 'Stabilization and Transition in Czechoslovakia', in O. Blanchard, K. Froot and J. Sachs (eds.) *The Transition in Eastern Europe*, Chicago: The University of Chicago Press, 93-118.

EBRD (European Bank for Reconstruction and Development) (1999), *Transition Report 1999; Ten years of transition*, London: EBRD.

The Economist (2002), *After the Chaos; A Survey of Finance in Central Europe*, September 14.

Fleischer, F. and K. Hornschild (1999), 'Innovation and the East German transformation', in M. Myant (ed.), *Industrial Competitiveness in East-Central Europe*, Cheltenham, UK and Northhampton, MA, USA: Edward Elgar, 169-186.

Hagen, J. von (1995), 'East Germany: The Economy of Kinship', *CEPR Discussion Paper*, No.1296.

Hagen, J. von and R. Strauch (2000), 'East Germany: Transition and unification – Experiments and Experiences', *CEPR Discussion Paper*, No. 2386.

Hallett, A. and Y. Ma (1993), 'East Germany, West Germany, and their Mezzogiorno problem: A Parable for European Integration', *Economic Journal*, **103**, 416-428.

Hedlund, S. and N. Sundstrom (1996), 'The Russian Economy after Systemic Change', *Europe-Asia Studies*, **48**, 887-925.

Heiner, R.A. (1983), 'The Origin of Predictable Behaviour', *American Economic Review*, **73**, 590-595.

Hodgson, G.M. (1988), *Economics and Institutions*, Cambridge: Polity Press.

Holesovski, V. (1977), *Economic Systems. Analysis and Comparison*, New York: McGraw-Hill Book company.

Imai, M. (1986), *Kaizen*, New York: Random House Business Division.

IMF (International Monetary Fund), *International Financial Statistics, various issues*.

Kaldor, N. (1972), 'The Irrelevance of Equilibrium Economics', *Economic Journal*, **82**, 1237-1255.

Knaack, R. (1996), 'The Collapse of the Russian Economy: An Institutional Explanation', in B. Dellago en L. Mittone (eds), *Economic Institutions, Markets and Competition*, Cheltenham, UK and Brookfield, USA: Edward Elgar, 252-273.

Knaack, R. (1999), 'De ineenstorting van de Russische economie' [The collapse of the Russian economy], *Maandschrift Economie*, **63**, 356-373.

Knaack, R. (2000), 'De Oost-Duitse sprong in het diepe' [The East-German leap into the deep end], *Economisch Statistische Berichten*, **85**, 179-181.

Knaack, R. (2001), 'De crisis van de Tsjechische economie' [The Crisis of the Czech Economy], *Tijdschrift voor Economie en Management*, **XLVI**, 81-108.

Ledeneva, A. and P. Seabright (2000), 'Barter in the post-Soviet societies: What Does it Look Like and Why Does it Matter?', in P. Seabright (ed.), *The Vanishing Rouble*, Cambridge: Cambridge University Press, 93-113.

Ledyard, J.O. (1991), 'Market Failure', in J. Eatwell, M. Milgate and P. Newman (eds), *The New Palgrave: The World of Economics*, London and Basingstoke: Macmillan, 407-412.

Lin, J.Y. (1989), 'An Economic Theory of Institutional Change: Induced and Imposed Change', *Cato Journal*, **1**, 1-33.

Maturana, H. and F. Varela (1984), *De boom der kennis* [The tree of knowledge], Amsterdam: Contact.

McDermott, G. (1997), 'Renegotiating the Ties that Bind: The limits of Privatization in the Czech Republic', in G. Grabner en D. Stark (eds), *Restructuring Networks in Post-Socialism*, Oxford: Oxford University Press, 70-106.

Munich, D. and V. Storm (1996), 'The Czech Republic as a Low-employment Oasis', *Transition*, 28 June, 21-25.

Myant, M. (1999), 'The Transformation of Czech Enterprises', in M. Myant (ed.), *Industrial Competitiveness in East-Central Europe*, Cheltenham, UK and Northampton, MA, USA: Edward Elgar, 145-168.

Nelson, R. and S. Winter (1982), *An Evolutionairy Theory of Economic Change*, Cambridge, MA: Harvard University Press.

Pareto, V. (1966), *Manuel d'Economie Politique*, Geneva.

Polanyi, K. (1992), 'The Economy as Instituted Process', in M. Granovetter and R. Swedberg (eds), *The Sociology of Economic Life*, Boulder: Westview Press, 29-51.

Samuels, W. (1988), 'Institutional Economics', in J. Eatwell, M. Milgate and P. Newman (eds), *The New Palgrave: A Dictionary of Economics*, London and Basingstoke: MacMillan, **2**, 864-866.

Samuelson, P. (1972), 'A Summing Up', in R.C. Merton (ed.), *The Collected Scientific Papers of Paul A. Samuelson*, Cambridge (Mass): MIT Press, **3**, 230-245.

Simon, H. (1991), 'Organizations and Markets', *Journal of Economic Perspectives*, **5**, 25-44.

Stiglitz, J.E. (1994), *Whither Socialism?*, Cambridge, MA: MIT Press.

Taylor, L. (1993), 'Stabilization, Adjustment and Reform', in L. Taylor (ed.), *The Rocky Road to Reform*, Boston: MIT Press.

Vroey, M. De (1998), 'Is the tâtonnement hypothesis a good caricature of market forces?', *Journal of Economic Methodology*, **5(2)**, 201-221.

World Bank (2002), *Transition – The First Ten Years: Analysis and Lessons for Eastern Europe and the Former Soviet Union*, Washington DC: The World Bank.

Williamson, O.E. (1985), *The Economic Institutions of Capitalism*, New York: The Free Press.

Index

Aaron, Henry 160–61
adverse selection 52
agency theory 56
Akerlof, George 47, 52, 68
altruism 69
American Economic Review 52
'anything goes' approach 28, 32
Aoki, Masahito 2, 8–9
Arrow, Kenneth 4, 41, 43, 66
Arthur, W. 44, 100
auctions 50, 205

Bala, V. and S. Goyal 45
Baldi, S. 46
banking industry, and model uncertainty 27
Becker, Gary 27, 55, 56, 68
behaviourism
    cooperation in social dilemmas 75–7, 203
    empirical research 70–71
    and Infonomics 166, 169
    information and future expectations 190
    preference falsification 77–9
    spontaneous social action 203–4
    see also individualism
Bergstrom, T. and J. Miller 58
Bertelsmann national ranking procedures 195
Bikhchandani, S. 45
Blaug, Mark 22, 28, 48–9, 66, 86, 99, 160
Blinder, Alan 48, 57
Boekaerts, M. 180
brainwashing claim 54, 79
business
    administration faculty complementarity 196, 197
    and general economics, merging 56
business cycle theory 50, 129

capitalism 66, 126, 127, 129, 189, 206
career advancement 85, 98, 109, 117, 121, 137, 163–4, 175
Central and Eastern Europe reform process 200–201, 206, 207–18
    Czech Republic *see* Czech Republic
    depression 208, 209, 213–14, 215, 217
    German unification *see under* Germany
    inflation 212, 213–14, 217, 219
    institutional vacuum 217–21
    privatization 211, 212, 214, 215, 216, 219
    productivity 210, 211, 212–13, 214, 215, 216–17, 219
    Russia *see* Russia
    SMEs 217, 219–21
    unemployment 210, 213, 215–16, 217, 219
    wage levels 209–10, 211, 216
    World Development Report 208, 219–20
    see also policy-makers; transition economies
Chandler, Alfred 47–8, 57
Chronicle of Higher Education (Rational Man article) 65
Coase, Ronald 1, 4, 12, 40, 41, 43, 47, 51, 52, 53, 55, 57, 59, 66
cognitive psychology 71, 125, 179
Cognitive Rejoinders 129–30
Cohn, S. and G. Schneider 125
Colander, David 3, 4, 14, 34, 42–3, 55, 102, 135
communication barriers across fields 35–6
Comparative Institutional Analysis (CIA) 2, 8–9, 12
competition
    in government departments 52
    and pluralism 42–4, 52

228 *Teaching Pluralism in Economics*

complexity approach to economics 44
constructivism 179
cooperation
  between firms 204–5
  partners, Bremen University 198
  in social dilemmas 75–8, 79
creativity 46–9
  and realism 47–9
  triggering new ideas 46–7
critical thinking skills 86, 128–9, 132–5
Czech Republic
  balance of payments deficits 213–14
  competitiveness 213–14
  currency devaluation 212, 213, 214, 219
  FDI 213, 214
  inflation 212, 213–14
  institutional economics 218
  migration 213
  privatization 211, 212, 214, 219
  productivity 212–13, 214
  reform process 207, 209, 211–14, 221
  structural flexibility 219
  tourist industry 213, 219
  trade balance 213–14
  unemployment 213

data analysis 118, 120, 133–4
David, Paul A. 95, 100–101
De Wit, B. and R. Meyer 153, 154
Debreu, G. 41, 43, 55
Denzau, A. 9, 10
disciplinary boundaries, crossing 55–6, 165–6, 169, 170–74
disciplinary training, advantages of solid 72–4
disciplined thinking, importance of 74, 166, 168, 169, 170, 171, 172–4
disciplining, excessive, dangers of 74–80, 85, 88, 108, 161, 164, 172–4
diversity 45–6, 47, 205
Dochy, F. 183
Dolmans, D. 180, 183
Dow, Sheila C. 3, 22–39, 42
dualism 24, 26, 28, 31
Durlauf, S. 44, 45, 71

eclecticism 24–5, 32
  research innovation 164–5
econometrics 4, 32, 118

economics
  basic principles, importance of 58, 127, 169
  behaviourism *see* behaviourism
  complexity approach 44
  experimental 2, 5, 6, 58, 70–71
  evolutionary *see* evolutionary economics
  flexibility 206
  heterodox *see* heterodox economics
  imperialism 13, 14, 47, 55–6, 169–72
  institutional *see* institutional economics
  mainstream *see* mainstream economics
  methodology, realism in 48–9
  neoclassical *see* neoclassical economics
economics curriculum
  and academic clusters 44, 131
  basic principles of economics, importance of 58, 127, 169
  benchmarking statement, UK *see* UK Economics Benchmarking Statement
  bias, lack of 73
  brainwashing claim 54, 79
  business and general economics, merging 56
  and career advancement 98, 109, 117, 121, 137, 163–4, 175
  change, attempts at 164–5
  change, conditions for successful 176
  change dynamics 176–84
  change, need for 176–8
  Cognitive Rejoinders 129–30
  constructivist view 179
  content change 160–76
  'content comes naturally' assumption 97
  content conveyed in historical processes 98–9, 100–101
  context and historical processes 99–100
  context, lack of 96–8
  and cooperation in social dilemmas 75–8, 79
  critical thinking skills 86, 128–9, 132–5